UNDERGROUND PHILADELPHIA

From Caves and Canals to Tunnels and Transit

Harry Kyriakodis & Joel Spivak

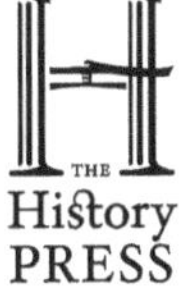

The History PRESS

Published by The History Press
Charleston, SC
www.historypress.com

Cover images: Front, bottom courtesy the Library of Congress. Back cover tunnel image courtesy of Chuck Denlinger.

First published 2019

Manufactured in the United States

ISBN 9781625859730

Library of Congress Control Number: 2018960964

Contents

Acknowledgements

The roots of this book go back to the year 2000, when I created a walking tour for the Preservation Alliance for Greater Philadelphia called "Underground Philadelphia: The Subways, Railways & Stations of the City." In the following years, the tour was often suggested as a good topic for a book. I also developed an expedition for the Society for Industrial Archeology of the post-industrial urban landscape sitting between Callowhill and Spring Garden Streets from the Delaware to the Schuylkill Rivers. This also became a tour for the Preservation Alliance; much about that corridor is included in this book.

Joel Spivak joined the research effort so that his vast knowledge of Philadelphia's transit infrastructure could be applied. He has written several books on the city's transportation resources and is a respected architect, artist, and community activist of the city. More importantly, Joel provided some of the transit-related images and captions in this text, including the cover photo.

I would also like to thank these individuals for their assistance: Nicole Joniec, formerly at the Library Company of Philadelphia; neighborhood historian Doreen Velnich; Philadelphia Water Department consultants Ed Grusheski and Adam Levine; Water Department engineer Mark Waas; archaeologist and Philadelphia Archaeological Forum president Douglas Mooney; archaeologist Jed Levin; Terry Buckalew of the Bethel Burying Ground Project website (https://bethelburyinggroundproject.com); Daniel Rolph of the Historical Society of Pennsylvania; the staffs of Bistro Romano and the Hill-Physick House; Joe Becton of Joe Becton Tours; Arcadia Publishing author Gus Spector; History Press authors and local historians Tom Keels, Kenneth Milano, and Rich Wagner; Hidden City Philadelphia (https://hiddencityphiladelphia.org) writers Michael Bixler, Nicholas Pappas, Sam Robinson, John Vidumsky, and Peter Woodall; Russell Jackson; and several others.

Lastly, thanks go to my brother George for his much-needed computer expertise and to J. Banks Smither and other members of The History Press for their general guidance.

—HARRY KYRIAKODIS

INTRODUCTION

Perhaps no American city has as close a relationship with the subterranean world than does Philadelphia.

The municipality's association with the underground started in the 1680s, when adherents of William Penn (1644–1718) came to live in the area between the Delaware and Schuylkill Rivers. This territory was sparsely populated by the Leni-Lenape Native Americans (the Delaware Indians), who had inhabited villages along the Delaware for a thousand years.

Newcomers to Penn's settlement were members of the Religious Society of Friends (the Quakers) who came to the New World to escape persecution in England. These early settlers resided in caves by the Delaware beginning in 1681; roughly one-third of Philadelphia's population was living below ground the following year. Part of the Quaker City's lore, these riverfront grottos allowed the colonists to survive while going about the business of establishing the City of Brotherly Love.

After dealing with the caves and buried creeks and sewers around Center City, the book turns to infrastructure associated with the delivery of water, gas, steam, electricity, and telephone service. Philadelphia was a national leader in most of these utilities during the nineteenth and twentieth centuries, and they were usually implemented first in the downtown area. These lifeblood utility services helped make Philly the "Athens of America" and the "Workshop of the World" during that epoch. All are functioning today, helping the modern metropolis work and prosper. The dawning of each of these utilities in the Quaker City is not only interesting but should also be venerated by modern Philadelphians as inseparable aspects of the city's history.

The book then investigates the downtown infrastructure of Philadelphia's railroads and the stations of these rail lines, past and present. Philadelphia was the railroad capital of the world in the mid-1800s, and it could be said that the mighty Pennsylvania Railroad helped bring the city to industrial prominence in the last half of the nineteenth and the first half of the twentieth centuries. Arterial infrastructure of both the Pennsylvania Railroad and the Reading Railroad still exists in the inner city and is coupled with the subterraneous groundwork of Philadelphia's capable mass transit system. The Chinese Wall, the Reading Viaduct, the Commuter Rail Tunnel, and Philadelphia's once great trolley system are also discussed as principal components of the city's considerable transportation history.

Center City's labyrinthine pedestrian concourse network is striking for its breadth and interconnectivity, a delight (for good or bad) to both city newcomers and old-timers, not to mention urban explorers. Philly subways that were never built for one reason or another are examined, as are intriguing connections to Benjamin Franklin, Stephen Girard, John Wanamaker, and other illustrious Philadelphians. Modern highway tunnels and a few vital bridges and viaducts in the Center City area are also included in this whirlwind virtual tour of Philadelphia's anatomy (new and old).

A book of this size cannot possibly delve into the entirety of Philadelphia's urban infrastructure, so only underground stories relating to Center City are covered, along with occasional forays out of that zone. Firefighting developments, local canals, the Underground Railroad, bus service, and cable TV are dealt with before a curious Victorian system for the delivery of mail is presented. The book then concludes with a look at some criminal activity underfoot and a description of archaeological efforts in the city.

Philadelphia's geology and paranormal matters are not discussed, and neither are burial grounds—except in cases where they relate to history, archaeology, or specific individuals. Various superlatives of the city are mentioned along the way of this subsurface trek through the hidden-most elements of the "Hidden City" of Philadelphia, especially in relation to utilities that Philly has played a key role in advancing for the United States and the world.

It will be seen that the history of Quaker City's secretive infrastructure is a fascinating topic and that the innovative spirits of William Penn, Benjamin Franklin, and other notable Philadelphians can still be detected in the city's underground experience.

CHAPTER 1

Caves Along the Waterfront of William Penn's Quaker Colony

The earliest underground human activity in Philadelphia must have been that of the local Leni-Lenape, who had long used dugouts along the Delaware River's western bank for temporary winter shelter. Perhaps jokingly, they told the city's first settlers that the holes had been created by muskrats and were then enlarged for human use.

But it was the stalwart Quaker colonists who really began the underground history of Philadelphia. Upon reaching Penn's settlement in the 1680s, they burrowed into the Delaware's western embankment for their initial refuge. As Philadelphia historian John Watson declared in his *Annals of Philadelphia, and Pennsylvania, in the Olden Time* (1844):

> *Most Philadelphians have had some vague conceptions of the caves and cabins in which the primitive settlers made their temporary residence. The caves were generally formed by digging into the ground, near the verge of the river-front bank, about three feet in depth; thus, making half their chamber under ground, and the remaining half above ground was formed of sods of earth, or earth and brush combined. The roofs were formed of layers of limbs, or split pieces of trees, over-laid with sod or bark, river rushes, &c. The chimneys were of stones and river pebbles, mortared together with clay and grass, or river reeds.*

Whereas Watson states that these shallow—but apparently substantial—subterranean dens were dug vertically (down) into the ground, other

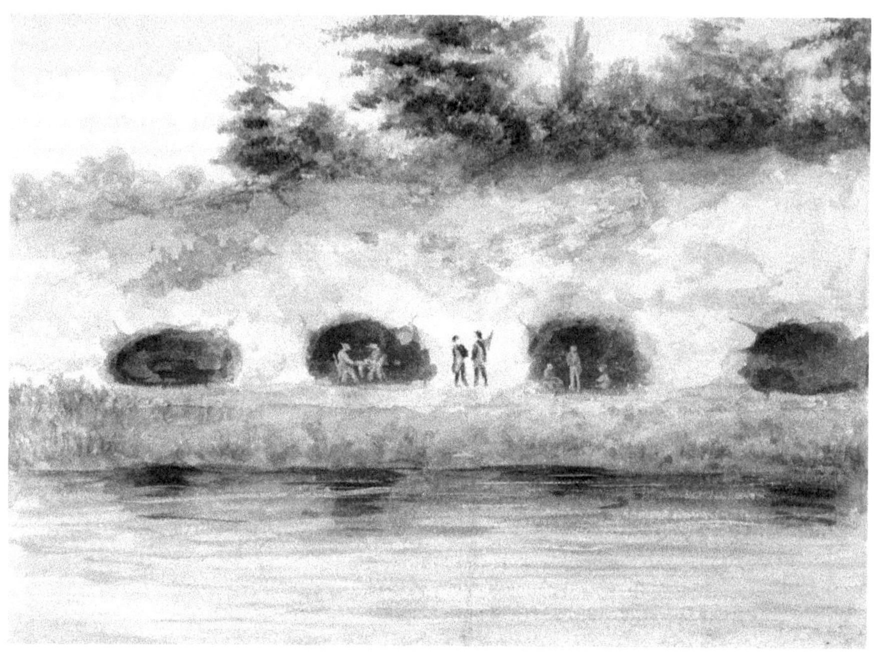

Caves along the east bank of the Delaware River, under what came to be Front Street, in the 1680s. The grottos sheltered Quaker newcomers while they built their homes close by or farther inland. However, it is hardly likely that the caves were so uniform in size and so regularly spaced apart as they appear in this nineteenth-century painting. *The Library Company of Philadelphia.*

evidence maintains that the caves were dug horizontally into the Delaware River embankment. Located within the space between where Front and Water Streets came to be, this bank was valuable river frontage that settlers had acquired or hoped to acquire from William Penn and the Pennsylvania Proprietary.

Surprisingly, some Quakers operated unlicensed taverns and illicit businesses in their riverbank caverns. Betting occurred wherever sailors gathered to eat and drink, and tavern owners conducted games of chance in secluded rooms to meet the demand. Plus, brothels flourished, as gambling went hand in hand with prostitution along the Delaware River. When families vacated the underground lairs for better housing, new families—or gamblers and prostitutes—often moved in.

The grottos ultimately emptied. Some were filled in, while others became part of the basements of houses and businesses that were built between Front and Water Streets, right over the caves. Others were converted into brick-arched hypogeums (vaults) beneath the east pavement of Front and then connected to newly dug basements.

It is fortunate that a group of urban homesteaders came to the block of Front Street between Vine and Callowhill in the 1970s and resuscitated what had been a row of derelict shops and warehouses. In doing so, they preserved what may be the oldest man-made (or muskrat-made?) things in Philadelphia. Today's homeowners use these underground chambers as storage closets and wine cellars.

Whenever a sidewalk is made of huge slabs of flagstone (as a rule gouged with diagonal hash marks), that suggests that the property's basement vault continues under the pavement; 3rd Street north of Market Street in Old City Philadelphia retains much of its original flagstone paving, spanning arched basement chambers. Sadly, these slabs and hypogeums are slowly disappearing with twenty-first-century development.

Some sidewalk-basement chambers were utilized as beer vaults by neighborhood brewers. Hypogeums like these provided cold storage space, using blocks of ice cut from the Delaware, before artificial refrigeration came to be. Other basement vaults stockpiled wood or bottles of wine.

Coal deliveries were also made into such subsurface rooms via circular openings in the sidewalk. Looking like large utility manholes, these apertures were where chutes from coal wagons would empty coal into basement bins. Most "coal-holes" were semi-cylindrical brick-arched structures under the pavement. The openings were covered by round cast-iron hatches, although other covers were rectangular in shape and still others were a set of metal doors in a building's front foundation wall. When contemporary residents find coal bins by breaking open old doors in their basements, they often say, "It must be a tunnel, maybe part of the Underground Railroad!" But this is not the case.

Something like this occurred in 1998 when a brick arch and passageway about eight feet below the pavement was exposed in front of 120 Chestnut Street during sewer work. Numerous explanations were offered: that it was used to hide runaway slaves, to smuggle things into the city from the Delaware waterfront, or to transport contraband alcohol during Prohibition. But it was doubtlessly a basement coal vault.

In 2016, two brick basement vaults beneath the walkway along 3rd Street were laid bare during excavation work at the southwest corner of 3rd and Market, their arched roofs about five feet below the surface. The owner of a building formerly there had boarded up these chambers with plywood. What could they be a remnant of?

It turns out that the "Old Stone Prison" stood there for much of the eighteenth century, consisting of a debtor's jail facing High (now Market) Street and a prisoner workhouse facing 3rd. Then again, the two hypogeums could be from a house that was erected at 3rd and Market in 1785. Or they may have been added when that house was later altered for commercial use. These possibilities are borne out by the fact that the jail and workhouse were constructed of stone and the surviving arches are brick. Without a full archaeological investigation, the true meaning of these now-reburied vaults will remain a mystery. But it's too late: the property is now new commercial space. Archaeologists Douglas Mooney and Jed Levin lamented there are hundreds of sites like this in Center City and the rest of Philadelphia that will probably never get unearthed or examined because of the city's ceaseless redevelopment.

Furthermore, the property diagonally across the prison site, at 303 Market Street, contained underground cells that held British prisoners during the Revolutionary War. And a tunnel ostensibly crossed under Market Street to that corner but disappeared when the Market Street Subway was built. Later chapters will further discuss the subject of tunnels under Old City and Society Hill.

Vaults under sidewalks interfered with the laying of conduits, pipes, and other municipal infrastructure. In 1902, the City of Philadelphia prohibited such vaults, except in cases where the ceiling was at least four feet below the walkway. The four-foot space could then be used for infrastructure purposes. It should also be pointed out that Pennsylvania's Underground Utility Line Protection Act of 1974 requires utilities to mark their buried lines to prevent infrastructure damage.

Many residential and business buildings also have horizontal or slanted bulkhead doors leading from the sidewalk down to the basement. These weather-tight steel doors allow for access to a house or store cellar without having to enter the first floor. In this way, deliveries can be made without soiling a living room or a salesroom and appliances can be readily moved in and out of the building. Called Bilco Doors (for the manufacturer), these and similar bulkhead hatchways are found throughout Center City Philadelphia and in other cities. Some people refuse to walk on them, since falling through has happened, although more often with wooden versions that had rotted. Conversely, children often take delight on jumping on Bilco Doors, considering the racket they make.

The last intact vestige of Philadelphia's colonial port heritage is along Delaware Avenue between Vine and Callowhill. The remains of a shipyard

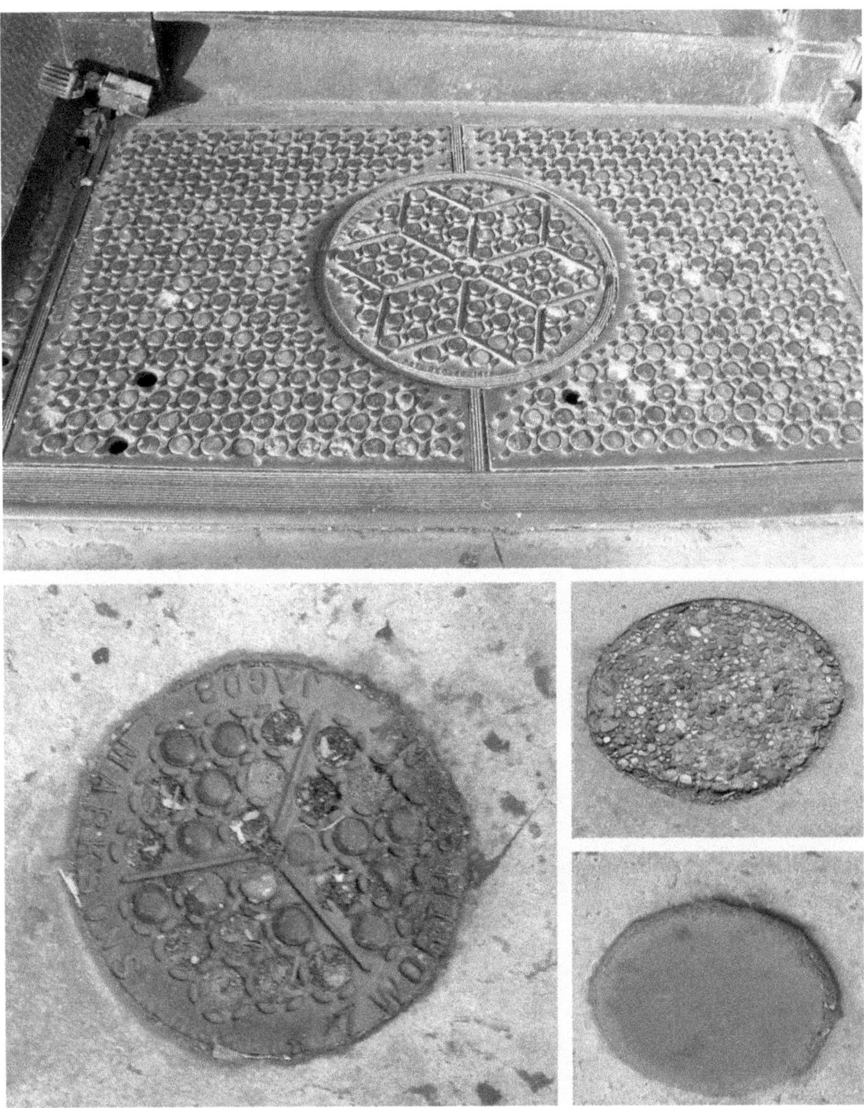

From the 1870s into the twentieth century, vault lights (basement skylights) became popular in large cities to help illuminate basements with outside daylight. Manhole-sized cast-iron grates were found in stone slab sidewalks, as were more larger and ornate fixtures, inlaid with small round pieces of lavender prism glass often arranged in a honeycomb pattern. This composite image shows vault lights on the north side of Chestnut Street, near 3rd. On the right are basement skylights that have been sealed with concrete or replaced with a metal plate. *Photographs by Harry Kyriakodis.*

are underneath the parking lot at the foot of Vine Street across from Pier 19. The West Shipyard was one of four local yards fabricating fishing craft, riverboats, and oceangoing vessels in the earliest days of Philadelphia.

James West (?–1701) set up his yard on the west bank of the Delaware River as early as 1676, years before the arrival of William Penn in America. In the days before dry docks, sailing ships needing repair would be dragged up slipways (ramps) to enable repairs to be made. New vessels were also built on slipways.

The West Shipyard had faded from memory by the early 1800s, and the old slipways and quays were filled as Philadelphia's waterfront developed. Disturbances at this site were relatively minor because the structures built there did not have deep foundations. By the early 1900s, a railyard of the Reading Railroad covered the block.

In 1987, a small archaeological dig was carried out on the West site. Remnants of eighteenth-century wharves and a slipway were among the findings. Paved over to keep it preserved, the old slipway is the only feature of its kind unearthed on the American East Coast. Another dig occurred there in 2012. Much valuable material is undoubtedly buried not far below the surface since the property escaped the havoc wrought by the construction of nearby Interstate 95.

It was normal in the late 1600s and early 1700s to see pirates of the Atlantic Ocean openly swagger along the Philadelphia waterfront. Pirates, including Blackbeard and William "Captain" Kidd, liked the city on account of the mild temper of Quaker justice, so much so that Philadelphia became a favored place to hide pirate plunder. Rumors of buried treasure along the Delaware River have lingered for hundreds of years. John Watson claimed that a pot of coins (roughly $5,000) was once discovered in the cellar of a tavern at Front and Spruce. Citizens also hunted for pirate booty around Front and Fairmount.

Starr Garden Playground at 6th and Lombard was the first children's play yard in Philadelphia. Before its creation in the 1890s, the site was crammed with dozens of small houses that made up a criminal community dubbed "Murderers' Row" that supported a gang called "The Forty Thieves." (The group was similar to bands of criminals in other cities like New York, and the name obviously came from the *Arabian Nights* tale.) Under the block ran a surreptitious tunnel that local pirates and ruffians used to stash their ill-gotten gains. This passageway began in the basement of 612 Lombard Street (one of the homes later demolished for the park) and terminated at a long-gone alley off St. Mary (now Rodman) Street. It was formally discovered in

1895 when Starr Garden was laid out and made a reappearance in 1907 when the ground above it collapsed. The tunnel had been sealed by The Forty Thieves and was never fully explored before Starr Garden's debut. Its possible Underground Railroad use is brought up in Chapter 15.

Moreover, the house at 616 Lombard had a backyard well, down which crude coffins were tossed that allegedly contained victims whom The Forty Thieves Gang had kidnapped, robbed, and murdered. Sure enough, upon the pit's excavation in 1895, a coffin was brought to the surface that held the bones of babies. While the story of pirates and neighborhood outlaws is no doubt true, the most plausible explanation is that the park was built atop the site of the Colored Presbyterian Church on St. Mary Street and that the infants were buried in unmarked graves by unscrupulous church sextons who had not given them proper Christian burials after being paid by indigent parents to do so.

Philadelphia's underground narrative may have started along the Delaware River, but the city's other cardinal waterway, the Schuylkill, also has subsurface tales to tell. (*Schuylkill*, after all, means "hidden river" in Dutch.) In particular, a duo of mystifying cave-related stories makes their home along the river and its tributaries.

As far back as 1694, Philadelphia's first mystics came to meditate and await the Second Coming inside a grotto above Wissahickon Creek near Hermit Lane. The band of German Pietists-scientists—variously called the "Mystic Brotherhood," the "Society of the Woman in the Wilderness," and the "Monks of the Wissahickon"—were dissatisfied with Protestant and Catholic ritual. Their leader, Johannes Kelpius (1667–1708), was a Transylvania-born astronomer/philosopher who was renowned as the "Hermit of the Wissahickon."

The "Kelpius Cave" may simply be an old springhouse, but the Rosicrucian Brotherhood—a veiled worldwide society claiming to have wisdom hearkening to ancient Egypt—installed a marker there in 1961 pronouncing that the chamber hosted the first theosophical community in the New World. Plus, the cavern gave the Roxborough neighborhood its name since it was referred to as the "Burrow of Rocks" (or "Rocks Burrow") by Kelpius's followers. The "rocks" is a type of bedrock in the Pennsylvania and New Jersey region termed Wissahickon schist.

Caves were excavated nearby by a team of colonial explorers seeking mineral (not mystic) fortune. At the intersection of Wissahickon and Gorgas Creeks, a tunnel reaches back twenty feet into rock, and a gap in the hillside blows cold air, hinting at larger spaces underneath. The caverns were quarried

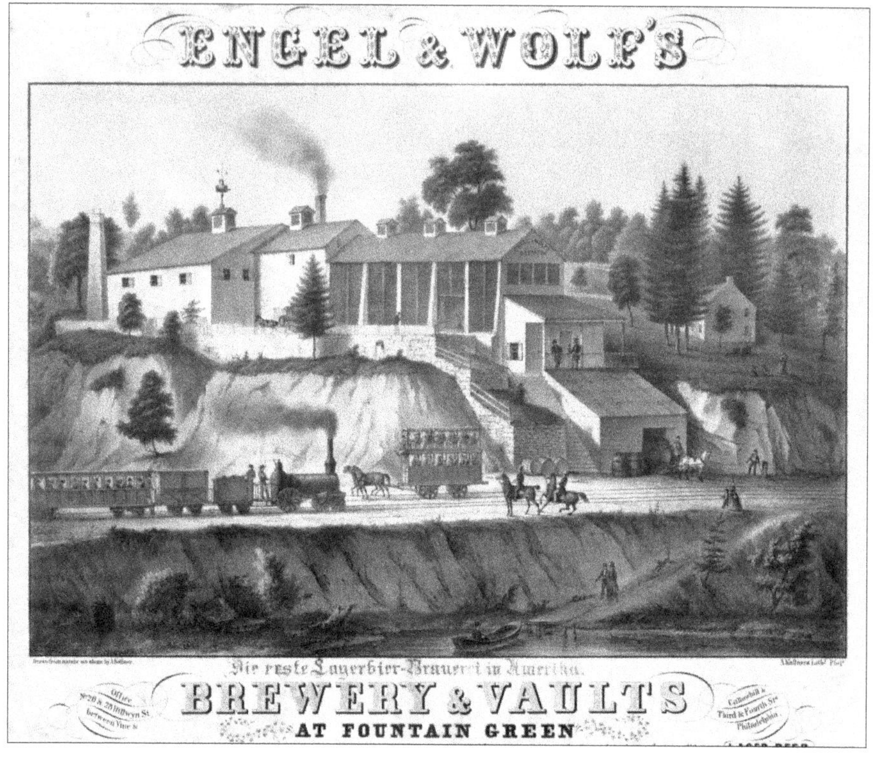

Back in the 1850s, when Philadelphia was the lager beer capital of America, the Engel & Wolf Brewery fermented and aged beer in seven underground vaults at Fountain Green, an area along the eastern bank of the Schuylkill River about a mile north of Fairmount Water Works. The hypogeums were carved out of solid rock and partitioned into cellars forty-five feet below ground, keeping beer at a constant forty to fifty degrees. This lithograph advertisement shows a passenger train on the Philadelphia & Columbia Railroad passing by the brewery. Engel & Wolf was forced to vacate the Fountain Green premises in 1870, when the city appropriated the land during Fairmount Park's creation. *The Library Company of Philadelphia.*

with hand-powered rock drills and black powder by the Roxborough Mining Company in 1763–64, making them among the oldest mines in North America. The rock contains nothing of value, so it is puzzling why the outfit chose to dig for gold there.

Not so inexplicable was "The Jungle," a collection of dugouts and shacks on the Schuylkill River's east bank near the Philadelphia Museum of Art. The riverside encampment was home to about a hundred homeless men in the early years of the Great Depression. The Jungle was cleared by the end of 1932 after the homeless decided to burn the shantytown before the Fairmount Park Guard could evict them.

Chapter 2

Major Underground Streams, Canals, and Sewers Around the City

Several streams once passed through current-day Center City Philadelphia. These creeks figured prominently in the city's primeval history until they were culverted or buried section by section in the 1700s and 1800s and customarily topped with a roadway afterward.

The most conspicuous of these streams was Dock Creek, a Delaware River tributary that provided colonists with a natural cove or tidal basin—hence its earliest name, the Dock. William Penn anticipated the creek to be a convenience to inland inhabitants of the Quaker City by affording easy transportation of food and goods into the center of town. Tides on the Delaware ebbed inward as far as Chestnut Street, and Dock Creek was navigable for sloops and schooners as far west as 3rd. Small ships with shallow drafts could pass beneath bridges at low tide. At 4th and Market, there was a duck pond with fish that had swam there from the Delaware.

Breweries, lumberyards, and slaughterhouses were built alongside Dock Creek, and leather tanners began using and abusing the stream, both to fill the vats in which they soaked animal pelts and as a place to dump foul water from the vats. The populace also used the tidal stream as a waste receptacle for chamber pots and the like, polluting the creek and making it sluggish.

As a result, Dock Creek's main branch was turned into a sewer and paved over in sections between 1765 and 1784. The eastern arm was enclosed within stone walls and arched with bricks, while the western branch and minor offshoots were filled with soil, all in keeping with a series of

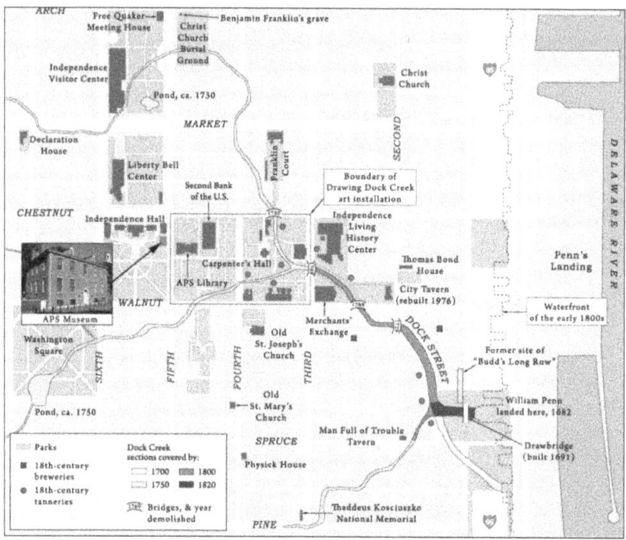

This modern map shows the path of Dock Creek and its branches as they flowed through the Old City and Society Hill neighborhoods of Philadelphia. It was created in 2008 by the American Philosophical Society for the temporary art installation called "Drawing Dock Creek." The stream's main course was laid out with bungee cords, patches of grass, and white lines over brick pathways. The work was designed to raise awareness of the many waterways that once crisscrossed Philadelphia. *The American Philosophical Society.*

ordinances enacted over the years. One in 1784 ordered the laying of paving stones to "form a public highway known by the name of Dock Street."

All this explains why Dock Street is a curvilinear street in a city reputed for not having curved streets: it follows the channel of an old waterway. Dock Street is also extremely broad (about a hundred feet), reflecting the original width of Dock Creek and the footpaths along its banks. Nearly 16 million square feet of surface land—approximately one-fourth of downtown Philadelphia—drained into Dock Creek Sewer in the 1840s.

Dock Street eventually became the Quaker City's primary food market and served in that capacity for almost a century. As such, the roadway became as dirty as the creek it replaced. The Pennsylvania Railroad even laid freight tracks on Dock Street that made their way to Market Street and out west. Food of all kind was unloaded from ships docked in the nearby Delaware River. Grimy warehouses and market stalls with tin roofs over the sidewalk lined both sides of the street for decades. Dock Street teemed with buyers and sellers and their horse-drawn wagons in the morning. By afternoon, it was deserted—except for the rats.

When larger motorized trucks took the place of wagons, the street was not able to handle the traffic. The frenzied state of affairs ended in 1959, when the Food Distribution Center opened in South Philadelphia. Society Hill Towers and the Sheraton Society Hill Hotel took over Dock Street and vicinity after the old warehouses and sheds were torn down. (In 2011, the Food Distribution Center was replaced with the Philadelphia Wholesale Produce Market, the world's largest indoor refrigerated produce complex, in Southwest Philadelphia.)

In 1955, Dock Creek Sewer was tied into the city's sewage interceptor system, which directs sewage to treatment plants. Seventeen years later, contractors erecting Penn Mutual Life Insurance Company's building at 510 Walnut were faced with a number of gushers that revealed that Dock Creek still flows intermittently below the earth's surface. To meet this engineering challenge, workers laid the basement floor atop iron pilings they had driven into the streambed, one hundred feet down to bedrock.

Dock Street from Front to Delaware Avenue is somewhat north of its original location owing to the upheaval caused by Interstate 95's construction. The street was reconstructed atop the concrete roof above the superhighway, as was Foglietta Plaza, which lies squarely at the historic location of the mouth of Dock Creek. The paltry greenery of this forbidding maze-like courtyard hardly camouflages the ventilation towers and fire suppression equipment required for the highway tunnel underneath. I-95 is further canvassed in Chapters 11 and 18, and a nefarious incident related to Dock Creek is covered in Chapter 17.

Other streams were gradually turned into sewers and roadbeds as the city developed. The District of Northern Liberties, for example, was initially bounded by two tributaries of the Delaware River: the Cohoquinoque Creek on the south and the Cohocksink Creek on the north.

Cohoquinoque Creek arose around the intersection of 15th and Spring Garden and was fed by a spring near 9th Street. The succeeding name of the creek, Pegg's Run, was derived from Daniel Pegg (circa 1660–1702), an affluent Quaker brickmaker who was an early landholder in the southern area of what became Northern Liberties. The creek was navigable as far west as Ridge Road (Avenue), about a mile in from the Delaware. Farmers would carry their meats and produce on flatboats to deliver them to Philadelphia markets via the river. Historian John Watson reported that young men and women had many romantic moonlit nights paddling rowboats along Pegg's Run.

Philadelphia's first major manufacturing sector was located on the banks of Pegg's Run, and these early industries—breweries, slaughterhouses, soap makers, tanneries, and so on—discharged their waste directly into the creek for outflow to the Delaware. As with Dock Creek, the channel became terribly polluted by the late eighteenth century. Heeding public outcry, the Commissioners of Northern Liberties ordered that a sewer be constructed in lieu of Pegg's Run from 6th Street to the Delaware. This work took place in stages in the 1820s. Industries along the way, however, obtained entrances into the sewer and continued releasing refuse into the underground stream.

Willow Street was laid on top of the creek-sewer in the 1820s. Then tracks of the Northern Liberties and Penn Township Railroad (aka the Willow Street Railroad) were placed on the street surface by 1834. This line ran from the Delaware River to Broad Street and there connected to the Philadelphia & Columbia Railroad (see Chapter 9). The united route later became part of the Reading Railroad.

The movement of freight trains on Willow Street caused subsidence of the sewer. On April 28, 1885, street workers were repairing the damaged culvert near 2nd Street when a heavy rainstorm unexpectedly arose. They scrambled to escape from the manhole, but the last man, one James Wright, wound up getting pushed through the sewer by a wall of water. As his screams echoed underground, his coworkers ran to the sewer outlet on the Delaware and saw Wright shoot thirty feet out into the river. He was found clinging to a plank, badly bruised and minus his shirt. Describing his journey through the Willow Street Sewer, Wright said that "the noise was absolutely frightful, and I was turned over and over again like a scrap of paper blown before a gale of wind."

The Callowhill East Redevelopment Project of the late 1960s eliminated most east–west streets and several north–south streets from the Philly street grid in that locale. Because of the expense of creating a substitute sewer, the Willow Street Sewer had to stay in place, which is why Willow Street itself was not stricken from the grid. But the railroad tracks on the street were removed during the redevelopment project since they had been abandoned by the failing Reading Railroad. Willow Street was then repaved with concrete. Nowadays, the surface of the street has many cracks and is sinking here and there, indicating that the sewer is subsiding.

Very much ignored these days, Willow Street stops at 2nd, having been severed from Delaware Avenue by Interstate 95. The creek-sewer still flows under the boulevard and I-95 to the Delaware River at Pier 25 (Cavanaugh's River Deck). Willow Street parallels nearby Callowhill Street, but since it traces the course of Pegg's Run, it does not fit neatly into Philadelphia's gridiron street layout.

A mile north is the other stream that once confined and defined Northern Liberties: Cohocksink Creek. This stream meandered through the marshlands of Northern Liberties and Kensington, separating the two districts as it flowed toward the Delaware. It arose at the confluence of two rivulets around the contemporary intersection of 6th and Thompson and entered the river at the foot of modern-day Brown Street.

The Pennsylvania Assembly in 1797 approved a statute declaring the lower Cohocksink a public canal from Front Street eastward to the Delaware. The forty-foot-wide waterway subsequently became used by the growing medley of industries and trades along its course. Then, in 1829, the legislature authorized the culverting of the upper Cohocksink (west of Front Street) so as to drain the neighborhoods being developed in those environs. Not much happened until after an act was passed in 1851 requiring the districts of Northern Liberties and Kensington to cooperate with the County of Philadelphia in burying the creek's upper channel.

By the 1870s, it was determined that "the Cohocksink sewer diverts the water from the bed of the canal, which is now filling up and becoming filthy and highly prejudicial to the health of the neighborhood." So the Cohocksink Canal was concealed, with streets placed on top, from Front Street east to the Delaware River. The creek still basically flows as a sewer under several streets in Northern Liberties.

Historically, the Cohocksink sewer, when overburdened with storm water, became more powerful and hazardous than Pegg's Run—a result of the sewer's wandering channel. A deep rumbling in the neighborhood would alert residents of Northern Liberties of the torrent underground. Sinkholes opened in the streets throughout the nineteenth century, and people would sometimes lose their lives, swept away along with great chunks of sidewalk and building foundations.

In 1889, one William Keppler was not as lucky as James Wright at Pegg's Run. Keppler was a sixteen-year-old youth who could not hear the water rushing below because he was deaf. When the Cohocksink sewer roof collapsed, this time at 3rd and Thompson, he fell in and drowned. The same thing happened to others who suddenly found themselves plunged into the creek-sewers of Philadelphia.

The story of an eleven-year-old boy found dead in a storm sewer in 1974 is similarly tragic and extreme. Allegedly, he was sucked into a pool drain at a city-owned recreation center in Northeast Philadelphia. Other accounts stated that the kid was exploring the facility's drainage system when he fell down a ladder inside the sewer and drowned underground.

At least these sewer incidents did not involve thousands of cockroaches. On July 16, 2017, countless cockroaches emerged from a manhole in the Bridesburg section of Philly and swarmed the neighborhood. Officials speculated that a nearby sewer inlet had clogged with food debris, attracting the insects, which multiply in warm weather.

Then there's the old Aramingo Canal in the Kensington quarter of Philadelphia, over the bed of a rambling creek called Gunner's (or Gunnar's) Run. A new harbor at the mouth of this stream where it emptied into the Delaware River was seen as beneficial—if the creek was first straightened, widened, and deepened and then lined with lumber. Ground alongside the channel could then be made available for wharves and other port facilities. All this was accomplished in the years following the incorporation of the Aramingo Canal Company in 1847.

A great deal of money was spent on this venture, but the work turned out to be fruitless because canal business was lackluster. By the 1880s, Aramingo Canal was a disease-spreading cesspool of industrial waste and residential refuse. The putrid tidal inlet was buried into a sewer by 1902. There is no surface evidence of the canal's port facilities (once situated near Interstate

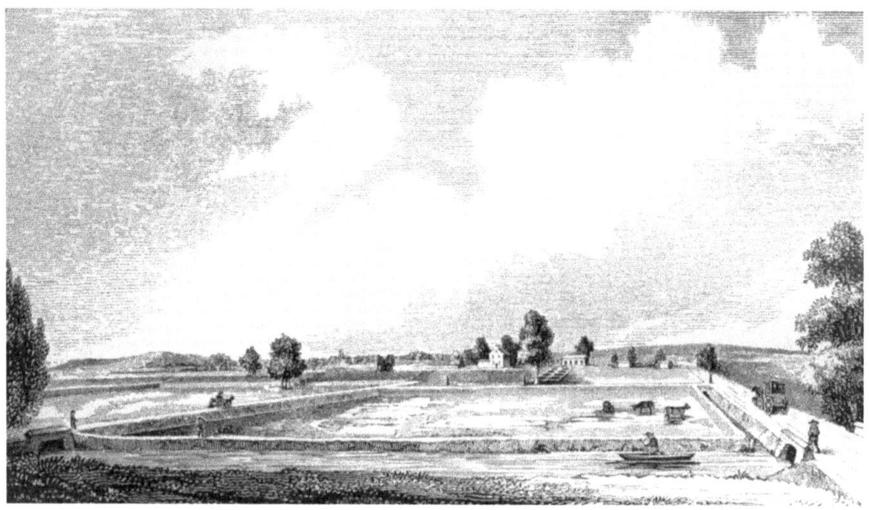

Cohoquinoque Creek, or Pegg's Run, flowed through the southern part of Northern Liberties, not far from Vine Street, the border with Philadelphia. This drawing shows the wooden causeway, dubbed Poole's Bridge, that was built over the stream at Front Street in the 1740s. Sluices permitted water to flow freely to the Delaware River. Several people straying from the causeway lost their lives in the mud, since land on both sides of Pegg's Run was low and swampy. Other bridges followed on 2nd Street and other north–south roads. *From* Annals of Philadelphia, and Pennsylvania, in the Olden Time *(1844), by John F. Watson.*

95's Aramingo Avenue interchange) or the canal itself (today the route of Aramingo Avenue). Yet bits of the wood-lined channel endure, as proved by an archaeological dig conducted for the Pennsylvania Department of Transportation in 2007–8.

Valleys that other creeks carved while tracing their way to the Delaware or Schuylkill Rivers were often filled with coal ash in the early twentieth century. Coal ash (or cinders) is an unstable material on which to build. When houses were later erected atop such newly graded landfill, they inevitably became unsteady, developing cracks in their foundations as they sank into the ground and making the houses unsafe to occupy. This is what famously happened in two Philly neighborhoods.

The twenty-foot-diameter Mill Creek Sewer in West Philadelphia was the largest sewer conduit in the world when built from 1869 to 1895. In the 1930s, thirty-year-old homes along Walnut Street between 43rd and 44th began to collapse. The neighborhood's disintegration continued into the 1960s, with several fatalities resulting when children and adults stumbled into sinkholes. This stretch of sewer was rebuilt in 1972 after the remaining houses were cleared away. A supermarket parking lot is now on the site.

A Valentine's Day gas main explosion and fire in 1986 destroyed several Logan houses and induced an exodus of the neighborhood. Furthermore, the subsidence of 1920s-built homes in the bygone floodplain of Wingohocking Creek necessitated their demolition in the 1990s. What remains is a forty-acre sprawl of grass and shrubs, called Logan Triangle, where nearly one thousand rowhomes once stood. Illegal dumping has occurred there ever since. The Philadelphia Redevelopment Authority, which now owns the land, has selected a developer to rebuild Logan Triangle. Furthermore, Wingohocking Creek-Sewer's outlet into Frankford Creek is over two miles away, by the intersection of Ramona Avenue and I Street. This open-air aperture is the largest in Philadelphia's sewer system, at about twenty-four feet in height.

Parenthetically, lower Frankford Creek was channeled into a new watercourse in the 1950s to eliminate bends that caused the languid, polluted stream to occasionally flood. Efforts to control flooding lopped off the length of creek that flowed through Bridesburg, with sewers built in the old creek bed and the old channel filled. Frankford Creek's updated mouth empties into the Delaware River about a mile and a half south of its natural mouth, which still exists as a storm water sewer outlet onto the river.

Sinkholes have also transpired in firmer parts of the city. In early 2017, a sinkhole developed in the Kensington neighborhood's East Boston Street when a sewer pipe developed a hole and began to take in dirt over several months. Continued erosion formed a void that caused the collapse and also broke a paralleling water main. The opening became a seventy-foot gash in the street that swallowed up parked cars—but no people.

Even city buses are not immune from the scourge of sinkholes. On March 9, 2018, a SEPTA bus fell into a sinkhole that opened up on Lombard Street between 16th and 17th. This incident gave rise to only minor injuries.

Happily, the growth of downtown Philly's sewer system—the city's first instance of underground infrastructure—has not always been as alarming as the preceding might imply.

Philadelphia is wholly within the Delaware River Basin, so all water runoff in the city discharges to the Delaware (and the Schuylkill, which empties into the Delaware). Direct drainage to the Delaware River from Philadelphia is only about forty square miles of the city. Before the region's urbanization, drainage to the Delaware was accomplished by means of an estimated sixty-seven linear miles of creeks and streams.

The city's first non-creek sewers, built around 1740, were constructed to convey only stormwater. Human waste was collected in privy pits, and most commercial waste was simply dumped into adjacent streams. After the city began to supply water to citizens in 1801, bathtubs and flush toilets came into wide use and domestic wastewater increased.

By midcentury, Strickland Kneass, Chief Engineer and Surveyor of Philadelphia, decided that something should be done. In 1857, he wrote in a report to civic leaders:

> *There should be a culvert* [i.e., sewer] *on every street and every house should be obliged to deliver into it, by underground channels, all ordure or refuse that is susceptible of being diluted.... The great advantage in the introduction of lateral culverts is...* [that] *our gutters would cease to be reservoirs of filth and garbage, breeding disease and contagion in our very midst.*

This was the inception of Philadelphia's "combined sewer system," in which storm water runoff *and* human and commercial waste all flow into the city's sewers. Larger-than-average sewer conduits that had been designed to carry only storm water began admitting waste. (As a means of averting sewer backups into living spaces, some rowhouses were built with toilets in their basements, a practice followed in other East Coast cities.) The "combined sewer" system still prevails in Philadelphia to this day, covering almost two-thirds of sewer service, including Center City.

Philadelphia's "separate sewer" system provides the remaining third of sewer service. Separate sewers consist of two distinct sewer conduits running alongside each other: a storm water pipe carrying water accumulated from building downspouts, street inlets, and other storm sewer pipes, discharged into the nearest stream, and a sanitary sewer conducting sewage collected from plumbing connections of homes, businesses, and industry to sewage treatment plants. The separate sewer system reduces water pollution.

As early as 1914, the Commonwealth of Pennsylvania passed a law prohibiting municipalities from building new sewers that would admit untreated sewage into streams. Accordingly, the City of Philadelphia published a report detailing proposed improvements to sewage collection and treatment. The plan required miles of intercepting sewers designed to transport sewage from neighborhoods just above the city's main water intake pipes to three downstream sewage treatment plants. This extensive system to keep sewage out of the Delaware and Schuylkill Rivers—and the city's water supply—took more than fifty years to complete.

In some Philadelphia homes, human waste, shower water, dish grease, and other stuff that belongs in the sanitary sewer goes down the wrong pipe, sending sanitary waste to waterways that feed the Delaware River. This may be because the homeowner or a lazy plumber connected a new fixture to the house's stormwater sewer pipe as opposed to its sanitary sewer pipe. The city actively searches for such improper sewer connections.

The Northeast Sewage Treatment Plant opened in 1925 at Richmond Street and Wheatsheaf Lane by the Delaware River. This 150-acre facility, now called the Northeast Water Pollution Control Plant, is home to a Biogas Cogeneration complex, a modern marvel that turns human waste into enough methane gas to power the plant's equipment.

The Depression and World War II delayed completion of the Southeast and Southwest Pollution Control plants until federal and state funding became available in the mid-1950s. The city also built a chain of large intercepting sewers and pumping stations along the Delaware and Schuylkill Rivers to collect waste from neighborhoods and direct it to the treatment facilities. The three plants clean and discharge nearly 500 million gallons of wastewater each day.

Waste matter from Center City flows by gravity to the southwestern part of the city and then crosses under the Schuylkill through dual fifty-inch-diameter horizontal syphons eighty feet below river bottom. The Central Schuylkill Pumping Station, visible on the river's west bank by the Schuylkill Expressway's Grays Ferry exit, merges this waste with waste from West

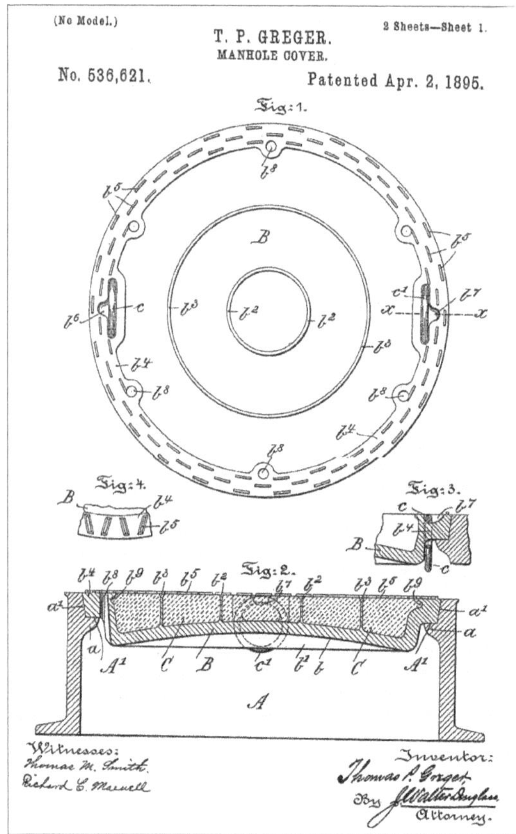

The Greger Noiseless Manhole Cover was a patented design that became embraced in Philadelphia and other cities at the turn of the twentieth century. Greger covers also contained asphalt in their centers, so that wagons rolling over them made little noise. They were designed by Inspector Thomas Greger, of Philadelphia's Board of Highway Supervisors, and were among the first to be circular. Older manhole covers were rectangular and tended to jump out of place under traffic; a circular cover is the only shape that will not fall through the hole. *Harry Kyriakodis's collection.*

Philadelphia. Colossal pumps inside the odd-looking round pump building then lift the collected waste about forty feet so that gravity can take it to the Southwest Pollution Control Plant. As they approach the treatment plant, sewers in West Philadelphia can be as wide as fourteen feet in diameter.

The end product of sewage treatment was initially sent to central Pennsylvania to reclaim strip-mined land. That stopped after statewide protests were heard about receiving Philadelphia's excreta. By the 1980s, all three plants were upgraded to "secondary treatment." This is a process whereby settleable solids are removed and organic compounds in sewage are eliminated via a biological process. Whatever waste remains is converted into burnable biofuel pellets.

Philadelphia's massive sewer system includes more than 1,600 miles of combined sewers, more than 1,200 miles of separate sanitary and storm sewers, 150 miles of intercepting sewers, 169 sewer regulating chambers, 75,000 curbside storm water inlets, and 85,600 manholes.

Storm water inlets in Philadelphia are often numbered "City No. 1 Inlet," "City No. 2 Inlet," and so on. The number refers to the style of inlet grate, a method of standardization for the Philadelphia Water Department (PWD), which manages the city's sewer system.

In recent years, urban scavengers have been removing manhole and inlet covers to sell the iron discs for scrap. A missing inlet or manhole cover could mean a seven-foot drop into the sewer below. This applies to other utilities too. In 2004, a fellow fell into an uncovered Philadelphia steam system manhole at 19th and Walnut and plunged eighteen feet, breaking his back. A homeless man had stolen the cover only minutes beforehand. The steam utility was found liable, and a jury awarded the man $18 million for his injuries. PWD and other utilities are now welding these covers shut to prevent such incidents.

The preponderance of today's sewers are of brick construction built at the turn of the twentieth century, as well as some newer ones made of clay and concrete. They are generally in satisfactory condition, with only pockets of deterioration that come with age. One example was the thirty-six-inch brick sewer underneath 3rd Street between Chestnut and Market that began to fail in 2011. Installed in the 1850s, its leakage had caused restaurant owners in Old City great anxiety, as did the 2012 work to replace it.

An enormous sewer project in recent times was the Dobson's Run Stormwater Relief Sewer project of 2007 to 2010. The neighborhood of East Falls had periodically flooded because an 8-foot storm sewer built in 1912 could no longer contain the buried creek called Dobson's Run. The modern sewer in its place now carries storm water directly to the Schuylkill River by way of a 12.5-foot-diameter bore.

Much of the $36.4 million cost of the Dobson's Run project was generated by the use of a tunnel-boring machine to drill through solid rock under Allegheny Avenue, Ridge Avenue, Laurel Hill Cemetery, Kelly Drive, and CSX Railroad tracks. The machine's application in Philly was uncommon, since most tunnels and conduits in the city, whatever their purpose, are produced using the cut-and-cover (or open cut) method of construction.

In cut-and-cover construction, shallow trenches are excavated (usually within the width of city streets) and then are roofed over with a series of arched concrete supports and scalloped side walls of concrete. Ceilings made of steel-reinforced concrete are upheld by steel beams perpendicular to the tunnels, about five feet apart at the arches. Wider tunnels also have steel columns in the center for ceiling support. Cut-and-cover is used in circumstances where the passageway to be dug is not far below the earth's surface, which is why almost all railway and subway tunnels in Philadelphia are built employing this technique.

Lastly, a group of intrepid urban adventurers in 1991 allegedly proved that it was possible to go from a point near Oxford Circle in Northeast Philadelphia all the way to South Philadelphia without ever coming above ground. The explorers traveled through restricted maintenance tunnels of the city's sewer, water, and transit (subway) systems using borrowed keys and maps, along with help from friends at PWD. Needless to say, the fourteen-hour unauthorized excursion across town was very dangerous and even more unlawful.

Chapter 3

Supplying Philadelphia with Water and High-Pressure Fire Service

For decades after the city's founding, Philadelphians drew water from backyard and public wells that were often too close to household privies, which were typically located in backyards, cellars, and alleys. The first two water wells were sunk before 1682, and the town was dotted with almost five hundred private and public wells by 1770. In that era, an ordinance governed the depth of both wells and privies to ensure that water would be drawn from a deeper strata than deposited waste, the two separated by a fortuitous (yet imperfect) layer of clay. Owners of wells were also permitted to charge for water pumped from them.

Benjamin Franklin was the first to call attention to the notion of watering the city from another source, urging that an abundant supply of wholesome drinking water would ensure the health of citizens. In his will, Franklin advocated conducting water from Wissahickon Creek into Philadelphia, using money he left to the city. He stipulated that this plan of action should be carried out one hundred years after he died. (This did not happen.)

A succession of yellow fever epidemics visited the Quaker City around the time of Franklin's death in 1790. Nearly 10 percent of the city's inhabitants succumbed during the worst outburst in 1793. The disease produced the morbid cry, "Bring out your dead!" as carts bearing corpses rumbled over Philadelphia's cobblestone streets. Thinking that yellow fever was waterborne and worried about polluted wells, civic leaders commissioned a "Watering Committee" on January 3, 1799, to determine how to provide city residents and businesses with a constant supply of uncontaminated water.

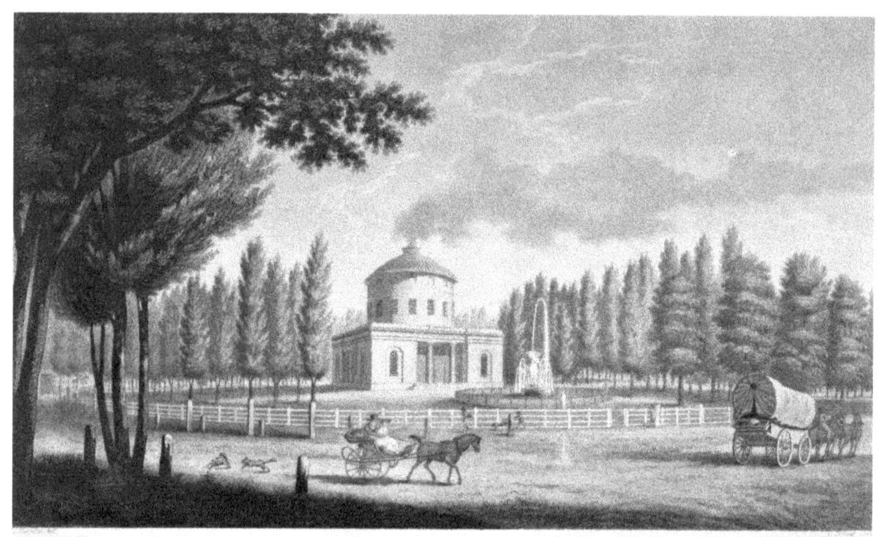

Penn (or Center) Square was once the site of the city's first waterworks. Completed in 1801 and nicknamed the "Pepper-Box," this unassuming structure was the nation's first municipal waterworks. An impressive fountain with the sculpture *Water Nymph and Bittern* (1809) by William Rush was in front of the building and was almost certainly the first publicly funded decorative fountain in America. The innovative water pumping station was abandoned in 1815 for the more capable Fairmount Water Works. *Library of Congress.*

The Watering Committee forged a plan that year. After convincing people that they could trust public water enough to forgo wells and rainwater cisterns on their property, the committee enlisted Benjamin Henry Latrobe (1764–1820)—a young English architect and engineer commended as the "Father of American Architecture"—to design and build a system in which water from the pristine Schuylkill River would be distributed through wooden pipes to the developing city.

The Philadelphia Water Works, dedicated in January 1801, was the first large-scale steam-driven water pumping assemblage in the country, as well as the nation's first major public infrastructure undertaking. *Poulson's American Daily Advertiser* called Philadelphia's water system the "tenth wonder of the world." The system consisted of two pumping stations, one at the Schuylkill River by Chestnut Street and the other at Center (or Centre) Square, now Penn Square.

At the Schuylkill Pumping Station, water was drawn into a basin at 24th and Chestnut that was eighty feet wide, two hundred feet long and three feet deep below low tide. This pool of water functioned as the intake into a well from which a steam engine pumped water to a sufficient height so that it could flow eastward by gravity beneath Chestnut Street through a six-foot-diameter brick-lined tunnel. The subterranean water passage then turned north at Broad Street toward Center Square—where Philadelphia City Hall now stands.

There, at the Center Square Water Works, another steam engine—the largest then in America—pumped Schuylkill River water up into two wooden tanks (with a combined capacity of twenty thousand gallons) inside a circular building that looked like a compact Greek temple. Made of marble, the pumphouse was nicknamed the "Pepper-Box" by reason of its shape. From thirty-six-foot-high water tanks, water flowed to an iron distribution tank and then by gravity under the city streets via thirty thousand feet of water mains. These mains were logs of spruce, white oak, and yellow pine that were hand-bored into hollow pipes and joined together with iron couplings.

Homeowners could have water conveyed into their abode if they installed a connecting lead pipe from the wooden main to a cedar cistern set in the ground near the curb. The flow of water was regulated by a copper ball, and a hand-operated pump brought water into the home. Residents paid a "water rent" of five dollars per year, and businesses were offered a corresponding deal. In fact, four breweries were among the first customers of the service, which began on January 21, 1801.

Fresh water from the meagerly populated Schuylkill watershed greatly abated waterborne disease. Pure piped water from the Philadelphia Water Works also mitigated yellow fever outbreaks by curtailing the need for cisterns, which had been breeding grounds for mosquitoes. Philadelphia suffered its last big yellow fever epidemic in 1805.

Still, the pioneering water system was abandoned as its insufficiency became manifest. The Schuylkill Pumping Station frequently delivered muddy water, the log pipes leaked, and the tiny reservoir tanks of the Pepper-Box held a mere twenty-five-minute supply of water for the whole city. Plus, the system's early steam engines required continual maintenance and were often inoperable.

In 1811, engineer Frederick Graff Sr. (1774–1847) recommended that the Schuylkill River's east bank north of Vine Street would be an excellent setting for a new water facility. Graff, who had been Latrobe's assistant at the Center Square Water Works, was then charged with designing and constructing the partially underground plant. Placed into service in 1815, the system first employed steam engines to pump water into the same distribution system used before. The engines were inside an engine house that still stands as a catering facility along the Schuylkill.

Latrobe's picturesque pumphouse at Center Square lingered as a water dispersal point until it was demolished in 1829. The city is commemorating the Pepper-Box with a pop-up beer garden in City Hall Courtyard, where the pumphouse had been. The warm-weather installation also emphasizes that the site straddles the demarcation of the watersheds of the Schuylkill and Delaware Rivers.

The use of steam engines at Fairmount ultimately proved inefficient and expensive. Plus, several boiler explosions that left three men dead triggered agitation to use the Schuylkill itself for power. To accomplish this, the city in 1819 invested $426,000 to build Fairmount Dam across the river in front of the Water Works.

Situated diagonally across the Schuylkill and completed in 1822, the dam—actually a spillway, since it allows water to flow over it—diverted water into a forebay at the east side of the Fairmount facility. The forebay, blasted out of bedrock, created a pool of water that flowed through slender flumes into the newly built pumphouse. An arch bridge controlled the flow into the artificial cove, which separated the Water Works from the shore of the Schuylkill, thus making a peninsula of the complex.

A short canal (with wooden locks) on the river's western bank, across from the Water Works, allowed boats to bypass the dam. Once known as the Fairmount Dam Canal, this channel was part of the Schuylkill Navigation Company, which in 1825 began operating a system of interconnected canals and slack-water pools within the river. The company once had thirty-two dams and seventy-six locks along 108 miles of the Schuylkill, which altogether were named the Schuylkill Canal. Schuylkill Navigation also had the right to supply Philadelphia with water, but that never happened.

Canal traffic, mostly coal barges, had diminished along the Schuylkill Canal by the twentieth century, but a lock-tender lived with his wife in an isolated cottage flanking the Fairmount Canal (for thirty years!) until the 1950s. The house was demolished in 1956, and the abandoned waterway was filled with rocks during the Schuylkill Expressway (I-76)'s construction, making room for West River (now Martin Luther King) Drive to pass alongside the river beside the new throughway.

Water flowed through the new pumphouse to turn several sixteen-foot-diameter water wheels. The first three wheels were made of wood; five that came later were cast iron with wooden buckets. The water wheels operated pumps that raised Schuylkill water via large mains to reservoirs atop a bordering hilltop. Traces of these pipes can still be seen in the hillside, which had been identified as a "faire mount" on a 1683 map Thomas Holme, the first Surveyor General of Pennsylvania, prepared for William Penn.

Releasing water for the first time on July 1, 1823, the five (later six) water-settling basins of the Fairmount Reservoirs were ninety-six feet above the Schuylkill River and had a 22-million-gallon capacity. Each twelve feet deep, the pools were at the apex of a gravity system that circulated water throughout Philadelphia via the system of hollow logs used since 1801.

No trip to Philadelphia was considered complete until the Fairmount Water Works were beheld. It was the second-most popular tourist attraction in America after Niagara Falls during much of the nineteenth century. Charles Dickens, who visited Philadelphia in 1842, was impressed and recorded, "The Water-Works, which are on a height near the city, are no less ornamental than useful, being tastefully laid out as a public garden.…The river is dammed at this point and forced by its own power into reservoirs, whence the whole city is supplied…at a very trifling expense." The ponderous water wheels, revolving thirteen times a minute with practically not a sound, were particularly remarkable.

Public gardens, promenades, and pavilions around the Water Works were the beginning of Philadelphia's Fairmount Park. In the 1840s, the city began purchasing estates on both banks of the Schuylkill to forestall industries from locating on ground close to the city's water supply. This clever strategy for protecting drinking water in Philadelphia was unprecedented in the world, since land fronting rivers had been, until then, privately owned. Fairmount Park consequently became the lungs of the city, providing fresh air to citizens and offering a new model for American parks—one in which public health took supremacy over private industry.

Frederick Graff was responsible for engineering the Fairmount compound—the buildings, the machinery, the distribution system, and even the facility's gardens. Becoming a national authority on water supply, he designed water works for dozens of American cities. Graff remained Chief Engineer/Superintendent of Fairmount Water Works until his death in 1847, after which time Philadelphia's bicameral City Councils ordered the placing of a monument to his memory in the south garden of the complex. It is still there, alongside the Schuylkill River Trail, an eleven-foot-wide, active multiuse footpath to Valley Forge.

Graff's son, Frederic Graff Jr. (1817–1890), served in the same capacity at Fairmount from 1847 to 1856 and again from 1867 to 1872, becoming a leading civil engineer in his own right and playing an important role in the evolvement of Fairmount Park.

After 1854, when Philadelphia expanded its borders to encompass outlying districts and municipalities, Fairmount Water Works was expanded to supply all the augmented city. The Spring Garden and Northern Liberties Water Works—later recognized as both the Schuylkill Water Works and the Spring Garden Pumping Station—were incorporated into the system. This water plant was located on the Schuylkill's east bank by the Girard Avenue Bridge and supplied water to the Districts of Spring Garden, Northern Liberties, and Kensington. It was put into operation on July 15, 1845, after dwellers of those precincts became unhappy with the high price of water obtained from Fairmount.

A fifteen-foot-deep reservoir was built at 27th and Thompson in 1844 for the Spring Garden and Northern Liberties Water Works. Called Spring Garden Reservoir, a portion of its 13-million-gallon supply satisfied the water needs of nearby Girard College and Eastern State Penitentiary. On November 11, 1848, the basin broke through its embankments and inundated the ground around 25th Street, worrying new homeowners of that burgeoning North Philadelphia neighborhood that Spring Garden Reservoir might rupture again. (It did not.)

Technological improvements continued at Fairmount with the installation of seven Jonval water turbines in lieu of the water wheels beginning in 1851. A new millhouse and pump-room were also built for these French-designed turbines, which were very efficient. They pumped water to the top of a fifty-foot-high standpipe erected at the Water Works.

From this standpipe, water could then be sent a mile away to the Corinthian Reservoir, an immense water basin that extended from Corinthian Avenue to 22nd Street and from Poplar to Parish Streets. This 120-foot-high pool was added to the water dispersing system in 1852 because the Fairmount Reservoirs were just barely above the roofs of many buildings in Philadelphia, causing water supply and pressure troubles on upper floors. The Corinthian Avenue Reservoir later became known for the freshwater sponges that grew at its discharge pipes as the result of many years in which it had not been emptied and cleaned.

Additional reservoirs were built on higher ground all over the Quaker City as water usage increased during the 1800s. Most were deemed redundant by the early twentieth century. The Corinthian Reservoir was abandoned in the 1920s, and the site thereafter became a housing development. The same thing happened to Spring Garden Reservoir, with

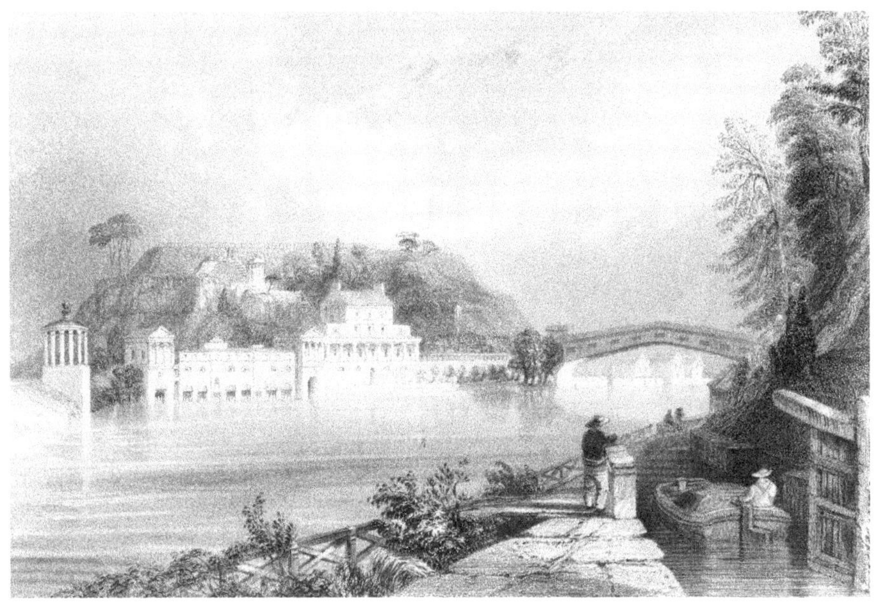

A view of Fairmount Water Works looking southeast around 1835, engraved by British artist William Henry Bartlett. At top are the Fairmount Reservoirs. The foreground shows the canal that used to bypass the Fairmount Dam on the Schuylkill River. The bridge in the background was called the Upper Ferry Bridge and later the Fairmount Bridge but was better know as the "Colossus" of Philadelphia. The 340-foot single-span wooden bridge was designed and built by Lewis Wernwag in 1812 and destroyed by fire in 1838. *Library of Congress.*

its associated waterworks mothballed around 1921. A few overgrown ruins remain at what is now Glendinning Rock Garden. The secluded garden, a hidden gem of Philadelphia, is off Kelly Drive, pretty much under the Girard Avenue Bridge.

East Park Reservoir in Fairmount Park, adjacent to the Strawberry Mansion neighborhood, is a still-functioning reservoir near Center City. Constructed by 1889, the giant brick-lined earthen pond, divided into three basins, could hold 750 million gallons of water and was an international engineering sensation.

While portions of East Park Reservoir have been deserted since 1970, a renewal project there is installing two concrete 30-million-gallon holding tanks for drinking water. A module of this work is the construction of a "Discovery Center" to furnish local children with a world-class educational venue and to preserve the unused section of the reservoir as a wildlife sanctuary and migratory bird habitat. Opening in 2018, the Discovery Center will nurture an oasis-like attraction in Fairmount

Park. Projects like this are why 10,000 Friends of Pennsylvania, the state's leading promoter of infrastructure policies and practices, honored the Philadelphia Water Department with its Excellence in Public Infrastructure Award in 2016.

Powered by its battery of Jonval turbines, Fairmount Water Works was a must-see attraction during the Centennial International Exposition of 1876. But by the 1890s, the Schuylkill River's pollution—from communities and industries beyond Fairmount Park—made continued operation of the Water Works untenable. The place was decommissioned as a water pumping station in 1909.

Fairmount Park Aquarium was thereupon inaugurated at the mostly underground site, opening on Thanksgiving Day 1911 with nineteen tanks set up in the old engine house. Some forty thousand people visited the attraction, one of the first aquariums in the United States, in its first six weeks. More widely known as the Philadelphia Aquarium, it boasted the nation's best tropical fish collection and was presumably the world's fourth-largest aquarium by 1929. One fish tank was thirty feet long, the largest on Earth.

A waterworks turbine and pump remained in place, but they were used only for a short time before repairs were necessary, causing their abandonment. Treated city water was healthier for the fish than untreated Schuylkill River water anyway. In 1925, an artesian well was drilled five hundred feet underneath the complex to provide fresh water; salt water delivery, on the other hand, proved costly and difficult to obtain. Seals and sea lions frolicked in the old forebay for a while, but the inlet was filled to become Aquarium (now Waterworks) Drive after the creatures became ill.

The Philadelphia Aquarium gradually became dank and decrepit, with worn-out displays, poor lighting and water leaking from the tanks and dripping from the ceiling. Despite nearly 750,000 visitors staring back at the fish as late as 1948, the cavern-like place shuttered its doors fourteen years later, a victim of city politics and civic apathy.

A practice pool for competitive swimmers was set up in the Jonval millhouse around 1961 with funds from the John B. Kelly Foundation. (Father of Grace Kelly, "Jack" Kelly was a nonprofessional expert in the sport of rowing, winning three Olympic Gold Medals for the United States.) School groups also used the Kelly Natatorium, which lasted until Hurricane Agnes devastated the site in 1972. The entire facility then closed.

In 1974, the Junior League of Philadelphia began a campaign to restore and preserve the waterworks. It nowadays functions as the Fairmount Water

Works Interpretive Center, an interactive museum attraction showing visitors their part in the use and preservation of the Quaker City's rivers. The facility occasionally floods when the Schuylkill River rises too much.

After the Fairmount Reservoirs were drained in 1911, "Faire Mount" hill was proclaimed a fine elevated spot for the city's new art museum. Seventeen years later, the Philadelphia Museum of Art was completed on the elevation.

Although Fairmount Dam's original purpose is no longer necessary, it does pool the Schuylkill River nicely for six miles behind it, thus making the waterway a superb recreational attraction. Sculling and boat races began on the tranquil "Schuylkill Pond" around 1835, and the houses of Boathouse Row were built for the "Schuylkill Navy"—the country's oldest amateur athletic governing body—beginning in 1860. The dam also marks the Schuylkill's northernmost navigable point and prevents saltwater intrusion upriver.

Several schemes were proffered for replacing the Fairmount Water Works in the 1890s. One by industrialist Joseph Wharton recommended building a system of reservoirs on land he owned in the New Jersey Pine Barrens, the

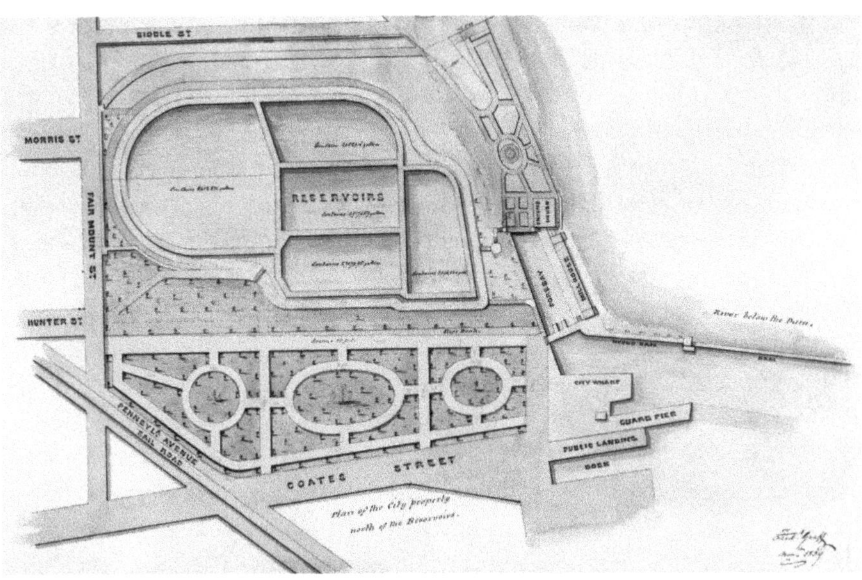

In 1839, engineer Frederick Graff Sr. drafted this plan of the fine walkways, manicured gardens, and water-settling reservoirs of the Fairmount Water Works. This was the start of Fairmount Park. (North is toward the bottom.) The Philadelphia Museum of Art now sits where the reservoirs were, and the surrounding landscape has been very much modified through the years. *Library of Congress.*

water coming from an aquifer. A tunnel under the Delaware River would deliver fresh water to Philadelphia. Opposition to Wharton's idea brought about a New Jersey law prohibiting the export of water from the state.

Instead, water treatment (or filtration) plants were constructed at several points removed from downtown. Water is cleansed by letting it slowly seep through large amounts of sand in huge underground chambers. Plus, chlorine started being added to water in 1913. Today, PWD collects raw water from the Delaware and Schuylkill Rivers and sends it to one of three treatment plants: Belmont Pumping Plant on the Schuylkill; Queen Lane Pumping Plant, a few miles upriver; and the Samuel S. Baxter Plant on the Delaware. About 57 percent of water comes from the Delaware and the balance from the Schuylkill.

Sand filtration plants and chlorine proved instantly successful in purifying water for the city's residential, commercial, and industrial consumers. Typhoid deaths in Philadelphia dropped from several hundred per annum to virtually none within just a few years after 1908; 56 percent of the city's water was filtered by that year.

The Baxter facility serves the Center City area and was at first called the Torresdale Filter Plant. Water from Baxter is carried 2.5 miles to the Lardner's Point Pumping Station via the Torresdale Conduit. This brick pipe, more than ten feet in diameter, was built alongside the Delaware River in the early twentieth century to convey filtered water to the city's distribution pipes. Lying approximately one hundred feet below the surface, the conduit was bored completely "in tunnel" rather than by open-excavation trench (i.e., cut-and-cover construction). Fourteen people died during the construction of this pipeline, which remains an indispensable component of the city's water circulation system.

Water treatment plants also supply water to the many fountains of Philadelphia, which has been labeled the "City of Fountains" for the number of decorative fountains and watering troughs dotting the landscape. The concept of watering the city with fountains followed the Roman tradition of regarding fountains as both beautiful and beneficial to health.

Water troughs began being installed along Philadelphia streets to relieve thirsty horses (and other animals) about a decade after the city's first horsecar routes commenced in 1858. Seeing the need to alleviate animal distress, a group of civic-minded downtowners, led by Dr. Wilson Cary Swann (1806–1876), founded the Philadelphia Fountain Society in 1869. Its first stone trough was placed at Washington Square near 7th and Walnut. This squat example still exists, minus its embellishments, on the opposite

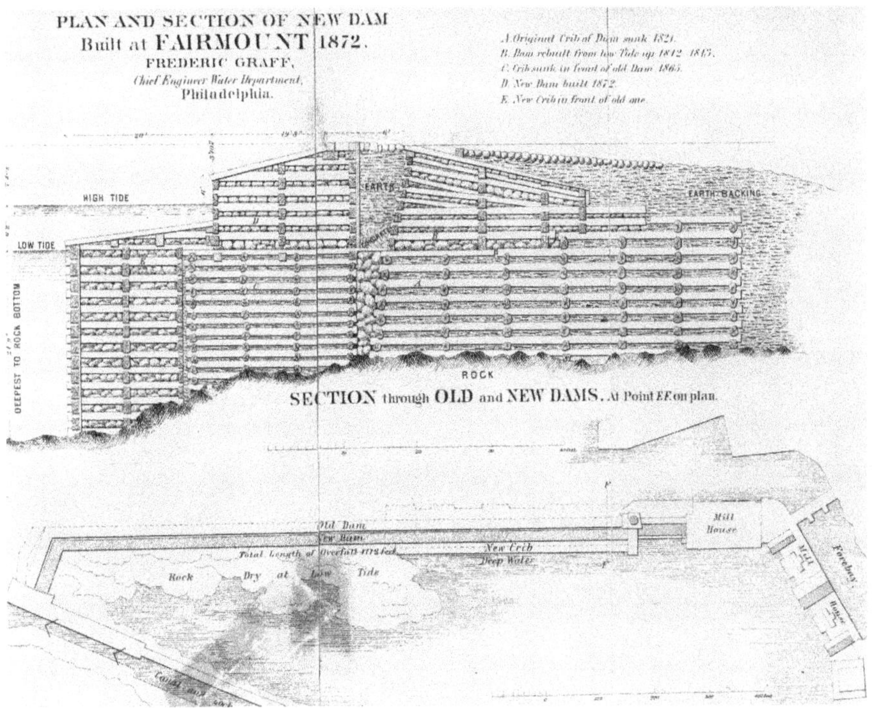

An assemblage of cribs of logs filled with stone, Fairmount Dam was originally 1,204 feet wide across the Schuylkill River, making it the longest dam (spillway) in the world at its completion in 1822. Angled in the river to permit the breaking of ice floes, the structure reaches down into bedrock, as this 1872 diagram by Frederick Graff Jr. shows. It was rebuilt that year. Lengthened to about 1,600 feet, the dam was replaced by a modern concrete structure in the 1920s. A 226-foot vertical slot fish ladder was installed in 1978–79. *Library of Congress.*

side of the Square, having been moved there in 1916 to improve traffic flow on Walnut Street. Watering troughs also promoted temperance, as the fresh, free water was for humans too. The Fountain Society installed more than eighty troughs and fountains throughout the City of Brotherly Love, some bearing engravings such as "A Merciful Man Is Merciful to His Beast." Other organizations dedicated to alleviating animal cruelty also sponsored these interesting examples of roadside infrastructure.

Decorative public fountains started appearing soon after the Fairmount Water Works opened. One of the oldest is *Franklin Square Fountain*, installed in the Square a year after it became a public park in 1837. Built per a city resolution calling for a fount of "grand dimensions," the elegant marble fountain served as Franklin Square's centerpiece until it was turned off in the 1970s. Historic Philadelphia Inc. restored the fountain's workings to modern technology as part of its makeover of the 7.5-acre park a number of years ago.

The city's most glorious fountain is *The Fountain of the Three Rivers*, familiarly called "Swann Memorial Fountain," in the center of Logan Circle. The Philadelphia Fountain Society had long wanted to honor its founder with a fountain; a bequest from Dr. Swann's widow funded the memorial. Ten thousand people danced in surrounding streets when it opened on July 23, 1924.

According to its sculptor, Alexander Stirling Calder, the Native Americans of the work correspond to the Quaker City's principal rivers: the mature woman holding the neck of a swan personifies the Schuylkill, the male reaching for his bow embodies the Delaware, and the girl leaning against a swan symbolizes Wissahickon Creek. The inclusion of swans was an obvious pun on Dr. Swann's name.

A pump room was initially located below ground on the south side of Logan Circle to service Swann Memorial Fountain. Every time an underwater light burned out or whenever a pipe needed repairs, the fountain had to be drained or the enclosing ground had to be excavated. In 1993, the fountain was rebuilt to incorporate a network of tunnels that provide unconstrained access to water pipes, electrical wiring, and light fixtures. Water is filtered and recirculated for about two weeks before the fountain is drained, cleaned, and refilled. This, of course, occurs during warm weather; this and other fountains are not in service during winter.

The Fountain of the Seahorses in back of the Philadelphia Museum of Art is another beloved decorative fount. Colloquially called the "Italian Fountain," the work was a gift from Benito Mussolini's Italy on the 150th anniversary of the United States but arrived too late for the U.S. Sesqui-Centennial Exposition and was assembled behind the museum in 1928. The travertine fountain was painstakingly disassembled and refurbished in 2013.

Philadelphia's fountains tie into the city's water distribution network. The system's log pipes were removed from service by the 1850s, substituted with cast-iron pipe starting in 1819. This was the first widespread municipal installation of cast-iron pipe in the United States. Old wooden pipes have been sporadically dug up since then, often in a good state of preservation.

These days, there are 3,200 miles of water mains in Philadelphia, primarily made of ductile iron, cast iron, and steel. While some active mains were installed in the mid-1800s, most were installed at the turn of the twentieth century. Regardless of their age, these water pipes are an unrelenting cause of the city's infrastructure woes. Keep in mind, however, that street collapses and sinkholes are ordinarily caused by failures of sewer pipes, not water mains.

Most water breaks occur with eight-inch or smaller distribution pipes. These pipes normally fail in colder months when the metal pipes contract and rupture. The smaller the pipe, the greater the inherent stress—let alone the stress of the contracting ground above and around these pipes.

Large water mains do break, but more often in the warmer months because higher demand for water places additional stress on pipes. Such ruptures often do cause sinkholes to develop, like the break that befell Northern Liberties on July 22, 2005. A forty-eight-inch main burst at the intersection of 3rd and Wildey caused water to gush out at one hundred pounds of pressure per square inch. The "Great Water Main Break of 2005" flooded the basements of two dozen Victorian rowhomes and modish condos.

Another such incident occurred seven years later to the day on the other side of downtown Philly. A ninety-six-year-old water main burst and

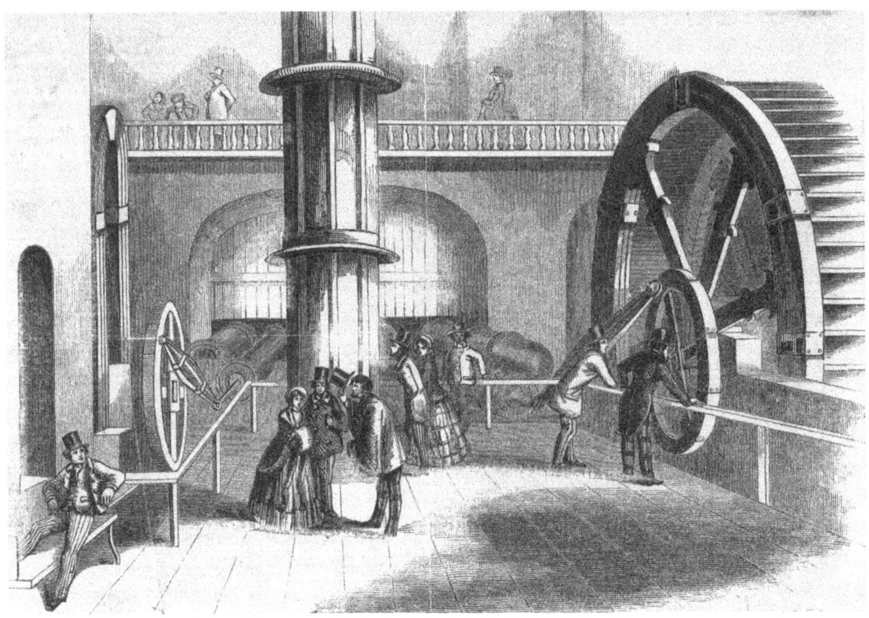

The operation of the Fairmount Water Works was a sight to see in the mid-1800s. Here, visitors are looking at a breast wheel inside the site's millhouse. From practically the day the waterwheels began turning, the Water Works was an international tourist attraction. Views of the Water Works were also transferred to porcelain and to pottery as a scene most representative of Philadelphia. *From the 1853 Collection of the Free Library of Philadelphia; Library of Congress.*

washed away the intersection of 21st and Bainbridge, leaving a fifteen-foot chasm. Four blocks of rowhouses were inundated during South Philadelphia's "Great Flood of 2012," which was followed by months of cleanup and street repair.

The Philadelphia Water Department has stayed ahead of water main breakage by employing inexpensive "trenchless" techniques to examine pipes before problems arise. Remote-controlled video inspection vehicles travel through pipes, requiring little or no ground excavation. The city has instigated a comprehensive inspection program, targeting two hundred to three hundred miles of the water main system every year for assessment.

In addition, PWD is a master in the field of "trenchless" repair techniques, through which the interiors of pipes are relined with concrete and other material. The 1980s saw the first local foray into this noninvasive method of sewer and water main repair, using cured-in-place pipe to rehabilitate an off-street location that would have made open-cut trench (cut-and-cover) methods difficult to use. PWD reinforces and repairs five to ten miles of pipe annually using trenchless techniques.

Philadelphians should be more troubled about lead contamination from their water supply. About sixty thousand houses in the city have lead pipes connecting household faucets to water mains. Lead gets into water when it sits in these pipes or when microscopic pieces of plumbing break off into the flow. In 1986, the Environmental Protection Agency banned pipes and fixtures made of the toxic metal, as it was found that about 20 percent of lead ingestion was received through water.

Lead contamination of soil is another problem Philly is facing lately, given the city's long industrial history. At one time, Philadelphia had more lead smelters than any other American city; fourteen of them operated along the Delaware River alone. When they were torn down, the lead they made often wound up in the ground. The city's current building boom is aggravating the situation by churning this tainted soil and spreading it around.

In particular, the Kensington neighborhood once had the city's largest lead smelter, more than eight acres on both sides of Aramingo Avenue. Demolition of the Anzon factory, which had been producing lead for 140 years under one name or another, began in 1999. Rubble was piled into a mound that was capped with a foot or more of dirt and grass. Children living near the site are six times more likely to have dangerous amounts of lead in their bloodstreams than the national average.

Returning to water, it should be noted that firefighting is a public service that had its universal genesis in Philadelphia. Before Benjamin Latrobe's

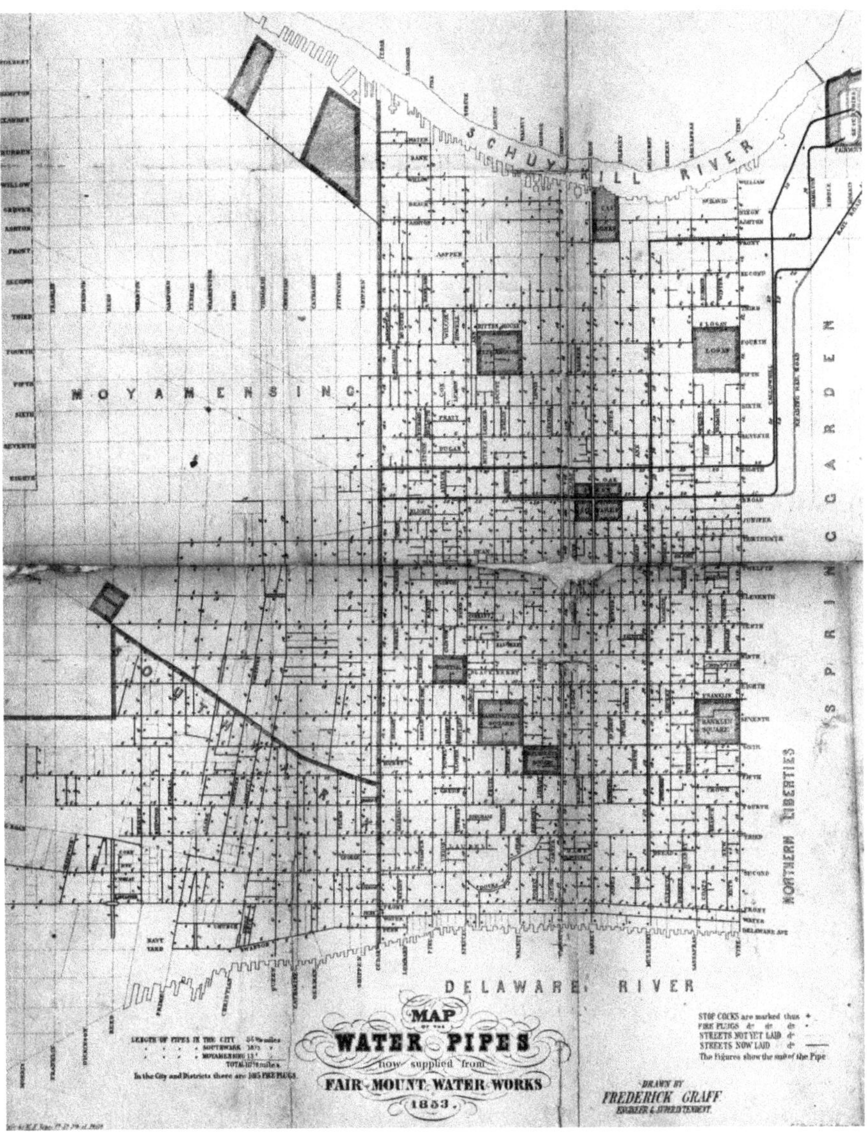

This 1853 map, drawn by Frederick Graff Jr. and issued by the Water Department of Philadelphia, shows the network of underground pipes that supplied the city with water pumped by the Fairmount Water Works and distributed from the Fairmount Reservoirs *(far right at top)*. *From* Annual Report of 1853 of the Water Department of Philadelphia*; Library of Congress.*

watering system of 1801 came into use, rainwater cisterns were used to store water for early firefighting purposes. But such "fire cisterns" were oftentimes inadequately filled.

But after 1801, whenever fires occurred, volunteer firefighters dug down to a wooden water main in the street and drilled into it with an auger. Water would fill the excavation, forming a "wet well" to either retrieve buckets of water from or to serve as a reservoir from which water could be pumped. When the fire was out, the hole in the pipe was sealed by driving a wooden plug into it. The plug's location was noted and marked before the pipe was reburied so that it could be used the next time instead of boring a new hole. This procedure is the basis of the term "fire plug," a name applied to modern fire hydrants in Philadelphia.

Frederick Graff then invented the first "post-type" fire hydrant made of wood and consisting of a combination hose/faucet outlet with the valve at the top. Philadelphia thus became the first city in the United States to have a fire hydrant system. Before long, cast-iron hydrants, manufactured by a local cannon maker, came into use. Philadelphia claimed to have 185 such hydrants by 1811, and by the mid-nineteenth century, there were 1,015 fire plugs in the unincorporated city. Cast-iron hydrants analogous to the ones used today were installed by 1865.

Fire hydrants and the city's watering system made possible the cleaning of city streets for the first time. Stephen Girard (1750–1831), a French-born merchant-banker who was the fourth-richest man in American history, bequeathed $500,000 to the City of Philadelphia for enhancing the Delaware River frontage. Girard's will directed, among other things, that water pipes and hydrants should be installed from Vine to South Streets for the purpose of regularly cleansing riverfront streets. The improvements were made, but it is uncertain if and for how long the streets were flushed as Girard desired.

As Philadelphia's water source changed from private wells and cisterns to a city-provided public utility, firefighting became a public service as a matter of course. Both William Penn and Benjamin Franklin would have been proud: Penn specifically planned Philadelphia to be fire-resistant, with buildings made only of brick and wide-open streets and parks to double as natural firebreaks, while Franklin formed the first organized volunteer fire company in the New World, the Union Fire Company, in 1736. These ideas, ingrained into or emanating from Philadelphia, soon spread (like wildfire) all through the nation and the world.

The Philadelphia Fire Department came into being on March 15, 1871, replacing the old system of volunteer associations and private companies

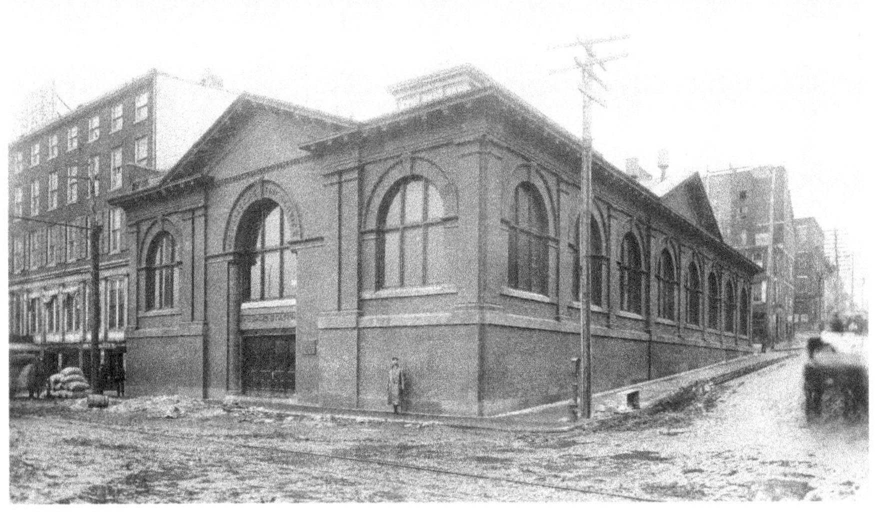

The High-Pressure Fire Service building in 1904, just after completion. It had the capacity of pushing ten thousand gallons of water a minute at up to three hundred pounds of pressure, with power to throw a two-inch stream 230 feet vertically. The modest building looks much the same today, although in recent years it has been transformed into a restaurant and office/performance space for the Philadelphia Live Arts Festival. *Philadelphia City Archives.*

with a unified entity with paid firefighters. But in terms of infrastructure, the Quaker City's development of High-Pressure Fire Service (HPFS) was more crucial.

Regular-pressure water had become ineffective in fighting fires amid downtown Philadelphia's increasingly larger and higher edifices by the 1900s. Years of prodding by insurance companies and the fire department spurred the city to install the world's first high-pressure water service in a major city. The High-Pressure Fire Service is the main reason why, unlike other cities, Philadelphia never suffered a catastrophic fire during the twentieth century.

The system delivered mass quantities of water, at high pressure and at a moment's notice, via independent pipes throughout downtown for use in fighting fires. The HPFS pumping station at Delaware Avenue (now Columbus Boulevard) and Race Street drew water straight from the Delaware River by way of a twenty-inch main beneath Delaware Avenue. Seven 280-horsepower pumps in the HPFS station supplied a network of twelve- and sixteen-inch mains all through Center City. Representatives from around the nation came to see the first demonstration in 1904.

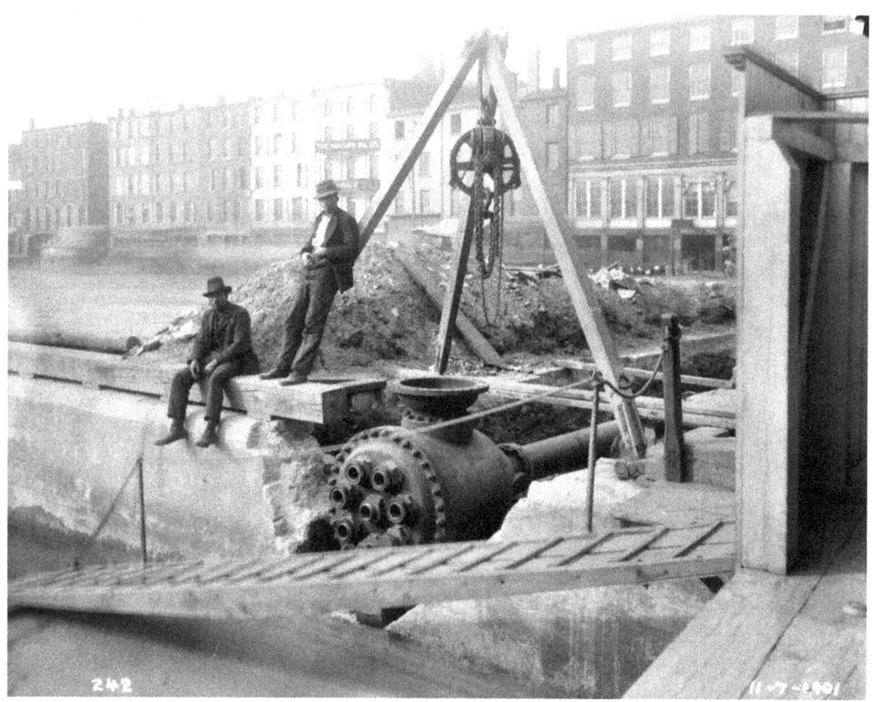

This 1901 photograph shows the installation of a large manifold that fireboats on the Delaware River could use to pump water into the HPFS pumping station when necessary for backup purposes. Today, this very same manifold remains a protrusion in the sidewalk across from the old HPFS station. Pumps normally used inside the building were powered by three-cylinder four-cycle engines operating on "coal" (or "city" or "town") gas—an early use of internal combustion engines for such work. Full pressure was available within two minutes from the time a fire alarm was sounded. (It would have cost the city a fortune in coal to use steam engines, as they would have had to be kept running all the time to provide such instant pressure.) *City of Philadelphia Department of Records.*

Pressurized water was accessed at hundreds of high-pressure fire hydrants on the blocks between Delaware Avenue and Broad Street from Race to Walnut. Red HPFS hydrants are larger than orange regular-pressure hydrants and are accompanied by one or two adjacent manhole covers that enabled access to underground mains. The covers always have "HPFS" marked on them.

Fire losses immediately declined after the HPFS system was operational, prompting the removal of extra insurance charges imposed on structures within the congested Center City area. Other pumping stations followed around the city when the system was expanded into peripheral neighborhoods. The HPFS system's success brought about high-pressure water systems in other American cities and municipalities across the globe. Philadelphia's was acknowledged as the best anywhere for years and years.

High-pressure water service in Philadelphia lasted until 2005, when the system was decommissioned after falling into disrepair. Water delivered at high pressure had become unnecessary anyway due to better firefighting equipment, high-rise sprinklers and fire-resistant construction material.

The High-Pressure Pumping Station at Columbus and Race still heroically stands. It has become a restaurant and office/performance space for the Philadelphia Live Arts Festival (aka Philly Fringe). HPFS hydrants and manholes are still found throughout Center City. But as the years pass, more and more are disappearing on account of Philadelphia's perpetual redevelopment.

In the context of underground Philadelphia, it should lastly be mentioned that the Rat Receiving Station of the Philadelphia Bureau of Health was located across from the HPFS building. Rats were a big problem along the Delaware, and officials sought ways to get rid of them and the diseases of the fleas they carried—bubonic plague in particular. Special agents rat-proofed riverfront buildings and maintained scores of rat traps alongside the river. They also inspected vessels docking beside the Delaware, enforcing a rule that mandated rat guards on mooring lines. Moreover, citizens were encouraged to bring rats to the Rat Receiving Station for a bounty: five cents for live ones and two cents for dead ones. The station was established in 1914 and collected more than five thousand rats by year's end.

Chapter 4

Center City's Gas and Steam Infrastructure

In the 1750s, Benjamin Franklin organized in Philadelphia the first municipal street cleaning effort in America. He then lived near the Jersey Market (a marketplace at Front and High Streets) and was instrumental in getting the streets around the market paved with stone so that people would not get muddy while shopping. Franklin further hired a man to sweep the footpaths twice a week. This raised a desire to have all of Philadelphia's streets paved and cleaned and made people willing to be taxed to accomplish that.

Yet Franklin's involvement with lighting Philadelphia's streets was more noteworthy. Also in the 1750s, the Pennsylvania Assembly passed a street lighting bill suggested by Franklin. Whale oil was the prescribed fuel. This is how the Quaker City became the first municipality in North America with streetlights. By 1757, Ben Franklin had invented an improved streetlamp superior to whale oil lamps of the day. Instead of being a fragile glass sphere that was often vandalized and that darkened from soot, the "Franklin Lamp" had four replaceable flat panes of glass and a funnel on top to draw out smoke.

Whale oil lanterns provided the best source of light into the nineteenth century, especially those that burned the precious spermaceti oil of sperm whales. Many species of whales were driven to the brink of extinction in the relentless pursuit of this lighting fuel.

Gas surpassed whale oil in the early 1800s and became the cutting edge of fuel technology for street illumination. The gaseous fuel was concocted from the "cooking" of bituminous coal at high temperature. The product of this distillation and refining process was referred to as "coal gas," although "city gas," "town gas," "illuminating gas," or "manufactured gas" were more common terms.

Coal was plentiful in Philadelphia by the 1830s, given the city's profound contribution to fostering the American coal industry in the nineteenth and early twentieth centuries. Coal gas was made from soft bituminous coal, deposits of which had been mined for decades throughout northern and western Pennsylvania.

On the other hand, anthracite, or clean-burning hard coal, was discovered in Schuylkill County in Northeastern Pennsylvania around 1791. The very first documented burning of anthracite occurred in Wilkes-Barre, Pennsylvania, on February 11, 1808. A Quaker tavern owner and judge named Jesse Fell burned anthracite in an enclosed fireplace at his inn by employing an open grate of his design. The experiment may have been conducted before, but Judge Fell's successful results were promulgated through him.

The realization that anthracite could be utilized as domestic heating and cooking fuel in lieu of wood revolutionized American life and started the American Industrial Revolution in eastern Pennsylvania. Plus, the ascent of Philadelphia as the "Workshop of the World" can be traced to Judge Fell's breakthrough. While not formulated from anthracite, coal gas became a beneficiary of the awareness of coal that anthracite produced.

Anthracite coal was introduced in Philadelphia around 1814, and promoters offered demonstrations of Fell's coal grate and other anthracite-burning devices to potential customers from New York to Baltimore. Philadelphia investors, like Stephen Girard, purchased large tracts of land in northeastern Pennsylvania for the coal in the ground. Scores of anthracite mines opened to provide Philadelphia and surrounding localities with all the coal needed to make the region a sprawling industrial center. Anthracite was shipped to Philadelphia and elsewhere via the Schuylkill Canal from the 1820s to the 1850s. The Reading Railroad then assumed this transportation function. Known also as the "Reading Lines," the railroad was distinguished for its "Black Diamond" logo, symbolizing anthracite.

Getting back to gas illumination, the first use of coal gas for lighting in America purportedly happened in Philadelphia when Italian immigrant Michael Ambroise made experiments with gas illumination in 1796. He advertised on August 2 that his firm would "show a grand firework by means of light composed of inflammable air." Specializing in the fabrication and exhibition of fireworks, Ambroise & Company also employed coal gas to

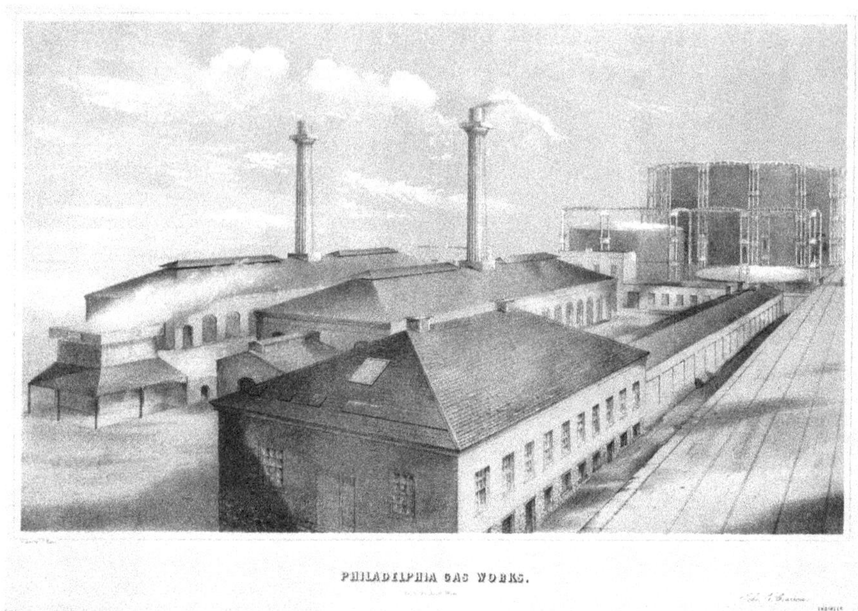

Opened in 1836, the Market Street Gas Works contained several gas retorts (where coal was distilled), cast-iron telescopic gasometers (or gas-holders, tanks that measured and stored gas), and other buildings used in the production of coal gas. The plant initially had a daily capacity of seventy-five thousand cubic feet of illuminating gas—more than sufficient for the private residences and businesses that had purchased gas service in the early years. As with the Fairmount Water Works, the structures were built in the classical/Greek Revival style. *The Library Company of Philadelphia.*

illuminate chandeliers at its amphitheater near 9th and Arch. This was the first instance of gaslight in America.

In 1802, the citizenry of Philadelphia was aggrieved by the vicious murder of a farmer by thugs along Market Street near the Schuylkill River—then a dark and sparsely settled zone of Philadelphia. Local mineralogist-inventor Benjamin Henfrey soon proposed lighting the city at night by burning jets of gas inside lanterns atop a series of tall towers. (About that time, he had been experimenting in Richmond, Virginia, with a single forty-foot tower, which did not generate any lasting approbation.) If Philly's bicameral City Councils had offered Henfrey encouragement, the City of Brotherly Love would have become the first municipality in the world to be illuminated by gas.

Gas *lamps* lit a public street in London in 1807, and Baltimore became the earliest American city illuminated with such streetlamps ten years later. Philadelphians Rembrandt Peale and Rubens Peale had set up the first privately owned gasworks in America there in 1816. The company's investors were wealthy and influential men of Baltimore.

In April 1816, a merchant, Dr. Charles Kugler, exhibited "gas lights, lamps burning without wick or oil" at the Philadelphia Museum, subsequently known as Peale's American Museum, on the second floor of the Pennsylvania State House (now known as Independence Hall). This demonstration proved so satisfactory that operators of the nearby Chestnut Street Theater introduced gaslights later that year. Formerly located at the northwest corner of 6th and Chestnut, the playhouse maintained a coal gas generator and a gas storage vessel in its basement. Illuminating gas made strip-, foot-, and border-lights possible for the first time, turning Chestnut Street Theater into the first gaslit theater in the United States. Its interior was utterly bathed in light as compared to the gloom of oil lamps.

Later in 1816, the first private home lit by gas in America was that of William Henry at what was then 200 Lombard Street, by 7th Street. Henry was a local coppersmith who had constructed the gas apparatus at Peale's American Museum and the Chestnut Street Theater. He invited city legislators to witness the use of illuminating gas in his house, but they were unimpressed, citing usual qualms of the risk of explosions (gas was said "to be as ignitible as gunpowder and nearly as fatal in its effects") and ambiguous health hazards from gas fumes (it was thought that citizens would die like flies). Another worry was that Philadelphia's rivers would be left with a nauseating smell from gas production and that tar waste would kill fish—this really happened in other municipalities.

Local businessmen used gas for demonstrations or to light their establishments over the ensuing years, but none could allay apprehension about the fuel. In 1825, after an unsuccessful attempt to induce City Councils to charter a company with license to manufacture gas and lay pipes in the streets, the *United States Gazette* denounced gas as being "folly, unsafe, unsure, a trouble, and a nuisance." Indeed, the application of gas to lighting, cooking, and heating in Philadelphia was considered absurd, showing the conservative mindset with which the Quaker City has been branded.

Gas lighting at length appeared in Philadelphia's principal streets in the 1830s. While privately owned gas factories had been constructed in other American cities by then, a *municipal* gasworks had not been attempted. Samuel Vaughan Merrick (1801–1870), an engineer and member of the city's Common Council, traveled to Europe in 1834 to inspect methods used for gas manufacturing. Upon his return, he submitted a detailed report to the Select and Common Councils of Philadelphia and lobbied for the creation of the first city-owned American gasworks. Pursuant to an ordinance of March 21, 1835, Merrick was entrusted with the facility's construction.

The Philadelphia Gas Company (later called the Philadelphia Gas Works, or PGW) began operating as a private company on February 8, 1836. Two days afterward, forty-six gaslights along Schuylkill 2nd (now 21st) Street between Vine and South were lit as a demonstration of the practicality of gas illumination. Nineteen burners inside two private residences that had signed up for service were likewise activated. Lamps fueled by gas so quickly eclipsed lamps fueled with whale oil that other districts in Philadelphia County soon clamored for their own gasworks. A bonus was that overnight crime markedly decreased on streets lit with gas.

PGW's original gas plant was located on the north side of High (Market) Street from the Schuylkill River to Schuylkill Front (22nd) Street, with wharf facilities on the south side of Market along the river to accept supplies of coal obtained from northern and western Pennsylvania. The Market Street Gas Works had an initial daily capacity of seventy-five thousand cubic feet of coal gas, and the structures were built in the classical/Greek Revival style, much like the buildings of the Fairmount Water Works. The plant was far enough away from the city's developed area that noxious fumes would not bother the populace.

Coal gas was distributed through the city via an underground system of cast-iron pipelines ("trunks") of varying diameter radiating below city streets about two feet deep. Filbert Street carried the cardinal trunk. Several hundred cast-iron lampposts lined city streets, and each and every gas lamp was daily lit and extinguished by hand (i.e., a lamplighter and his stick). By 1837, 268 downtown buildings were connected to the system via eight miles of pipes.

Northern Liberties Gas Company went into operation at about the same time. The Commissioners of Northern Liberties established the gasworks on March 15, 1838, with an authorized capital of $100,000. In 1844, it was incorporated to serve a zone bordered by the Delaware River and Vine, Thompson, and 6th Streets. The Northern Liberties gas plant was on the south side of Laurel Street by Canal Street.

PGW built a more capable gas facility in the 1850s at Passyunk and Schuylkill Avenues in South Philadelphia. The Point Breeze Works were able to distill 3 million cubic feet of gas per day and contained the largest telescopic gas-holder in the United States (maybe the world). At 160 feet in diameter and 95 feet tall, it could hold 1.8 million cubic feet of gas. Placed into operation on December 13, 1854, the plant fed underground mains that conveyed gas to the existing pipeline system. Other gasworks were built elsewhere in Philadelphia as the value of gas for lighting, cooking, and heating became accepted.

The city bought out PGW's stockholders for $173,000 in 1841 and took possession of the Market Street Works. Upon the consolidation of Philadelphia and the County of Philadelphia in 1854, PGW purchased all other gas plants within Philadelphia County (except the Northern Liberties Gas Company, not fully absorbed until 1955). Operation of the Philadelphia Gas Works was then transferred to the Bureau of Gas, within the Department of Public Works.

In 1897, the City of Philadelphia contracted with the United Gas Improvement Company (UGI) to administer the gasworks. UGI was established in Philadelphia in 1882 as the world's first utility holding company. UGI offered the city $25 million in 1905 to lease the gasworks for seventy-five years. The plan was withdrawn after public outcry about this "gas grab," as it would have resulted in a loss of gas rents for the city and a profit of $900 million for UGI.

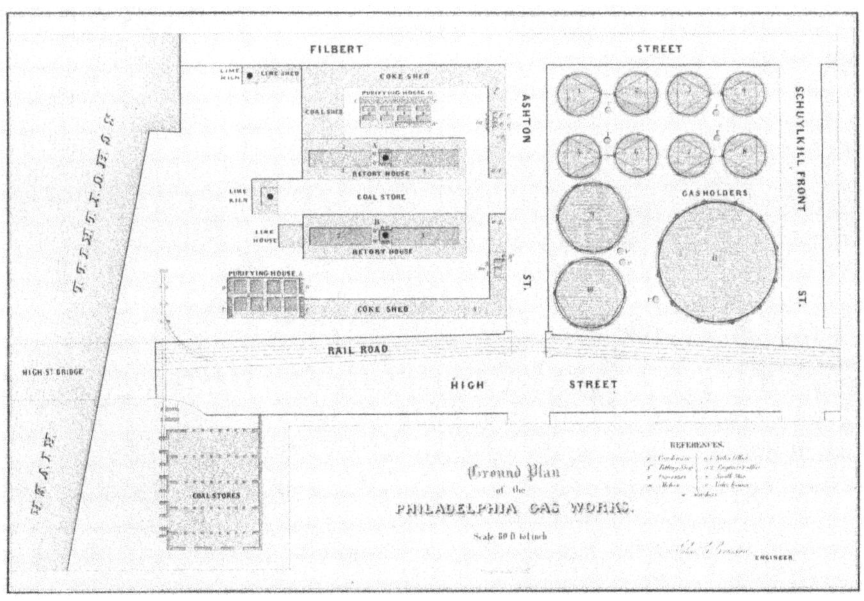

Superintendent and engineer John C. Cresson (1806–1876) drew this "Ground Plan of the Philadelphia Gas Works on High (Market) Street" soon after the eight-acre facility opened in 1836. The rate for gas in Philadelphia was $3.50 per one thousand cubic feet of gas, which was half the price demanded in New York City. *The Library Company of Philadelphia.*

People would stop by the UGI Building at the northwest corner of Broad and Arch to pay their gas bill for decades. The ornate Renaissance-style edifice was enlarged toward the west and is now twice as wide as when built in 1898. It has since been renamed One City Plaza.

Girl Scout cookies were first commercially sold anywhere at the UGI Building. In November 1932, the Girl Scouts of Greater Philadelphia Council persuaded PGW to allow its Scouts to bake shortbread cookies in company ovens on the first floor. Passersby on Arch Street were enticed by the aroma and begged to buy the cookies. So began a national tradition.

The making of gas has always been an intrinsically dangerous process. Eight workmen at the Point Breeze Works were instantly roasted to death on May 12, 1905, when a holding tank containing 2.5 million cubic feet of gas and oil vapor exploded. A dozen more men also were injured, some dying from their burns.

Use of the hemmed-in Market Street Works on the Schuylkill River dwindled until it was shut down in 1898, although its gas-holders were still utilized for years afterward. The old plant was dubbed the "City Works" or the "Ninth Ward Works" by then. In 1907, part of the site was used for the western portal of the Market Street Subway; the balance eventually came under control of The Philadelphia Electric Company (PECO). The electric firm's "Tower of Light" headquarters skyscraper was built there in the late 1960s. Nothing survives of the old gas plant.

Production of coal gas at Point Breeze ended in the 1950s as natural gas from southern states became available. A large gas-holder, built around 1910, continues to store gas there for distribution around the city.

On April 15, 1959, Mayor Richardson Dilworth extinguished the final gas-illuminated streetlamp in Philadelphia. The last gas lantern was located on 45th Street just south of Osage Avenue in West Philadelphia. Residents applauded as the mayor, with great ceremony, climbed a ladder and used a lamplighter's stick to snuff out the city's 123-year gas lamp epoch. Victorian-era gas lanterns can still be seen as decorations on the front lawns of some Philadelphia homes. Gas service, using natural gas, has remained in the city for cooking and heating use.

Whereas more than thirty-nine thousand gaslights once illuminated Philadelphia's streets, fewer than seven thousand were left by the time the city decided to spend $3 million to convert its streetlamps to electricity. While this was happening in the 1950s, Philadelphia was planning the revitalization of Society Hill, the first residential historic preservation initiative in a major American city. Society Hill's streets would be lit by lamps modeled on whale oil lanterns that Ben Franklin devised—only powered by electricity.

The Bureau of Gas supervised UGI until 1972 when the city contracted with Philadelphia Facilities Management Corporation to administer PGW. Today, the Philadelphia Gas Works is the largest publicly owned gas utility in the United States. In 2014, Philadelphia City Council declined a deal to sell PGW for almost $2 billion to UIL Holdings Corporation of Connecticut.

A notorious abandoned building in downtown Philadelphia is the Willow Street Steam Generation Plant at 9th and Willow. Built in 1927 by The Philadelphia Electric Company, the plant burned coal to produce steam for the underground district steam system, which still operates to this day in Center City. Coal was brought in via railcars that ran along Reading Railroad tracks once on Willow Street (the Willow Street Railroad). The plant's smokestacks are 163 feet high, making the lumbering building a prominent landmark in the city's downcast (but improving) Callowhill precinct.

Accompanied by manhole covers stamped with "STEAM" and deserted since the 1980s, the Willow Street Steam Plant is no longer part of Philadelphia's subterranean steam system. Easy alteration for its reuse is precluded because there are no floors inside the structure; the large interior space held nothing but gigantic coal-firing boilers. As of late, rumors have circulated of remedying the asbestos and selling the building for redevelopment.

The Pennsylvania Railroad built its own steam generation plant in the railyard adjoining 30th Street Station to meet the heating needs of that station and Suburban Station, about a mile away. Interconnected with the city's steam network, the facility was razed in 2009 after a spirited existence in which its protuberant smokestack was identified as the "Drexel Shaft" by students of nearby Drexel University. (There are YouTube videos galore of the chimney's destruction.)

A comparable smokestack monolith stood a few blocks away by the South Street Bridge at the Schuylkill River, built in 1924 by the University of Pennsylvania as a new electrical power plant. Now known as the Hollenback Center, the building (minus its chimney) has housed office space for Penn since 1968, when the university decided to purchase electricity rather than generate it on campus.

That 1924 plant replaced Penn's Central Light and Heat Plant at 34th and Spruce, where the Irvine Auditorium is today. Erected in 1891, the old electricity and steam facility was taken down in 1925. Legends about

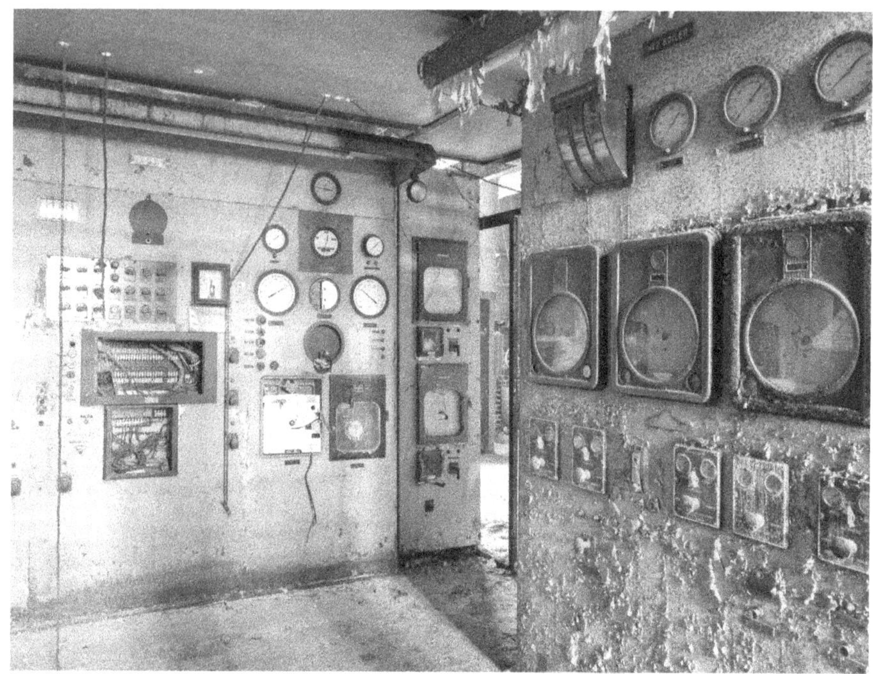

Dials and gauges relating to steam generation inside a control room of the vacated Willow Street Steam Generation Plant. The sixteen-story industrial ruin would be prohibitively expensive to demolish, as it is filled with asbestos. The Philadelphia Fire Department has sealed the plant because it is so dangerous. Serious proposals to convert the facility into a trash-to-steam plant and also to screen it with wraparound advertising have gone unfulfilled. *Peter Woodall.*

underground corridors between College Hall and Logan Hall likely relate to when the plant sent steam to those buildings. More Penn utility tunnels are beneath the adjacent Perelman Quadrangle and its flanking collegiate buildings. Adventurous students have found entrances and decorated the walls with graffiti and other marks.

Returning to the city's steam system: the roots of this underground steam network date to March 5, 1889, when the Edison Electric Light Company of Philadelphia began generating electricity at 908 Sansom Street. This was the site of Edison Generating Station, put up in the late 1880s under the personal direction of Thomas Edison. Exhaust steam from the plant's steam engines was used to heat a house at 917 Walnut, producing an additional revenue stream for the firm with trivial outlay.

The Philadelphia Electric Company established a vast below-ground steam network to serve a diverse clientele of local institutions. Other generating plants, including the Willow Street Steam Plant and the Edison Steam Plant on the site of Edison Generating Station, were later erected. The replacement Edison Steam Plant began service in 1958, produces 720,000 pounds of steam an hour, and is still in operation.

Philadelphia Thermal Energy Corporation purchased the steam network from PECO in 1987 for $30 million. A series of subsequent sales concluded when Veolia Energy bought the steam system in 2007. Today, Veolia manages a network that delivers steam through forty-one miles of underground pipes to some three hundred customers throughout Center City and University City in West Philadelphia. About 4 million pounds of steam per hour are produced at three steam production facilities and one chilled water facility.

Philadelphia's steam loop—more a grid than a loop—supplies steam and hot water to hundreds of businesses, universities, hospitals, hotels, and residential buildings (the Comcast Center, the Franklin Institute, and the United States Mint, to name but a few). These customers use steam for heating, cooling, and hot water production, among other purposes. The business is demanding, as many institutional patrons have switched to natural gas service since the 1970s. Market share is also lost when older steam-heated buildings are substituted with modern ones heated by natural gas or electricity (heat pumps).

At any rate, Philadelphia's steam network is the third-largest district steam heating system in the United States. The majority of steam is generated at Veolia Energy's Schuylkill Station at 26th and Christian, alongside the Schuylkill River near southwest Center City. Erected by PECO and once called the Grays Ferry Cogeneration Plant, this is a combined-cycle base load cogeneration facility with a combustion turbine and an extraction/condensing steam turbine. The plant generates both electricity and thermal energy by recapturing heat previously lost to the environment.

In 2012, Veolia invested $60 million in replacing Schuylkill Station's old oil burners with natural gas boilers to gain more efficiency. This has enabled Veolia to produce eco-friendly "green steam." Plus, the new boilers can come online in nine minutes instead of being operated on standby at all times, as with the oil burners. (Schuylkill Station is further discussed in the next chapter.)

Veolia Energy also owns and operates a seven-thousand-ton chilled-water facility for Thomas Jefferson University and Hospital. The water used at the chiller is generated initially as steam at Schuylkill Station. It is piped to the Edison Steam Plant at 9th and Sansom and changed to chilled water there.

Since 2000, the University of Pennsylvania has had its own chiller plant at the Grays Ferry exit of the Schuylkill Expressway (near the Central Schuylkill Pumping Station). The Module 7 Central Chiller Plant supplies chilled water to half the Penn's buildings, which consequently no longer need rooftop air conditioners. The $64 million plant is cloistered behind a sixty-foot-tall perforated-steel fence that makes it look like a work of art.

Millions of gallons of water are boiled to create steam for Philadelphia's steam network every day. Steam is sent under pressure between 165 and 205 pounds per square inch at an unchanging temperature of about 450 degrees throughout the year. Insulated carbon-steel pipes range in size from 1.5 to 20 inches in diameter, with 14-inch pipes being the most customary. Over time, the flow of steam will cause rust and corrosion, so mains near manholes are inspected every year, although most are inaccessible for routine review. Whenever a steam main has to be altered in any way, technicians inspect the pipe to check its integrity and may even send a remote-controlled device through to test the pipe's thickness with ultrasound waves.

Generated steam rarely escapes. Blasts of vapor often rise through pavement vents and manhole covers to surprise unsuspecting pedestrians, but this is merely the result of groundwater seeping into conduits carrying steam pipes and then boiling away. Chimney stacks have been placed throughout town to direct steam vapor up to street level without harming pedestrians. These protective upright pipes are typically found atop sidewalk metal grates, usually over places where buried steam pipes intersect—where steam typically escapes.

Many explosions of underground steam pipes have occurred in New York City in recent years. One of the most significant was on August 19, 1989, when a twenty-four-inch pipe exploded under a Manhattan street, killing three and injuring nineteen. Unlike New York, steam pipes in Philadelphia run eight feet beneath city sidewalks and are topped by heavy concrete. As such, they are also spared vibrations from vehicular traffic above. These factors account for why steam blasts are rare in the Quaker City.

The last time a major steam pipe burst in downtown Philadelphia was on September 14, 1989, at 15th and Wood Streets. A pipe had developed a twelve-inch fissure when it was re-pressurized following a shutdown during construction of the Vine Street Expressway. The explosion caused no injuries, but it spewed mud around the intersection and damaged cars. As a result of this incident, steam pipes are kept hot ("energized") at all times or are replaced whenever they are taken out of service for any length of time.

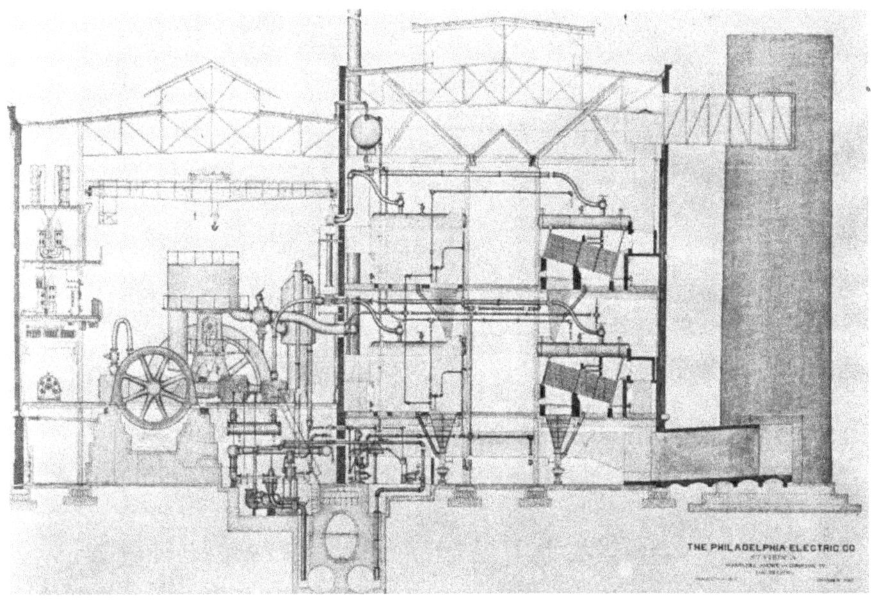

An early schematic of Philadelphia Electric Company's Schuylkill Station, Station A (later A-1). Constructed on a nine-acre plot, Schuylkill Station was planned to be the largest electricity generating station in the world, with a capacity of nearly 100,000 kilowatts. The plant generated AC current by burning coal received from barges and from both the Pennsylvania Railroad and the Baltimore & Ohio Railroad. *From* The Philadelphia Electrical Handbook *(1904).*

A boiler explosion at the Grays Ferry Cogeneration Plant on June 15, 2016, showed that steam generation is not for the faint of heart. The blast was felt and heard for miles and produced a great cloud of smoke above the plant. Safety valves had activated to relieve excess pressure, but the explosion happened anyway. Fortunately, injuries were few: a Veolia employee with minor burns and a bystander struck by flying glass.

Subsurface fires and explosions are more common with electrical conduits. Here are just two recent events involving buried PECO lines: On July 9, 2015, smoke billowed from manholes in the Old City/Society Hill neighborhood after an underground transformer fire near 2nd and Walnut left about a hundred PECO customers without power. And on May 22, 2016, a malfunctioning PECO cable at 6th and Pine led to a fire and then a blast that caused shattered windows and evacuations in the area. Nobody was hurt in these episodes, but it is only a matter of time before serious injuries occur as age catches up with Center City's buried infrastructure.

The Philadelphia Electric Company bored a $650,000 tunnel through bedrock about seventy feet below the Schuylkill River to carry both steam pipes and electrical transmission lines. The fifteen-foot-diameter passage was burrowed in 1946–47 after concerns arose that PECO's electrical cables might be severed by tankers on the Schuylkill. Armored submarine cables had previously transmitted power from Schuylkill Station under the river to the Pennsylvania Railroad's nearby catenary lines via the Arsenal Bridge Substation, located by the tunnel's western entrance. That end of the tunnel is inside a shack on the river's west bank next to the Schuylkill Arsenal Bridge; the tunnel's eastern end is a small structure at the intersection of Christian Street and Schuylkill Avenue. Veolia still uses this 1,070-foot-long utility tunnel, which also passes under the Schuylkill Expressway.

Nearby is the Arsenal Bridge, a two-track truss swing span erected in 1905 by the Pennsylvania Railroad. The moving section has been fixed in position for some time. The bridge passes above the past location of the Schuylkill Arsenal, for which it was named. Once located on the east bank of the Schuylkill in the Grays Ferry neighborhood, the facility was a manufacturing/supply depot for the U.S. military, built around 1800. The complex closed and was demolished by 1962, whereupon PECO secured the site and turned it into an electrical substation yard.

The west end of the Arsenal Bridge connects to the West Philadelphia Elevated Branch, which allows freight trains to completely bypass the 30th Street Station complex by using an elevated trestle—the "High Line"—just west of the station. Completed by the Pennsylvania Railroad in 1904, the Philadelphia High Line is a nearly two-mile-long, fifty-foot-high viaduct that runs along the west bank of the Schuylkill River, paralleling the Schuylkill Expressway.

The Arsenal Bridge's east end sends freight trains to the 25th Street Viaduct. This raised concrete structure carries railroad traffic over 25th Street to Greenwich Yard in South Philadelphia. Constructed by the Pennsylvania Railroad from 1926 to 1928 to aid in the abolition of grade crossings, the ponderous elevated line has been shedding chunks of concrete onto the roadway below for decades. CSX recently announced a multi-year project to restore the 25th Street Viaduct's condition and appearance.

Another Philadelphia arsenal complex is Frankford Arsenal, many miles from the downtown area. Closed since 1976 after 160 years as one of the nation's largest ordnance production centers, Frankford Arsenal is crisscrossed with miles of passageways filled with all sorts of electric and telephone conduits beneath the compound and its streets, as well as for interconnecting individual buildings. Several high-tech firms have leased bygone munitions factories there in recent years.

The Philadelphia State Hospital for the Insane was yet another complex of buildings outside Center City with myriad tunnels. The site was leveled around 2007, but throughout much the twentieth century, this institution was one of the largest and one of the leading mental hospitals in the nation, the standard by which other such hospitals were judged. Known locally as Byberry State Hospital, the fifty-plus building conglomerate was constructed between 1910 and 1950 on both the north and south sides of Roosevelt Boulevard in Northeast Philadelphia, near Byberry Road. Long subject to political corruption, mismanagement, and patient abuse, the asylum was finally shuttered by 1990. Byberry was then left to deteriorate, an urban-industrial ruin of huge medical structures interconnected by tunnels. There were disturbing stories that ex-inmates lived on the premises and that the complex was haunted, not to mention reports of occult activity. A housing development is now on the site.

Chapter 5

Connecting Philadelphia with Electricity, Telephone, and Cable Television Service

Few people are aware of the many contributions that Philadelphia is directly and indirectly responsible for in the realm of electrical generation and distribution. Much of the exploration and propagation of electricity's potential during the nineteenth and twentieth centuries transpired in Philadelphia under the auspices of The Philadelphia Electric Company and its predecessor firms. Furthermore, Philadelphia may justly be called the home of the phone, notwithstanding Boston's association with the telephone's inception.

The Centennial International Exposition of 1876 in Philadelphia heralded the modern age of electricity and telephones, as written in *Philadelphia: A Story of Progress* (1941):

> *The Centennial had two dramatic sequels which developed quickly. A telephone here and there was seen fastened against the wall in the business office. At almost the same revolutionary hour in world progress, a sputtering electric lamp amazed residents in this city. What those two products of wizard brains effected in Philadelphia was enjoyed in all forward looking communities. We know now that they changed completely in a few years manner of living and method of carrying on business intercourse.*

The local study of electrical energy began in the mid-1700s with Benjamin Franklin's research into the mysterious "ether" called electricity. With his kite and key experiment, Franklin conclusively confirmed that lightning and electricity were one and the same. It may have been only a theoretical experiment for Franklin, but it was successfully carried out by several European "electricians" (men who probed the secrets of electricity). The greatest scientific breakthrough of the eighteenth century, the experiment was celebrated through the world as "The Philadelphia Experiment."

Seeking to demonstrate that the "ether" could be employed for practical purposes, Franklin supposedly gave a public exhibition of the use of electricity for cooking in 1748. He declared that "[a] turkey is to be killed for our dinner by electrical shock, and roasted by the electrical jack, before a fire kindled by the electrified bottle." Franklin may have been joined by his fellow electrician friends (Ebenezer Kinnersley, Thomas Hopkinson, and Philip Syng) if this "electrical feast" actually happened.

The pragmatic application of electricity had to wait until the work of Thomas Edison in New Jersey about ninety years after Franklin's death. By the 1880s, Philadelphia electrical engineers Elihu Thomson, Edwin J. Houston, and William D. Marks had served in crucial roles in electricity's development. Plus, Philadelphian Coleman Sellers II designed the 1880s electric dynamos of the hydroelectric plant that first harnessed the power of Niagara Falls.

At the Centennial Exposition the decade prior, Charles Brush, an engineer from Cleveland, Ohio, demonstrated his invention, an efficient dynamo that generated electricity by steam power. The Franklin Institute in 1878 judged it superior to other dynamos due to its uncomplicated design and maintainability. Brush also devised his own version of an "arc lamp," a primitive apparatus that made light via an electrical current jumping between two sticks of carbon. The jump, or arc, produced a white glare that was immeasurably brighter than that of gas lamps then in use. His lights also were easier to maintain, had automatic functions, and burned twice as long as other arc lights. In 1880, Charles Brush established the Brush Electric Light Company, which licensed his dynamo and arc lamp system to enterprising individuals across the United States.

Industrialist Thomas Dolan (1834–1914) founded the Brush Electric Light Company of Philadelphia in 1881, funded by ten of the city's wealthiest merchandisers and manufacturers. One of Dolan's investors was John Wanamaker, who had already introduced Brush electric arc lamps at his Grand Depot department store at 13th and Market in 1878.

Opened in 1876, Wanamaker's Grand Depot was an old freight depot of the Pennsylvania Railroad. (It had grown into the largest retail store in America, if not the world, by the 1880s.) For $10,000, Dolan arranged for Charles Brush to install an eight-dynamo plant in the Grand Depot's basement to power twenty-eight Brush devices throughout the emporium. Wanamaker's retail store was the world's first with electric (arc lamp) lighting. Within months, stores and factories all over the United States rushed to have arc lights installed. (The Grand Depot was a precursor to the 1911 Wanamaker Building erected at the same spot across from City Hall.)

In 1881, Thomas Dolan tried to persuade Philadelphia's City Councils to enter a contract by which the city would pay his company $5,000 to illuminate Chestnut Street between the Delaware and the Schuylkill Rivers. Unsuccessful, he offered to string up the poles, wires, and arc lights and to provide the electricity at his expense as a demonstration. The equipment would be removed after a year if the city was not pleased.

Councils agreed, and more than 120 cast-iron lampposts were fixed along Chestnut to carry wires for forty-nine arc lamps. Dolan also built, at 20th and Ludlow, a Brush generating station, one of the first central electrical generating facilities in the nation. Four seventy-three-horsepower Babcock & Wilcox coal-firing boilers along with eight Porter-Allen steam engines provided power to eight Brush dynamos.

The Brush lights on Chestnut Street were first illuminated on December 3, 1881, at 1:30 a.m., attracting great curiosity and far outshining the typical gas streetlamps of that era. Interestingly, Chestnut Street's old gaslights burned along with the arc lamps during the successful yearlong trial; somebody had probably forgotten to cancel the gas contract for the street. The city was satisfied with the performance of Dolan's system, so it entered into an agreement with his company. Soon, other Philadelphia streets were lit with Brush equipment. (Thomas Dolan later dabbled in supplying the city with gas as president of the United Gas Improvement Company.)

The world's first international exhibition devoted to electricity and its use was held in Philadelphia for a five-week period beginning on September 2, 1884. Sponsored by the Franklin Institute, the International Electrical Exposition of 1884 took place at 32nd and Lancaster Avenue and was a great success. Nearly everyone in the city attended and became acquainted with Edison's incandescent lamp and his system of direct current (DC) power supply. The National Conference of Electricians was also convened at the Franklin Institute during the exhibition. This was the first national convention of electricians in the nation.

By the mid-1890s, Philadelphia had almost as many arc lights above city streets as New York, Chicago, and Boston combined. And with power lines now passing by their front doors, Philadelphians began running wires into their homes and started swapping gas lamps with electric lights.

It was not until the 1920s that incandescent bulbs surpassed arc lamps on lampposts. In current times, the city is seeking to replace high-pressure sodium lamps on light posts with LED lights. Street lighting is the biggest user of electricity in Philadelphia, accounting for 32 percent of public energy use. Switching to LEDs will cost tens of millions of dollars and take years to accomplish but should reduce the city's carbon emissions by 13,700 metric tons annually.

The Brush Electric Light Company of Philadelphia merged with its competitors to form Philadelphia Electric Company. The firm had incorporated in New Jersey on October 5, 1899, but a separate The Philadelphia Electric Company (with "The" as part of its name) was incorporated in Pennsylvania three years later to act as a subsidiary comprised of firms such as Brush Electric. A merger of that company with the Philadelphia Suburban-Counties Gas & Electric Company and three other utility companies in 1929 created a much larger Philadelphia Electric Company (PECO). Unicom Corporation of Chicago and PECO merged in 2000 to form Exelon Corporation, based in Chicago.

The Philadelphia Electric Company demolished the old Brush Station on Ludlow in 1909 and replaced it with a one-story building. The plain brick structure now functions as the Ludlow Substation for PECO, converting high-voltage electricity into a lower voltage that circulates through Center City's electrical grid. It is also used by SEPTA as a power converter facility.

The Edison Generating Station at 908 Sansom Street was erected by the Edison Electric Light Company of Philadelphia as the world's largest electric power plant, as well as the country's first generating facility specifically built as an Edison station. Enough machinery was installed and twenty-eight miles of underground conduits were laid to supply direct current (DC) to any home or business in Philadelphia's downtown. The eight-story plant went into operation on March 5, 1889.

Demand for lighting was so overwhelming that the Edison Station's capacity was repeatedly boosted until a 100,000-light electrical output was reached. Of this amount, one-third was used to power machines operated by electricity, such as elevators, printing presses, and ventilation fans. What's more, exhaust steam from the Edison Station's engines warmed a nearby house, thus inaugurating Philadelphia's district steam heating system.

Alternating current (AC) triumphed over direct current (DC) in electrical production by the early twentieth century, and given that the dynamos of

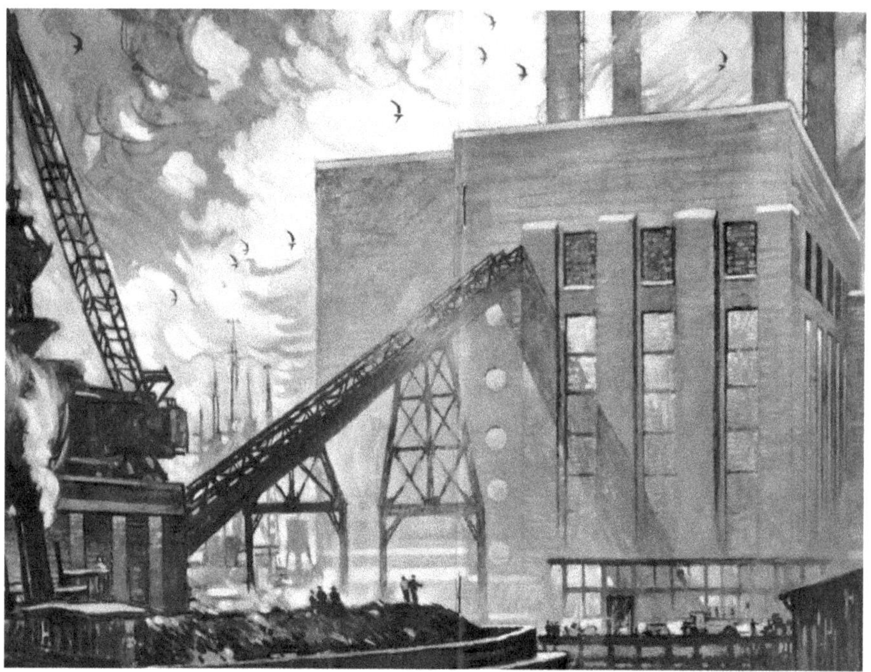

This bustling illustration of the Southwark Generation Station, depicted by "T. Oakley," appears in *Southwark Electric Generating Station*, a late 1940s promotional brochure for the power plant issued by Philadelphia Electric Company. Built for $45 million, it is still in use today. The station's exterior was designed by French-born Philadelphia architect Paul Crét. *Harry Kyriakodis's collection.*

the 1880s Edison Station could produce only DC current, the facility was withdrawn from service in 1930. It was torn down twelve years later, with its structural steel going to World War II scrap drives. Since 1958, the Edison Steam Plant—put up by PECO but now owned by Veolia Energy—has been at 908 Sansom Street.

Immediately next door, at the southwest corner of 9th and Sansom, is PECO's onetime headquarters building, built in 1927 and designed by Philadelphia architect John Torrey Windrim (1866–1934). The twenty-three-story structure is still called the Edison Building, even though it is now owned by Thomas Jefferson University. Exhaust smoke can sometimes be seen issuing from the exceedingly tall smokestack attached to the tower's west side. The smoke comes from Veolia's adjacent steam generation plant.

The first electrical generation plant that The Philadelphia Electric Company erected rather than inherited is the aforementioned Schuylkill Station at 26th and Christian. Built in 1902–3 on the site of a former streetcar powerhouse, the station had two electrical generating units: A-1 and A-2. Unit A-1's original equipment included a two-megawatt generator and a five-megawatt generator, both powered by steam from thirty-two coal-fired boilers, fed by hand. Three vertical turbines replaced the original generators in 1906. The boilers were converted to oil in 1935 so as to avoid supply problems caused by striking coal miners.

Unit A-2, added in 1914, provided two more generators: a thirty-five-megawatt generator for general power production and a thirty-megawatt generator for furnishing current to the Pennsylvania Railroad and the Philadelphia Rapid Transit Company, among other large power consumers. In 1950, PECO began cogeneration operation at Schuylkill Station, using exhaust steam to supply steam for heat in the city's steam distribution network. Conspicuous from the Schuylkill Expressway, Schuylkill Station is now primarily a steam generation plant operated by Veolia Energy. Its last electrical generating unit was shut down in 2012.

Schuylkill Station was the first of a series of palatial power plants built to service the greater Philadelphia area in the early 1900s. PECO conceived them to convey a sense of solidity and permanence in a time of public skepticism about electricity. The generating stations were all positioned along the Delaware River to access a constant supply of water and coal (via barges):

- Chester Station: One of the most magnificent power plants in the world, this facility was built in Chester, Pennsylvania, by the Delaware County Electric Company before its merger with PECO. The plant opened in 1918 as PECO's first expansion outside Philadelphia, providing electricity for one of the nation's largest manufacturing centers. Shuttered in 1982, Chester Station has been transformed into an impressive business/conference center called "Wharf at Rivertown."
- Delaware Station: This plant was constructed during World War I on a 16.4-acre site next to Penn Treaty Park, not far from the center of town. Looked on with amazement when new, it was placed in service on October 31, 1920, complete with the words "Philadelphia The Electric City" lit by light bulbs in seventeen-foot-tall letters on the roof facing south. ("The Electric City" was an old Philly nickname.) There are plans to give Delaware Station a new life as an event venue and hotel, as it was mothballed in 2004.

- Richmond Station: Entering service in 1925 as the world's largest coal-firing electric plant, the station is located at the foot of Lewis Street near the Northeast Water Pollution Control Plant. Besides its distinctive Neoclassical exterior, Richmond Station's interior was defined by tremendous open spaces, including a cavernous Turbine Hall with curved skylights along a cruciform ceiling. Among many customers, the facility supplied electricity to the Pennsylvania Railroad, powering electrified trains from New York to Washington, D.C. Desolate since 1985, it has since been used for motion picture locations, such as *12 Monkeys* (1995), *Transformers 2* (2009) and *The Last Airbender* (2010).
- Southwark Station: This smaller power plant opened in 1948 at Oregon Avenue in South Philadelphia. Built to generate 338 million watts of power through burning either coal or oil, Southwark Station is still in use, now firing only oil.
- Eddystone Station: The nation's most efficient power plant when it commenced service in 1960, this facility was erected on forty-five acres of riverside property at Eddystone, Pennsylvania. Its two coal-burning units were retired by 2012; Eddystone now generates 820 million watts of power by burning natural gas and oil.

Resembling public libraries or train stations, the first three of these metropolitan PECO complexes were designed by John Windrim with the notion of making the city more aesthetically appealing. (This interest in adorning Philadelphia sprang from the Progressive era's City Beautiful movement and the Columbian Exposition of 1893 in Chicago.) Windrim's imperial electrical plants burned coal, making PECO the city's dominant coal user into the 1970s. In spite of their size, efficacy, and architectural merit, each one was vacated after alternative methods of power generation came to the forefront.

The Crown Lights electronic messaging board encircling the top of PECO's "Tower of Light" headquarters at 23rd and Market is a Philadelphia institution. The message system originally consisted of 2,600 individual thirty-watt light bulbs that rendered a scrolling display of white letters and numbers. On July 4, 1976, the lights went live, displaying community missives for and about local organizations. An enhanced display using light-emitting diodes, for color and energy savings, was installed atop the twenty-seven-story tower in 2009.

PECO owns some 1,067 miles of high-voltage transmission lines, roughly 15,200 square miles of subterraneous distribution cable, and nearly 13,000 miles of aerial distribution lines. The company further maintains hundreds of electrical vaults and substations throughout Philadelphia. Many are around the large power plants mentioned earlier, while others are located within the city neighborhoods they serve.

One downtown electrical substation is along both sides of Noble Street, between 11th and 12th, within the split of the Reading Railroad's tracks leaving Reading Terminal. Built around 1960, Noble Street Substation feeds electricity to about 20 percent of Center City. It would have been buried at great cost if a Phillies baseball stadium had been built there, as was bandied about in the 1990s.

In 1966, Independence Mall Substation was built as a subterranean substation at the southeast corner of 6th and Arch. It is the first underground substation-vault ever attempted, as well as one of the largest, becoming necessary when construction of the William Green Federal Building meant demolition of Philadelphia Electric's 1920s Franklin Substation at 52 North 6th Street. Since Mall Substation had to supply the power needs of Old City while preserving the neighborhood's historic ambiance, it was concealed within the footprint of Independence National Historical Park.

Mall Substation is a concrete box-vault, 75 feet wide by 225 feet long, with 21-foot ceilings and 18-inch-thick walls. It was constructed in two sections separated by a concrete wall, allowing one side to operate in the event of a malfunction in the other. Its floor is 30 feet below ground, while its roof is 8 feet below to allow for plantings on the surface. An entrance for personnel and equipment is screened with red brick walls near Arch Street to blend with the colonial character of Independence Park.

Only a stone's throw away is the Federal Reserve Bank of Philadelphia, one of the twelve regional Reserve Banks that make up the Federal Reserve System. The building has a Cash Operations section forty feet below street level, with a cash vault the size of a football field. Billions of dollars in cash could be stored in this highly secure vault; some of the nation's gold reserves are stockpiled here too. The United States Mint (the fourth Philadelphia Mint), on the east side of Independence Park, also contains immense vaults partially underground. These oversized federal government facilities were constructed in the 1960s and '70s.

Between the Federal Reserve Bank and the U.S. Mint is the National Constitution Center (NCC), which opened on July 4, 2003. Two years before, a major telephone trunk line was unearthed passing through NCC property between 5th and 6th. The concrete-encased conduit, about twenty feet across and likely about as deep, had not appeared on any city utility maps. It was evidently laid in the early twentieth century underneath Cherry Street, a roadway that was eliminated in the 1960s for the creation of Independence Park.

The conduit was first thought to be carrying the hotline between the White House and the Kremlin, but that turned out to be false. Nevertheless, Verizon deemed it important enough to demand moving it at a cost of $10 million. The NCC balked at this figure and agreed to merely build around it for $2 million. Still below the National Constitution Center today, the telephone trunk in all likelihood heads toward and under the Delaware River on its way to New York City. (Chapter 18 describes archaeological digs at the NCC.)

It was at the Centennial Exposition that Alexander Graham Bell first publicly exhibited his telephone instrument and transmitted "To be, or not to be" over electrical wires. These words were distinctly heard by the emperor of Brazil, who cried out (possibly in Portuguese), "My God! It talks!"

In 1877, Thomas E. Cornish (1838–1924), a Philadelphia "electrician," returned to the Quaker City from Boston with examples of Bell's invention and a franchise to form a telephone company in Philadelphia. He set up one

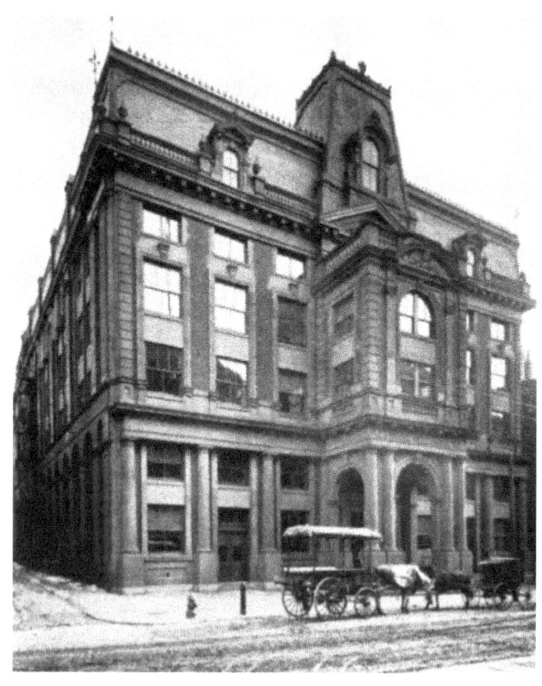

The Keystone Telephone Company was once headquartered in this building along 2nd Street near Walnut. This was originally the site of the "Slate Roof House," where William Penn lived from 1699 to 1701. The house was demolished in 1867 to make way for the Commercial Exchange Building, used by the Philadelphia Chamber of Commerce and sold in 1901 to Keystone to become the Keystone Telephone Building. Bell Telephone eventually came to own the structure but sold it in 1944. It was abandoned in 1961 and torn down in 1977–78. The site is now Welcome Park, an open recreational space in Old City Philadelphia. *From* The Philadelphia Electrical Handbook *(1904).*

Bell telephone in his home and the another at his office at 1111 Chestnut Street. Cornish also added a switchboard from which he ran wires to promising financial supporters. The Pennsylvania Railroad was one of his first telephone subscribers.

Cornish chartered the Bell Telephone Company of Philadelphia on September 18, 1879, and was elected its president. Within five years, at least four competing telephone companies were established in the city. Bell Telephone would ultimately own them all. The firm established its first headquarters at 4th and Chestnut Streets and became Bell Telephone Company of Pennsylvania in 1907.

The world's first intercity telephone call was made from a building at the northwest corner of 10th and Chestnut, then Western Union Telegraph Company's quarters. Elisha Gray, Alexander Graham Bell's great rival in telegraphy, used his "telegraphic reed transmitter" on April 2, 1877, to send a signal over ordinary telegraph wires to New York City. The call was, in reality, the world's first long-distance telephone concert, for a piano was played in the Western Union building that was heard by an audience at New York's Steinway Hall.

Wanamaker's Grand Depot store was the first retail establishment in the world to install Bell telephones for public use. This was in 1879, in the same store that John Wanamaker had introduced Brush arc lights the year before. The Grand Depot further instituted the world's first (and eventually largest) private store phone system by 1900. Wanamaker's was the first store to offer twenty-four-hour telephone service for order taking in 1905.

With miles of telephone and electric power lines interweaving downtown Philadelphia by the early 1880s, the city was virtually littered with wooden "telephone" poles carrying a maze of telegraph, telephone, and electric light wires of competing companies. Trolley wires also added to the untidy mess of cables over the streets of Philadelphia. The hanging wires made the streets ugly and increasingly hazardous, as storm damage frequently caused lines to fall, oftentimes short-circuiting other lines.

Compelled to act, City Councils voted on June 13, 1882, to notify the owners of overhead wires between Vine and South Streets to begin placing them underground. Councils took up the issue again two years later, resolving to require the installation of all electrical cables in conduits by January 1, 1885. Existing poles were removed, and additional ones were not permitted to be erected. Yet another wire and pole ordinance in 1885 strengthened the initial ones. The outcome of these edicts is that downtown Philly is generally free of hanging wires and poles that support them. Philadelphia was one of the first cities anywhere to mandate the placement of electrical wires underground.

One may ask: Why does PECO not place all its wires—the ones outside Center City—underground? The answer is that the cost of doing so would more than double rates for electricity, since stringing overhead wires is five to ten times less expensive than burying them. Moreover, underground cables are more difficult to repair and are subject to breakage when trees are uprooted or when streets, sewers, or water mains are excavated.

The Keystone Telephone Company was a late competitor to Bell Telephone in Philadelphia. Founded in 1900, Keystone installed the world's first phone system with all wires in underground conduits. The company subsequently implemented the first large-scale automatic system for telephone switching in America in about 1921.

In 1904, Keystone's 10.5 million feet of conduit were accessible via 5,200 manholes, many of which are still around (stamped with "KTCo"). The Philadelphia Electric Company that year needed a network of conduits to supply its growing consumer base with electric service. So, PECO simply purchased the Keystone Telephone Company's underground conduit system. The agreement was viewed as protective for Keystone, since PECO was not permitted to enter the telephone business as part of the deal.

Keystone operated only seven central exchanges at its peak and assigned one number to each exchange. As a result, its telephone numbers were only five digits long, one for the exchange and four for the extension, as opposed to seven-digit numbers used by Bell. Print ads highlighted this feature, billing Keystone's as "the fastest telephone in Philadelphia."

The Quaker City therefore had two independent telephone systems in the first half of the twentieth century, along with separate networks of wires, conduits, and exchanges. Keystone chiefly catered to business clients, which is why most city businesses maintained and advertised both a Keystone and a Bell number. The firm also handled municipal, police, and fire communications; for years, city workers phoned each other "on the Keystone."

Philadelphia was the last large city in the United States with competing phone companies. Keystone was one of Bell Telephone's last rivals when it was finally absorbed by Bell in 1944. Service ended on September 17, 1945.

Bell Telephone Company expanded its service to the national level in the early 1900s. It began by laying an eighty-seven-mile-long underground cable that would allow the nation's first intercity telephone conversation not carried by hanging wires. Occurring between Philadelphia and New

York City in 1906, this phone call inaugurated the countrywide telephone network known and used today.

On February 11, 1915, the Liberty Bell—that iconic symbol of American independence—was used to demonstrate Bell Telephone's new transcontinental telephone service. At its display setting in Independence Hall, the historic bell was tapped with a mallet, and its sound was electrically amplified and sent over telephone wires to San Francisco, with amplifiers along the way. This was the first official transcontinental telephone call in America.

The Liberty Bell has its own subterraneous saga. Two stories about the bell arose after British troops occupied Philadelphia in 1777, when it was feared that the city's bells would be melted to make cannonballs. One account is that the then-named State House Bell was taken from the Pennsylvania State House (Independence Hall) and hidden by being sunk into the Delaware River with other bells from local churches. The other is that the not-yet-famous bell was placed onto a cart and furtively whisked off to Allentown, Pennsylvania, accompanied by other bells, and then concealed in the basement of Allentown's Zion's Reformed Church. Whatever the case, all the bells were returned to their regular venues after the British left in 1778.

During the early years of World War II, the Insurance Company of North America offered to fabricate a fireproof and bombproof vault for the Liberty Bell's protection in Independence Hall. The City of Philadelphia accepted the overture, as it would cost the city nothing, but the War Production Board would not allocate steel for the undertaking, despite letters of support from around the country. By 1943, the threat of German bombings had passed, so no shelter for the Liberty Bell was made.

The Cold War renewed thoughts about the Liberty Bell's security, with the Philadelphia Civil Defense Council calling for a concrete vault to preserve the bell from nuclear attack. Furthermore, a lift would swiftly lower the relic into the ground with the push of a button. Once more, no action was taken.

Underground protection for the Liberty Bell was contemplated yet again after the 2001 terrorist attacks. The National Park Service also suggested a tunnel under Chestnut Street for visitor access to Independence Hall. This passageway was rejected due to the expense and other reasons. The Liberty Bell was left to fend for itself—on display, with no underground safeguards—inside the new Liberty Bell Center (erected in 2003) on 6th Street, between Market and Chestnut.

Christ Church was one of the local houses of worship that dispatched its bells to Allentown. In 1909, the church was the subject of national newspaper articles about a tunnel that was discovered leading to a hardware store basement at 211–13 Market Street. Described as more than two hundred feet long, three feet wide, seven feet high, and seventeen feet below ground with a paved floor, the so-called Revolutionary Tunnel supposedly began under the steeple tower and passed beneath Church Street. A blocked stairwell into the tower was found, as were (allegedly) the skeletons of eight men. The bodies were in casual stances, as if they had died there, trapped underground.

News of the find proliferated until it became speculated that the purported tunnel solved the puzzle as to how Christ Church's eight bells were spirited away during the first night of Philadelphia's 1777–78 occupation, while British soldiers patrolled around the church. But the passage had surely not been burrowed for that reason.

The footprint of 211–13 Market is now parkland for Independence National Historical Park, so this north–south tunnel is long gone, and its precise intent remains a mystery. Notwithstanding many explicit news articles, the "Revolutionary Tunnel" story and its unsettling details were never broached again anywhere after 1909. The overall account, then, is probably apocryphal, perhaps stemming from a brick-lined cavern or vault of some kind discovered there.

Getting back to Bell, the company in 1880 laid a submarine cable on the bed of the Delaware River to facilitate telephone communication between Philadelphia and Camden, New Jersey. For decades afterward, such cables on the riverbed were often mangled by ship anchors. The problem was rectified after World War II when Bell buried twelve replacement cables in a V-shaped trench ten feet below the Delaware, off Arch Street. The armored cables were three thousand feet long and weighed thirty tons apiece.

Bell Telephone had developed and installed a long-distance coaxial telephone/television cable between Philadelphia and New York City by 1936. The experimental cable proceeded through Philadelphia and Bucks County, Pennsylvania, to the Delaware River, opposite Trenton, New Jersey. It crossed over the river via an extant bridge and then continued through the New Jersey countryside to New York, with booster stations five to ten miles apart. Bell used the line to transmit the 1940 Republican National Convention, held in Philadelphia, to New York—the first time a major political event was carried via television signal between major American cities.

On their way to New York, the signals passed through the Bell Telephone Central Telephone Building on the southwest corner of 9th and Race.

Rising eleven stories above Philly's Chinatown, the eye-catching structure was designed by John T. Windrim in the early 1930s and is now occupied by Verizon. Windrim drew up imposing edifices for Bell Telephone as he did for PECO.

Indeed, Bell's headquarters buildings in Philadelphia have been noteworthy for their size and handsome appearance. Bell Parkway Building at 17th and Arch was completed in 1915 in anticipation of the Ben Franklin Parkway's construction. It was the most modern telephone switching building in the world at the time. Besides having five large switchboards and a dozen smaller ones, it had two floors that served as dining and rest areas for the seven hundred female operators who manually routed calls. (A good operator made five to ten phone connections per minute with precision.) Bell Parkway Building continues to serve as a switching hub and office space for Verizon and is now called the Parkway Central Office Building.

Two other Bell Telephone skyscrapers along the Ben Franklin Parkway were designed long after Windrim's death. The $15.5 million Bell Telephone Company Building, with its distinctive stainless steel façade, is at 16th and Arch. Finished in 1961, it was renamed One Parkway years ago. And the fifty-five-story Bell Atlantic Tower was completed in 1991 on Arch Street. The red granite edifice has been renamed Three Logan Square.

John Windrim also drew up scores of smaller telephone exchange buildings for Philadelphia neighborhoods in the early twentieth century. Exchanges housed complicated switching equipment and were often staffed with operators who connected telephone calls. Many are still around, though generally not assigned to telephone service anymore.

In 1967, Bell Telephone commissioned what is currently called the Verizon Building at 24th and South, beside the east bank of the Schuylkill River and CSX Railroad's East Side tracks (Chapter 9). Voice and data communications pass through it for the entire Atlantic coast. Finished in 1974 and known also as the AT&T Communications Building (or Data Center), the telecom monolith serves as a centralized hub for the region's phone system and houses what may be the world's most advanced automated switchboard system. The ungainly brick and glass structure, looking like a futuristic fortress or prison, was erected at that location because telephone trunk lines run along the bordering CSX tracks. Since the Verizon Building may also be a covert telecommunication surveillance facility for the U.S. National Security Agency, its front doorway is hidden, seemingly on purpose, behind a plaza at the corner of 27th and Lombard. Only a few workers use the building, which has walls five feet thick to withstand a nuclear blast.

Bell Atlantic merged with GTE Corporation to establish Verizon in 2000, and then the telecom conglomerate decamped to New York City.

Cable television arrived relatively early in Philadelphia. In 1966, City Council passed a bill dividing the city into six cable zones, each with a cable franchisee. But only one was able to devise a working system. Thirteen years thereafter, City Council approved an ordinance that created four service areas in the city and required franchise winners to afford full cable service to customers within five years after securing bids.

In the 1980s, cable TV became a hot potato in Philly, with political favoritism, redrawn service boundaries, and other issues—not to mention the royal mess created around town for years when sidewalks were dug up to install telecom wires. The city was at last wired for cable television by the late 1980s, and one of the franchisees, Comcast Cablevision of Philadelphia, was the clear winner of the turmoil.

Comcast Cable had grown into one of the world's leading telecommunications companies by the 1990s. The company's acquisition of AT&T's Broadband cable business in 2002 shifted the center of the cable universe to Philadelphia by forming the world's largest cable and high-speed Internet company. In 2011, Comcast concluded a merger with NBC Universal.

Rectangular covers made of fiberglass provide access to electrical and cable vaults and tunnels running below city sidewalks. These lids cannot withstand the weight of a motor vehicle. One cable service cover gave way in 2009 when the wheel of a telescoping lift machine broke through while being used on the pavement at 21st and Walnut. The lift toppled over and hurled its unlucky operator to his sudden death.

Chapter 6

The Pennsylvania Railroad, Broad Street Station, and The Philadelphia Improvements

The Pennsylvania Railroad Company (PARR) was chartered by Philadelphia tradesmen in 1846 to build a trunk route from Philadelphia to Pittsburgh. This rail line would compete for freight traffic that had started to bypass Pennsylvania in favor of New York due to the Erie Canal.

From that modest beginning, the Pennsylvania Railroad evolved into an eleven-thousand-mile behemoth running through the cities of New York, Washington, Chicago, and St. Louis. It became the largest railroad in the United States in terms of traffic and corporate assets from the last quarter of the nineteenth century until the decline of northeastern and midwestern manufacturing. The conglomerate owned its own shops, coal mines, power plants, and hotels—plus hundreds of depots, thousands of passenger cars, tens of thousands of freight cars, and a substantial fleet of steam, electric, and diesel locomotives. At its zenith, the PARR employed 280,000 people who moved five thousand trains per day! *Fortune* magazine once called the mighty Pennsylvania Railroad a "nation unto itself." The city of Philadelphia served as the PARR's headquarters and base of operations from the outset.

On December 5, 1881, Broad Street Station opened as the Pennsylvania Railroad's main passenger station in Philadelphia along Filbert Street (now JFK Boulevard). This majestic Victorian Gothic–style station brought the PARR's tracks from West Philadelphia right into downtown Philly directly across from City Hall, then under construction. Designed by Wilson Brothers & Company, Broad Street Station initially had eight tracks that entered the station on the second floor. The bustling place handled an average of 160 trains a day in 1889.

The terminal was enlarged toward the south (to Market Street) by eminent Philadelphia architect Frank Furness in the early 1890s, about the time that Wilson Brothers added a colossal glass and steel trainshed overhead. This was the world's largest single-span roof above a train station, covering sixteen tracks and making Broad Street Station one of the largest railroad passenger terminals on Earth.

The huge trainshed burned down on June 11, 1923, in one of Philadelphia's most destructive blazes. An alert conductor of a switch engine outside the station remembered that passengers were sleeping in Pullman cars under the shed. As flames spread, he had his engineer back the engine into the trainshed and then heroically jumped out to connect it to the sleeper cars. This enabled pulling the Pullmans out of the shed, thus saving the lives of some two hundred travelers. The trainshed was replaced with numerous platform shelters, most of which burned in another fire in 1943.

Broad Street Station's headhouse contained a main waiting room (often with a raging fire in its hearth) and a ladies' waiting room, together with a restaurant reachable by stairs and dumbwaiters from the kitchen above. Influential men and women from around the world made their way from the lobby to the train concourse on the second floor. The third and fourth floors were used as office space for the Pennsylvania Railroad, and a pedestrian passageway crossing over Market Street connected Broad Street Station to the Arcade Building across the street. Service was steadily expanded until more than 450 trains operated in and out of the terminal every day.

But as a stub-end station, Broad Street Station was not operationally efficient. Through-trains had to be reconfigured or run backward to join the PARR mainline headed to West Philadelphia, which created an intolerable level of congestion by the early twentieth century. The Pennsylvania Railroad critically needed a main through-station to improve service in the swelling Philadelphia market. Since plans for the Benjamin Franklin Parkway blocked any northern expansion of Broad Street Station, the PARR resolutely decided to supplant the terminal—as well as a too-distant station in West Philadelphia.

The unpretentious West Philadelphia Station was located on Market Street east of 32nd. It was opened in 1903 to address the awkwardness of Philadelphia's chief train station, as trains traveling from New York City to Washington, D.C., would avoid backing into Broad Street Station. West Philadelphia Station superseded the Pennsylvania Railroad's Centennial

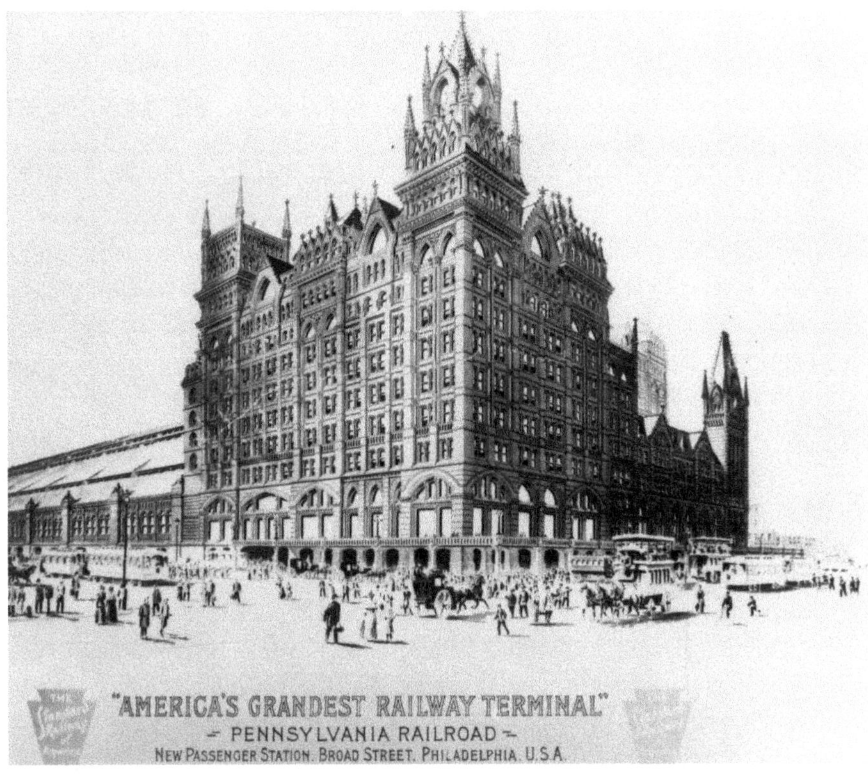

Broad Street Station brought the Pennsylvania Railroad's tracks into the heart of Philadelphia, directly across from City Hall. The terminal became among the world's largest railroad stations when it was expanded by Frank Furness in the early 1890s. (The Furness expansion is the larger portion in the drawing's center.) Wilson Brothers & Company also added the colossal train shed. This promotional depiction came out in 1893, after the Pennsylvania Railroad designated Broad Street Station as "America's Grandest Railway Terminal." *Library of Congress.*

Station, an elaborate depot built at 32nd and Market for the Centennial International Exposition of 1876. Centennial Station brought thousands of visitors to the World's Fair, dropping them off near the exposition's entrance gate at Belmont and Parkside Avenues. It burned down in 1896, and West Philadelphia Station replaced it in 1903.

Centennial Station, incidentally, took the place of a PARR station at 30th and Market Streets, more or less on the spot where the Market Street (Subway) Line's 30th Street Station is today. The Pennsylvania Railroad completed its *original* 30th Street Station in 1864 because a city ordinance banned steam locomotives from entering Philadelphia's downtown area. Trains stopped on the west bank of the Schuylkill River, where the locomotives were uncoupled, and passenger cars were then pulled into the city by teams of oxen and horses. Early PARR depots at 13th, 11th, and 8th Streets were then accessed by railroad tracks on the surface of Market Street. This is how the PARR entered downtown Philadelphia from the west through much of the 1800s. However, the situation became untenable as Center City developed.

The 1864 station at 30th and Market replaced the very first PARR station in West Philadelphia, a small depot at 31st and Chestnut dating to the 1850s.

These stations were all in the vicinity of the Thirty-Second Street Tunnel, the first instance of below-grade transit infrastructure in Philly. Still regularly used by SEPTA Regional Rail trains heading to and from points south, the two-tracked passageway goes beneath 32nd Street for just over a block from JFK Boulevard to Chestnut Street through Drexel University. Quite a bit of blasting was done to create the tunnel, which is encased by strong masonry. The route continues south through the University of Pennsylvania campus as an open-air trench. Outdoor seating for a restaurant is directly above the southern portal.

Known originally as the Junction Railroad Tunnel, the Thirty-Second Street Tunnel was built in the mid-1860s by the Junction Railroad Company, a rail line owned jointly by the Pennsylvania, the Philadelphia & Reading, and the Philadelphia, Wilmington & Baltimore Railroads. The right-of-way was part of the PARR's Grays Ferry Branch, which (in the days before 30th Street Station) was used by through-trains between New York and Washington that saved time by stopping at West Philadelphia Station instead of heading to Broad Street Station. (West Philadelphia Station had passenger platforms inside the tunnel.) The Junction Railroad route came under the PARR's full control in 1881 and was eliminated by merger in 1908.

The Pennsylvania Railroad substantially reconstructed the Thirty-Second Street Tunnel in 1926 in anticipation of greater use with the expected opening of 30th Street Station. The tunnel was enlarged from twenty-four to thirty-one feet wide and from sixteen to eighteen feet high. It needed this enlargement for the pantographs of trains, since the Pennsylvania Railroad had electrified its lines about that time (to be discussed).

In the 1950s, the tunnel was lengthened after Pennsylvania (later JFK) Boulevard was built immediately west of 30th Street Station; part of the roadway sits atop the tunnel. The lengthened segment, now partially discarded, continues north to SEPTA's "Powelton Yards" railyard behind 30th Street Station. The tracks are removed, but the tunnel fragment is still intact and visible from SEPTA trains turning into the station. It is slowly being filled with crushed rock and will disappear in time.

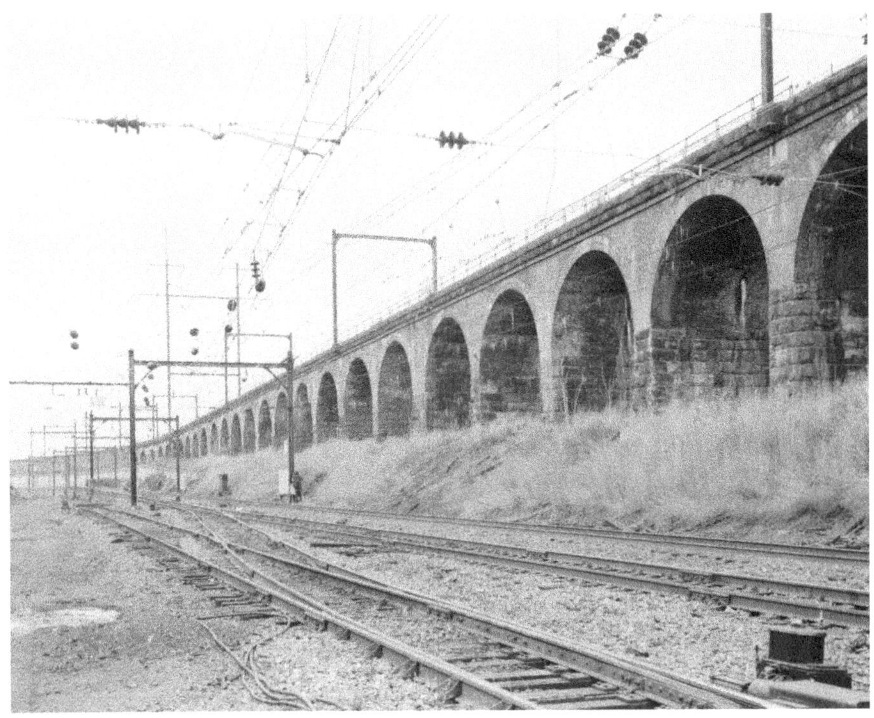

Freight trains completely bypass the 30th Street Station complex by using an elevated trestle called the West Philadelphia Elevated Branch—the "Philadelphia High Line"—just west of the station. Completed by the Pennsylvania Railroad in 1904, the High Line is a nearly two-mile-long, fifty-foot-high viaduct that runs along the west bank of the Schuylkill River, paralleling the Schuylkill Expressway. North of 30th Street Station, the two-track elevated steel trestle incorporates the longest brick arch bridge in the United States. *Library of Congress.*

PARR facilities throughout the city had become woefully inadequate by the 1920s. After several attempts at enlargement and modernization, a plan developed to not only drastically revamp the Pennsylvania Railroad's rail system in and around Philadelphia but also correct some railroad-created eyesores—including the elimination of Broad Street Station. This mammoth undertaking was christened the "Philadelphia Passenger Terminal Improvements Project," or simply "The Philadelphia Improvements."

The project encompassed the eradication of the formidable viaduct that carried PARR tracks to Broad Street Station from West Philadelphia. Derogatorily dubbed the "Chinese Wall" in view of its resemblance to the Great Wall of China, this grim elevated structure was a block wide at places and supported by earth fill between two immense stone retaining walls. Warehouse and office space for shipping companies was also between the walls. Properly called the Filbert Street Extension, the Chinese Wall upheld nine main tracks, more than a dozen spur tracks in a railyard, and a locomotive turntable. Heading west from Broad Street Station, three rail bridges over the Schuylkill brought trains to the Penn Coach Yard in West Philadelphia, on the west side of the river. (Now used by Amtrak, the Penn Coach Yard was laid out by the PARR starting in the 1850s.)

The Chinese Wall effectively divided Center City Philadelphia across the middle along Market Street from the Schuylkill River to 16th Street. North–south pedestrian and vehicular traffic was discouraged by the structure's squat underpasses that conducted numbered cross streets beneath the structure. These low-arched stone tunnels were not below the ground, but the effect of walking through them was very subterranean in nature. Aside from being long and dark, the passages were claustrophobic and continually dripped coal-sooted water that leached down from the tracks above. They helped make the western part of Center City unpleasant for seventy years. (But the arched tunnels did have exceptional acoustics; doo-wop groups sang inside them in the early 1950s.)

The precarious underpasses of the Lehigh Avenue Viaduct in Philadelphia's Port Richmond neighborhood give an inkling as to the bleakness of the old Chinese Wall's under-passages. The block-wide rail right-of-way runs over a mile alongside Lehigh Avenue from the railyards of Port Richmond west to Kensington Avenue (and beyond). Formally called the Richmond Branch Elevated, the viaduct lies within the block-wide space between Lehigh and Somerset Avenues.

From 1848 until the 1960s, the Richmond Branch of the Reading Railroad brought coal trains from the country's richest seams of anthracite in eastern Pennsylvania to Port Richmond along the Delaware River. The viaduct was once the world's busiest coal transport line, with one segment carrying as many as two dozen railroad tracks to the Port Richmond Yards, for generations the world's largest privately owned railroad tidewater terminal.

A remaining coal-loading dock at the former Port Richmond Yards is now known as "Graffiti Pier." Abandoned by Conrail in 1991, old Pier 18 has been reclaimed by nature, and its collection of concrete pillars has become a wildly popular destination for urban adventurers. Graffiti writers have turned the industrial ruins into an ever-changing, unsanctioned, open-air folk art museum along the Delaware's western bank. (This is somewhat appropriate, for the subversive art of modern graffiti began in Philadelphia.) Philadelphia police have recently started cracking down on trespassers because of the site's popularity and inherent danger.

The Lehigh Viaduct was built in the years before World War I to abolish grade crossings along the Richmond Branch. It was considered a rather everyday occurrence to be struck by a train or a trolley in Philadelphia in the late 1800s and early 1900s. While this could be explained by the myriad train and trolley lines on city streets before the automobile came to be, train and trolley dodging was deemed a fine sport, and general carelessness seems to have ruled the day. Children were the most common victims.

Railroads operating on city streets were especially problematic in Philadelphia into the twentieth century, reflecting an age when local railroads were an integral part of the city's day-to-day affairs. The railroads did provide crossing watchmen and gates at some major street-rail intersections, but this was not enough to avert innumerable accidents each year. Hundreds of people were killed or maimed at rail crossings annually in the City of Brotherly Love.

The city began encouraging railroads to eliminate grade crossings in the 1880s, although the effort really took off in the early 1900s. Railroad lines could be elevated or depressed. Either way, such projects were expensive and disruptive, involving the construction or reconstruction of retaining walls, abutments, embankments, temporary trestles, new passenger terminals, freight depots, coaling stations, and other railroad infrastructure. They additionally included street regrading and repaving, reconstruction of water mains and sewers, and strengthening of building foundations (aka underpinning). The city and the railroad usually shared the cost of these improvements.

The Richmond Branch is among the best examples of grade crossing abolishment in Philadelphia. It was accomplished through a combination of raising the tracks (about five to eight feet) and lowering the surrounding streets. This is why houses and streets on both sides of the Lehigh Viaduct look as if they were elevated: existing streets were actually regraded downward, foundations were bolstered, and steps were added to enter the homes. The Reading Railroad did this for hundreds of properties within the neighborhoods lining the Richmond Branch tracks.

The Market-Frankford Elevated transit line crosses over the Lehigh Viaduct with an impressive truss span at Kensington Avenue, and Aramingo Avenue ducks under the Richmond Branch where the Aramingo Canal used to pass. Fictional fighter Rocky Balboa jogged on the Reading trestle during a training routine in one of the *Rocky* movies. Today, the Lehigh Viaduct is a disheveled industrial relic, with just one or two remaining active tracks, hemmed in by brownfield sites and urban decay. Underneath are the fearful pedestrian/vehicular underpasses.

The Richmond Branch route to the west, between Kensington Avenue and 2nd Street, becomes submerged and secluded and has been in nationwide news for the outdoor heroin den that had subsisted along the right-of-way for decades. In 2017, the city worked with Conrail to clean up "El Campamento," removing mountains of trash (including used syringes) and overgrown vegetation. A greenway will replace what was once the Eastern Seaboard's biggest open-air drug market.

Railroad tracks on nearby Trenton Avenue in the Kensington sector were elevated off the earth's surface in the more traditional way: a steel viaduct. The Trenton Avenue Highline was originally part of the Philadelphia & Trenton Railroad (P&T), which began in 1834 between the two cities. The route had its Philadelphia terminus at Front and Berks and followed Frankford Avenue northward out of town. Abraham Lincoln traveled to Trenton on this railroad to convince the New Jersey legislature to support the Union cause, and his funeral cortege subsequently made its way out of Philadelphia via the line.

The Philadelphia & Trenton was authorized in 1839 to build its line southward, through Northern Liberties, to the northwest corner of 3rd and Willow. But that never happened, mostly because Kensingtonians resented the railroad appropriating public streets, to the point of rioting and ripping up freshly laid tracks on Front Street. The citizens in due time ceased their efforts to quash the P&T, but they were clearly on to something, considering the appalling amount of life and limb later lost to trains on city streets.

In 1871, the Pennsylvania Railroad purchased the Philadelphia & Trenton and proceeded to elevate the tracks over Trenton Avenue in about 1908–10 to abrogate thirty-seven grade crossings. Much of the old Philadelphia & Trenton Branch is now part of Amtrak's Northeast Corridor, and segments remain for freight traffic near the Frankford neighborhood. The raised portion over Trenton Avenue was dismantled decades ago.

Getting back to the PARR's Chinese Wall, the Pennsylvania Railroad's downtown viaduct was three-quarters of a mile long on some of Philadelphia's most potentially valuable property. Removing the objectionable structure would be an economic opportunity for the railroad, as eighteen acres of downtown land would be available for office, commercial, and recreational development.

The Improvements project was also prompted by the Philadelphia Art Commission's aspiration of bettering the city's looks, inspired by the early twentieth century's City Beautiful movement. The Art Commission had recently undertaken the Benjamin Franklin Parkway and the Philadelphia Museum of Art, two monumental endeavors of beautifying the Quaker City.

The technology of the 1920s—predominantly the push for electrification—also gave impetus for The Philadelphia Improvements. Underground rail stations became feasible once quiet electric-powered locomotives replaced loud steam locomotives and their problematic exhaust. A large portion of the PARR's commuter system had already been electrified: the mainline as far as Paoli in 1915; the Chestnut Hill Line in 1918; and the Media and West Chester Branch in 1928. Mainline tracks were electrified between New York City and Washington by 1935 and west to Harrisburg by 1938.

On July 13, 1925, the Pennsylvania Railroad entered into an agreement with the City of Philadelphia in which the railroad would release the corridor occupied by the Chinese Wall for development, plus some property north of Broad Street Station for the Ben Franklin Parkway. In return, the PARR gained subway tunnel rights in the space between Filbert and Cuthbert Streets from the west to 15th Street, near where the railroad would build an underground commuter station serving downtown. Furthermore, the city would construct a new bridge over the Schuylkill River on the line of Market Street so the street could be heightened to clear the through-tracks that the new station at 30th Street would require. The city would also widen Filbert Street west of Broad to ninety feet and rename it "Pennsylvania Boulevard," at the PARR's request, to serve as a dignified avenue to 30th Street Station. (The bridge carrying pedestrian and vehicular traffic over the Schuylkill on Pennsylvania Boulevard would not be built until the 1960s.)

Two years passed before The Philadelphia Improvements started in earnest. The project finally began on July 28, 1927, with a ceremony at 20th and Cuthbert. With that, the city was soon to look very different. Apart from removing the Chinese Wall and Broad Street Station and then building two new passenger stations and a connecting right-of-way between them, the PARR would also dismantle its extant railway bridges over the Schuylkill River, erect a new bridge over the river, raze West Philadelphia Station, and build a fourteen-story office building at 32nd and Market (now used by Drexel University), among other tasks. (West Philadelphia Station was removed in 1931 during construction of 30th Street Station.)

The ground fronting the west bank of the Schuylkill held a gigantic abattoir until the land was needed for the new main Philadelphia station and its tracks. The West Philadelphia Stockyard Company's slaughterhouse and 172 cattle pens were built in 1885, occupying twenty-one acres and designed by Wilson Brothers & Company. More than a thousand head of cattle and three thousand sheep could be butchered there daily. The facility in time became befouled, and a massive heap of manure graced the Schuylkill's western embankment for decades. Health authorities attacked the place as a public menace in the 1890s, but the Pennsylvania Railroad used its clout (on account of an ownership interest) to keep the stockyard going. Livestock facilities were relocated by 1931 to 36th and Gray's Ferry Avenue on the opposite side of the Schuylkill River, where they remained until the 1960s.

Long before the abattoir, the tract was home to two potter's fields known as the Lower Burying Ground and Upper Burying Ground, resting places for the city's earliest Quakers. These graveyards had likely been those of the Centre Square Meeting of Friends, which was built in 1685 at site of today's City Hall and abandoned a few years later. A 1930 newspaper article reported that numerous coffins and skeletons were found near the Schuylkill's western shore when 30th Street Station was excavated.

The Pennsylvania Railroad erected 30th Street Station from 1929 to 1933. Designed by Graham Anderson Probst & White, the building is a stately mixture of Greek and Roman Revival and Art Deco aspects, 637 feet long on the side facing the Schuylkill River and 327 feet wide east to west. Construction coincided with the onset of the Great Depression, resulting in slower progress than projected. Securing the foundation necessitated some five thousand poles to be driven down eighty feet to bedrock.

The exterior of 30th Street Station is faced with Alabama limestone. Its main arcade is 290 feet long and 135 feet wide, with a coffered ceiling rising 95 feet above a Tennessee marble floor. The reinforced concrete roof was designed to allow landing space for autogiro (experimental helicopter) service to the facility. The station incorporated other novel features, such as a chapel and a mortuary.

Named "Pennsylvania Station" when built, it was one of the last of the old glorious "gateways" to a major American city. It is now owned and operated by the National Railroad Passenger Corporation, doing business as Amtrak. A federal law was passed in 2014 that will one day change the station's name to "William H. Gray III 30th Street Station" in honor of the late U.S. congressman. Only a few years ago, there was a movement to rename it after Benjamin Franklin.

The commuter section of 30th Street Station is attached to the north side of the building several floors above the main terminal. It was the first part of the station to open (on September 28, 1930) for the PARR's suburban lines, which flow east–west through the station. Passengers had to walk through a tunnel past construction to get to the commuter facilities until the main station opened.

National passenger service began on March 12, 1933. Unlike Broad Street Station, 30th Street Station routed mainline (national) passenger trains underneath the building. This layout created a very efficient traffic flow by permitting the through-routing of trains traveling north and south without the need to reconfigure engines and cars. Even today, the arrangement keeps Amtrak's Northeast Corridor trains from interfering with local commuter traffic, since the tracks are perpendicular and at different levels. The station was fully opened on December 15, 1933.

There were plans to integrate the Market-Frankford Elevated transit line with 30th Street Station in the 1920s. Since the Market Street Line (Chapter 11) ran as an elevated alongside the terminal, a new stop at 30th Street would have been attached to the south side of 30th Street Station, symmetrical with the commuter rail station attached on the north side. These plans were dropped when the city announced it would extend the Market Street Subway into West Philadelphia and remove the elevated tracks to 44th Street. Due to the Depression and World War II, this additional subway construction did not take place until the 1950s.

The Market Street Line's 30th Street Station is therefore not directly connected to Amtrak's 30th Street Station. A winding underground passageway linking the two facilities once allowed travelers to walk underground between the Market Street Tunnel and 30th Street Station without having to brave the elements or traffic on 30th Street above. This passageway—a sequence of hallways at right angles, each one a blind corner where a mugger could lurk—has been closed since the 1980s after a passenger was assaulted. The eastern end of this corridor is under the floor of Bridgewater's Pub, a saloon inside 30th Street Station. Locked gates in front of a stairwell leading to the tunnel's western end are at the northeast side of the concourse of SEPTA's (i.e., the Market Street Line's) 30th Street Station.

The passageway will surely be restored as part of plans to develop the railyards around 30th Street Station. The name of this ambitious $6.5 billion project is "30th Street Station District," and it will entail constructing buildings over Amtrak's Penn Coach Yard and SEPTA's Powelton Yards while keeping trains running—over a duration of thirty-five years. (The same railyards, with a comparable plan of action, were unsuccessfully proposed in the 1960s as the site of the nation's Bicentennial festivities.)

Amtrak is planning to spearhead the redesign by converting the tangle of streets around the station into a landscaped "Station Plaza." In addition, Drexel University has just broken ground on "Schuylkill Yards," a $3.5 billion hotel-retail-residential development that will transform fourteen acres of the Schuylkill River's west bank over twenty years.

These days, Amtrak 30th Street Station is the nation's third-busiest train station in terms of national traffic. Congressman William Gray secured more than $100 million for cleaning and remodeling the structure in the 1990s. The landmark station is brought up in many bestsellers and is a favorite movie location, with several classics containing scenes shot within, including *Blow Out* (1981), *Trading Places* (1983), and *Witness* (1985).

The former Philadelphia Main Post Office is directly across Market Street from 30th Street Station. These two majestic monolithic structures were planned and built at about the same time, with underground passageways connecting them. Dedicated on May 25, 1935, the Main Post Office was the second-largest U.S. post office when it opened. Like 30th Street Station, it was constructed over a web of train tracks, thus allowing postal employees to access postal railcars through various stairwells and tunnels.

Ships could drop off mail at the Schuylkill River, and autogiros delivering airmail could land on the spacious flat roof. (Futile experiments with gyrocopter mail delivery between Philadelphia and Camden, New Jersey, occurred in the 1930s.) So this was the first post office in the world accessible by air, water, roadway, and rail. More than a million pieces of mail were distributed through the Main Post Office every day until the University of Pennsylvania purchased the building in 2004 and postal operations moved to a new facility in South Philadelphia. The renovated building has since been leased to the Internal Revenue Service.

Both 30th Street Station and the old post office are practically standing on stilts, thirty feet above ground level. New buildings—the FMC Tower (730 feet tall), Evo (an 850-bed student dorm), Cira Centre South, and its parking garage—have been built in recent years over onetime Pennsylvania Railroad property along the west bank of the Schuylkill, creating a new skyline for downtown Philadelphia. This batch of construction began with Cira Centre North across from 30th Street Station in 2004–5. Streets from JFK Boulevard to Walnut Street, between 30th Street and the Schuylkill River, are also elevated. Ground level is a labyrinth of isolated roads and railroad tracks that people are dissuaded from exploring.

One Drexel Plaza, immediately west of 30th Street Station, was originally the last headquarters of the defunct *Philadelphia Bulletin*. When built in 1955, the Bulletin Building was billed as the world's most modern newspaper plant and housed the longest line of presses in the world. These presses could churn out 50 complete newspapers every second, close to 250,000 an hour. An underground freight line ran into the basement level, and fourteen cars loaded with newsprint could stand at a rail siding there. The building is now owned by Drexel University and is set to be reconditioned as part of Drexel's Schuylkill Yards development.

Suburban rail lines come together at 30th Street Station's commuter station and then proceed east through Center City. Six tracks merge to four and cross the Schuylkill Expressway and Schuylkill River on a stately stone-faced bridge designed by French-born Philadelphia architect Paul Crét and built in 1930. The tracks also cross over the CSX's East Side tracks before heading east over a five-block elevated length of track paralleling JFK Boulevard (aka Filbert Street and Pennsylvania Boulevard). This had been the route of the Chinese Wall.

The four tracks start off on an elevated structure (a miniature Chinese Wall, so to speak) and then go downhill on a grade of 2.2 percent, causing 21st Street to stoop considerably. They then enter a five-block subway at

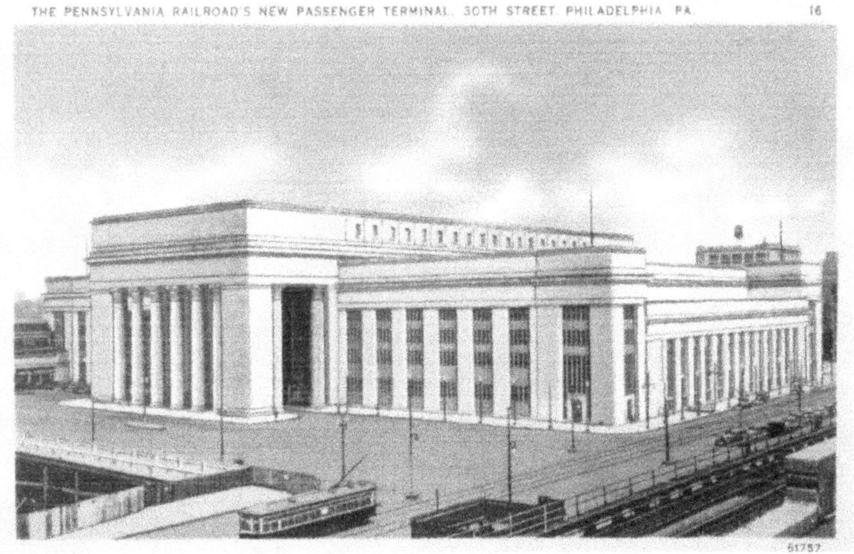

This chic postcard features the Pennsylvania Railroad's 30th Street Station, opened in the early 1930s on the west bank of the Schuylkill River. The Classic Revival station was the last great train station built in the United States. 30th Street Station still serves as Amtrak's passenger station in Philadelphia and also serves SEPTA commuter trains. *Union News Company postcard.*

20th, fanning into eight tracks as they approach Suburban Station. Several large buildings were built over the tunnel on the blocks between 20th Street and the station. One of them is Kennedy House, a thirty-story co-operative apartment completed in 1969 at 1901 JFK Boulevard. Insulation devices arrest the noise of hundreds of daily subsurface commuter train movements from disturbing residents. A line of air vent grates are on the southern sidewalk of Cuthbert Street between 19th and 18th.

Suburban Station is a sprawling underground SEPTA Regional Rail station between 18th and 15th Streets. The station was originally planned to have twelve tracks, but the Chinese Wall's foundations to the south hindered it from being built that wide. Tracks pass thirty-five feet underneath Suburban Station. There are seven floors below the platform level that afford access to utilities; the bottom two are reportedly flooded.

The twenty-two-story office edifice above Suburban Station is situated between 16th and 17th Streets and between Cuthbert Street and JFK Boulevard. This comely structure is one of the finest examples anywhere of the 1920s and '30s Art Deco architectural style and is also a standard of an integrated office building and passenger terminal, a new concept at the time. The PARR leased twenty floors of the building as downtown office space and used it as the company's nerve center for a while.

The PARR opened Suburban Station on September 28, 1930, the same day it placed 30th Street Station's commuter station into service. A mezzanine level above the tracks provides ample space for all manner of shops and eateries for commuters and visitors, together with a succession of sunken courtyards and a connection to the downtown concourse system, with links to the city's mass transit lines.

The concourse and station are now under SEPTA's control. SEPTA added two glass headhouses from the courtyard of Penn Center when it modernized the "MetroMarket at Suburban Station" in 2007, as well as illuminated sculptures to brighten up the courtyard hollows. The MetroMarket also provides a post office and, more importantly, restroom facilities.

Since the station's subterranean concourse is a destination for homeless people to escape the winter cold, SEPTA has equipped a facility along the underground route that provides showers, laundry, meals, and social services to the homeless. Opened on a large scale in late 2017, the "Hub of Hope" is designed to help transition people out of homelessness.

The pedestrian concourse system begins at the southeast corner of 18th and JFK at a stairwell descending under the boulevard's south sidewalk. The entry to these steps still displays signage reading "Pennsylvania Railroad

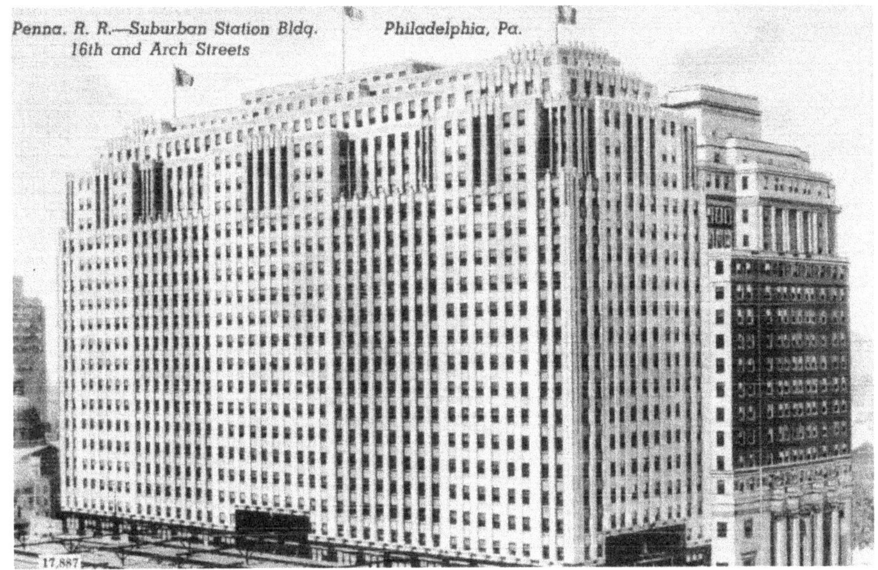

On September 28, 1930, the Pennsylvania Railroad opened Suburban Station, a sprawling underground terminal for commuter rail traffic. The Art Deco edifice above the station is a model of an integrated office building and passenger terminal. For many years, the complex was called "Broad Street Suburban Station," mainly for continuity with Broad Street Station. The twenty-one-story structure was renamed "Suburban Station" in the early 1950s and then "Penn Center Suburban Station" in the late 1960s. Now called "One Penn Center at Suburban Station," the office building above has been made economically and operationally distinct from the station below. *Colourpicture postcard.*

Suburban Station"—a half century after the Penn Central Railroad's insolvency following the PARR and New York Central merger of 1968.

The northeast corner of JFK Boulevard had an entry stairwell leading to a separate concourse, but both stairwell and concourse were removed in 1986–87 when the Philadelphia Centre Hotel (formerly a Sheraton) there was demolished. The headquarters of Comcast Corporation is now there. The Comcast Center tower includes 16,500 square feet of high-end food and retail space underground that is part of the city's pedestrian concourse network—although the portion owned by Comcast is kept under lock and key at night. Comcast Center faces a plaza that sits over SEPTA's buried commuter railroad tracks between 30th Street Station and Suburban Station. This is why the building was not built alongside JFK—it would have been too expensive to construct such a lofty edifice over the tracks. Furthermore, Comcast's nearby Technology Center in 2017 became Philadelphia's tallest building and will soon extend the city's pedestrian concourse west to as far as 19th Street. A concourse will also connect the two buildings underground.

Above the east end of Suburban Station's track layout is a surface park that has served as the Ben Franklin Parkway's eastern terminus since 1967. Philadelphia architect Vincent Kling designed the park, whereupon it was named "John F. Kennedy Plaza" to honor the slain President. The city also changed the name of Pennsylvania Boulevard to "John F. Kennedy Boulevard" as a memorial to Kennedy.

John F. Kennedy (JFK) Plaza is better recognized as "Love Park" after the globally famous *Love* sculpture that it features. Love Park was originally crowded with granite risers and consequently became an internationally renowned skateboarding spot by the 1990s. But it lost this status when the city added benches and greenery to make the place more welcoming for office workers and tourists.

The flying saucer–shaped structure within Love Park is the old Hospitality Center of the Philadelphia Convention and Visitors Bureau, consummated in 1961 across from Suburban Station. In 2006, the unconventional structure became the Fairmount Park Welcome Center; more recently, fans of mid-twentieth-century architecture have successfully rallied to save the building. It will become a café.

A multi-level underground parking garage is within the borders of Love Park, and several ventilation grates for the garage and for SEPTA trains beneath the surface punctuate the park. The city has completed a $26 million overhaul of the park emanating from the need to waterproof the leaking parking garage roof and has lately sold the garage for $29.6 million. The plaza's new design leveled most of the concrete stairs and walls previously within the site, replacing them with trees and water features that mask an eight-foot grade change. Now paved with bricks and granite, the flatter Love Park is anticipated to fulfill its role as a vibrant public space in Philadelphia. Programming to include music recitals, line dancing and table games will enliven the mix.

The completion of Suburban and 30th Street Stations should have been the end of Broad Street Station and the Chinese Wall, but the Depression and World War II delayed their demolition until the 1950s. The station and its viaduct had been around so long by then that their demise was regarded as fantasy. "Old Broad" remained a more convenient way into town anyway, and 30th Street Station did not have enough tracks to handle capacity until the 1950s.

Philadelphians had a love-hate relationship with "Old Broad." The push to eradicate Victorian structures throughout the nation after World War II

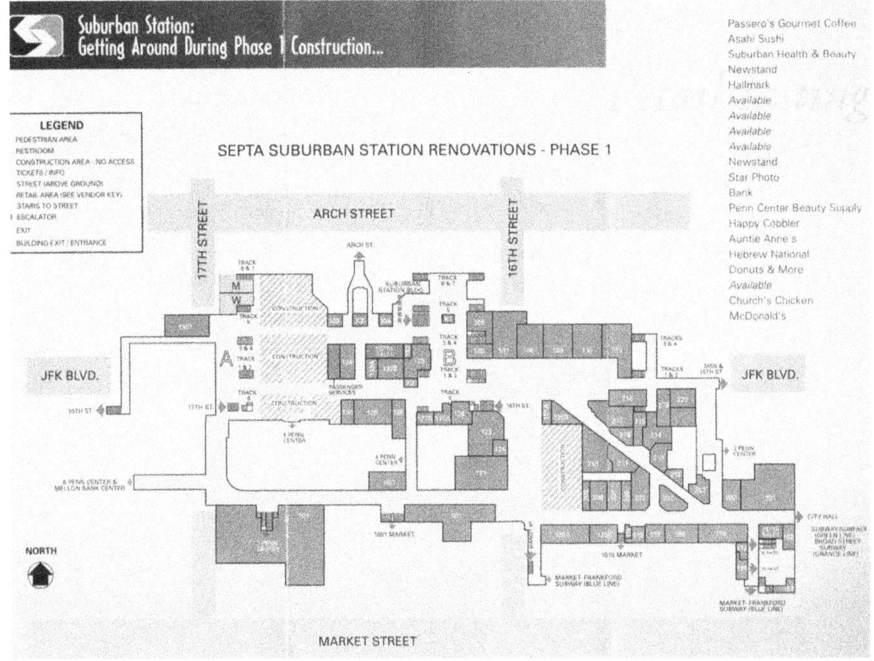

SEPTA issued this pamphlet showing the layout of the underground shopping zone surrounding Suburban Station (the "MetroMarket") around 2002 when the station and its concourse level received a $42 million makeover. Elevators, air conditioning, and a doubling of the number of stores were just some of the improvements. Plus, a new concourse entrance, with a large glass shelter and escalators, was built facing City Hall at 15th Street. *Harry Kyriakodis's collection.*

at last spelled the station's end. On April 27, 1952, the last train departed Broad Street Station, accompanied by Eugene Ormandy conducting the Philadelphia Orchestra, playing "Auld Lang Syne" and other compositions, in a farewell concert. The ceremony was attended by a few old-timers who had witnessed the first trains to enter the terminal.

Broad Street Station's demolition started within hours, showing how eager most parties were to remove the terminal. There was no lament over the station's destruction as there was with New York City's Pennsylvania Station in 1963. Rubble from "Old Broad" and the Chinese Wall was dumped into the Delaware River in South Philadelphia to facilitate construction of new piers at the PARR's Greenwich Yard. Even the Food Distribution Center of 1959 was built atop stones from the Chinese Wall.

If Broad Street Station had managed to persevere another twenty years or so, it would still be across from City Hall today, no doubt remodeled as a deluxe hotel. Only a historical marker across from City Hall indicates Broad Street Station's old setting. A remnant of the Chinese Wall supports JFK Boulevard and some green space from the Schuylkill River to around 22nd Street, paralleling the modern rail approach to Suburban Station. Sadly, the reconstruction of JFK Boulevard in 2018 might obliterate this last bit.

Much of the space the Chinese Wall occupied was to be developed into the Penn Center campus of (somewhat) tall office buildings. The Philadelphia Improvements had always assumed that an assortment of office towers would be built on the site of the old viaduct, but formal plans for Penn Center did not appear until 1947. That was the year of the Better Philadelphia Exhibition, a large display of models showing grand plans for Center City from the fledgling Philadelphia City Planning Commission and other reform-minded organizations.

Penn Center is Philadelphia's version of Lower Manhattan, a canyon of mid-rise towers from City Hall to 20th Street along both JFK Boulevard and Market Street. Visionary Philadelphia city planner Edmund Bacon (1910–2005), the "Father of Modern Philadelphia," included in Penn Center's design a weather-protected underground concourse that connected office, transportation, and retail facilities. The network was to have been an audacious esplanade eighteen feet below street level, open to the sky and studded by retail shops. But plans changed, and the esplanade was raised to the surface and placed between the buildings at Penn Center, with large openings down to passageways connected to pedestrian tunnels built decades earlier alongside the Market Street Subway and the Broad Street Subway.

The underground passageways around Penn Center were built differently than the city's earlier transit tunnels and concourses, which were created through the process of cut-and-cover construction. The 1960s tunnels were dug from below, utilizing the city's original transit tunnels for the movement of building material and equipment. This method of construction did not interrupt the flow of traffic at street level.

From the start, Philadelphians did not know what to make of the pedestrian concourses underfoot. The idea of such tunnels in the heart of a city was considered strange, and some people thought that they had to pay for their use. Others were more comfortable relying on familiar landmarks above ground; diminutive directional signs below grade were just not the same. Despite the system costing several million dollars and being one of the world's most extensive underground walks, newspaper editorials in the 1940s often suggested sealing up the concourses.

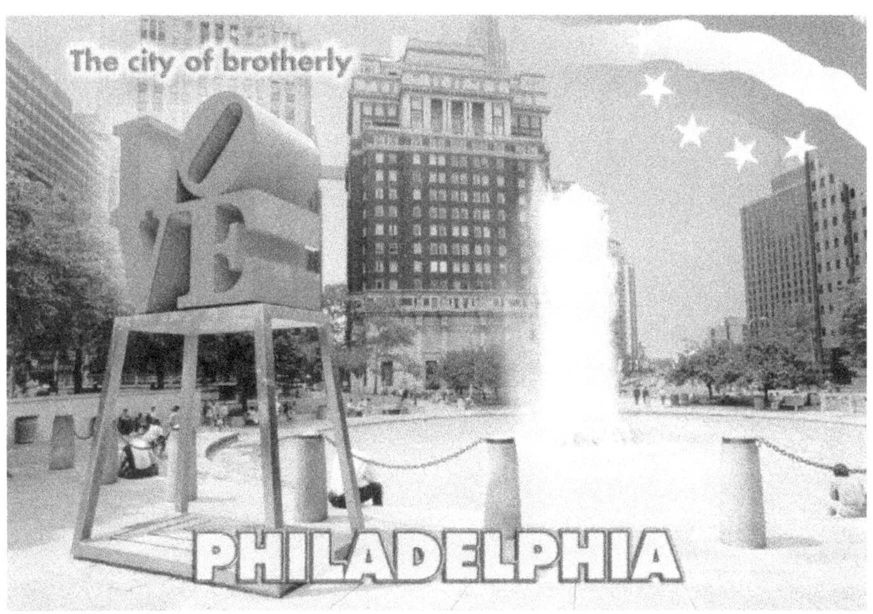

Open space on the eastern end of the Benjamin Franklin Parkway was dedicated in 1967 as John F. Kennedy Plaza. With its eye-catching fountain and pool, the square is better known as "Love Park" after the globally famed *Love* sculpture. Versions of this work of pop art can be found all around the nation and the world, but the City of Brotherly Love's example is surely the most prestigious. Supposedly, the "O" is tilted because love is imperfect. *The Postcard Factory postcard.*

In *Philadelphia: A Story of Progress* (1941), what must have been prevailing questions as to the need of the pedestrian concourses (as they existed by 1941) were succinctly asked and answered:

> *Philadelphia owns a city beneath the city which is another public achievement often criticized. What good does it perform? Why construct miles of subterranean walks beneath and around City Hall, which towers so majestically above? Why create streets beneath surface streets for blocks north, east, south and west?*
>
> *That city under a city cost millions of dollars and no doubt it will in time yield handsome dividends. These underground streets are now daily used by many thousand pedestrians who thus escape the delays of surface walking, plus the real hazards in congested automobile traffic. At any rate, this labyrinth of walks far below the surface of the city constitutes a definite portion of the average citizen's ownership in the municipality.*

And by the 1970s, the Quaker City's pedestrian concourse network was acclaimed as being innovative and influential in the design of other cities, and even Philadelphia's Market Street East Redevelopment project of the 1980s. Center City Philadelphia today has three and a half miles of pedestrian mezzanines underneath city streets, usually allied with retail stores. The concourse includes more than 500,000 square feet of underground space from JFK Boulevard to Spruce Street and from 8th to 18th. No transit fare is necessary to take advantage of the network, which is particularly useful in times of poor weather. Now being branded as the "Downtown Link" in their entirety, the pedestrian tunnels will be further discussed in subsequent chapters.

Penn Center also includes an underground roadway used to service and supply surface buildings. The entrance to this no-outlet road, Commerce Street, is on 19th Street between Market and JFK. An indispensable facet of Edmund Bacon's design for Penn Center, the subterranean street leads to loading docks under the buildings of Penn Center. These docks significantly lessen the number of trucks on surface streets, which accounts for the rarity of traffic jams caused by trucks loading and unloading in the Penn Center quarter.

The construction of Penn Center generated much excitement in the 1950s and '60s, as Philadelphians saw the complex as a progressive vision of civic renewal. Six Penn Center (at 17th Street) was put up by the Pennsylvania Railroad and became the company's home office. Two and Three Penn Center were constructed in the space once occupied by Broad Street Station's trainshed and tracks.

Four, Five and Seven Penn Center came later, along with an ice skating rink on either side of 17th Street at JFK. The rink was intended to attract suburbanites into the city. Many still recall how entertaining it was to skate and people-watch at this Rockefeller Center–style rink in the shadow of City Hall.

A Transportation Center was also built between 17th and 18th on Market. This office tower, like other Penn Center buildings, provided direct access to the Market Street Subway and Suburban Station via passageways to the pedestrian concourse network. This access, along with a Greyhound Bus Terminal on its ground floor, was the derivation of the building's name.

The Greyhound Terminal at Penn Center was a genuine denizen of downtown Philly during its short existence of just over thirty years. For instance, a watercolor sketch by Pablo Picasso was recovered in a public storage locker there in 1966. Two youths were arrested for the theft from the

Philadelphia Museum of Art, and an accomplice was shot dead by police during the investigation. Thirteen years later, more than 1,700 people were forced to flee from Six Penn Center when the building filled with carbon monoxide from the abutting bus terminal after a power failure.

The ice skating rink and the Transportation Center Building have been supplanted by other buildings of Penn Center, and the other major office towers that have arisen along and in between Market and JFK. Plus, Greyhound relocated to 10th and Filbert in 1987. The Philadelphia Greyhound Terminal serves as the primary bus station in Philadelphia, providing berths for several regional, inter-regional, and intercity bus lines, besides Greyhound. One of the busiest long-distance bus stations in the United States, it is steps away from Chinatown, next to the Pennsylvania Convention Center, and close to Center City's historic attractions.

Alas, the Pennsylvania Railroad compromised Bacon's plan for Penn Center—with enlarged buildings and less open space—to be more economically rewarding to the company. Penn Center and the underground

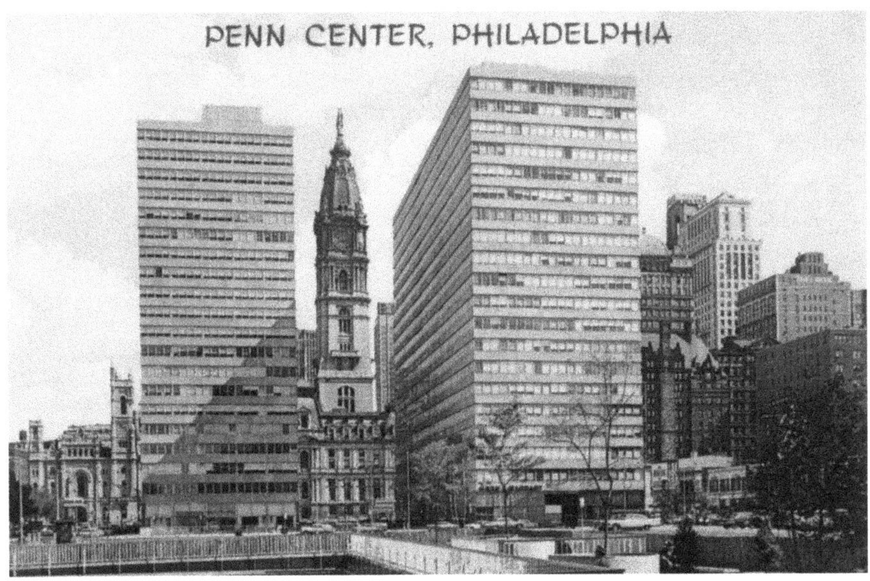

Built from the 1950s through the 1970s, Penn Center occupies space formerly taken up by the Pennsylvania Railroad's elevated tracks (the "Chinese Wall"). City planner Edmund Bacon included Penn Center as part of the Better Philadelphia Exhibition, accommodated in Gimbels department store and viewed by nearly 400,000 people. The city's underground pedestrian concourse system is prevalent throughout this area; an opening is shown at the bottom left of this postcard. *WYCO Products postcard.*

concourse network in due course became less pedestrian friendly and less attractive overall. Legitimate worries about crime and homelessness in the area became evident as the years passed. This type of overwhelming city-sculpting has been pretty much discredited since Penn Center's construction. In fact, Penn Center has been cited as a dreadful archetype of city planning for its disregard of the vitality of traditional city streets.

The PARR merged with the New York Central in 1968 to form the Penn Central Railroad. Two years afterward, Penn Central failed, and its freight, passenger, and commuter services were severed. Its freight lines eventually became Conrail (with the addition of a few more railroads), passenger service went to Amtrak, and local commuter lines went to Conrail and then to SEPTA in 1983.

With the longstanding competition between the Pennsylvania Railroad and the Reading Company eliminated by the financial collapse of both railroads, SEPTA began operating its Regional Rail service over the two systems without distinction.

A few years thereafter, in 1984, Suburban Station changed from a stub-end terminal to a through-station when the Commuter Rail Tunnel (Chapter 8) united the formerly opposed Pennsylvania and Reading Railroad systems. The tunnel basically continued the subway that the PARR built in the late 1920s. The Commuter Rail Tunnel was, in effect, the final component of The Philadelphia Improvements.

Chapter 7

Reading Railroad Company and Reading Terminal

Whereas remembered primarily as a railroad, the Reading Company was a multifaceted industrial giant at its peak. It was originally chartered in 1833 as the Philadelphia & Reading Railroad (P&R) to transport anthracite coal to the Quaker City. The Reading's ninety-three-mile right-of-way passed alongside the Schuylkill River from the mining town of Pottsville, Pennsylvania, through Reading to Philadelphia. Upon its completion in 1843, this was the first double-track mainline in the United States.

The pioneering railroad leased, purchased, or merged with numerous smaller lines, thus growing into a robust corporation serving the densely industrialized areas of eastern Pennsylvania, New Jersey, and Delaware. With its complex of shops for locomotive and car building and repair and its relentless advancement of railroad technology, Reading Railroad held a position of leadership in the railroad industry for more than a century. In its heyday, the P&R offered more than 2,600 miles of track for freight and passengers and carried 25 million riders annually.

The P&R in the 1870s established a subsidiary, the Philadelphia & Reading Coal and Iron Company, to gain control over vast anthracite deposits being mined for shipment over its lines. When the Reading attempted to further expand by controlling rail lines into New England, New York financier J.P. Morgan pulled the financial rug out from under the company. The P&R went into receivership on February 20, 1893, with Morgan restructuring the company three years later. This was the first of several bankruptcies during the Reading's long and tortured history.

At that time, the Reading was seeking to build a large passenger station in downtown Philadelphia. Driven by stiff competition with the Pennsylvania Railroad, the P&R built Reading Terminal as the company's headquarters and as the base for its expanding passenger rail system. The station's headhouse—an eight-story Italian Renaissance palazzo with a terra-cotta façade designed by Francis Kimball—was situated at 12th and Market to create a suitably regal entrance for the public.

There was controversy as to whether the right-of-way to the station should be elevated or underground. Since a subsurface route would be too costly, the Reading elected for an elevated right-of-way to bring trains to the terminal's second floor. It would be ninety years before the Commuter Rail Tunnel removed the route underground. (See the next chapter.)

Purchasing property on the 1100 block of Market was problematic for the Reading, since the site had been in continuous use as a public marketplace for decades. Back in 1860, the Butchers' and Farmers' Market (aka the

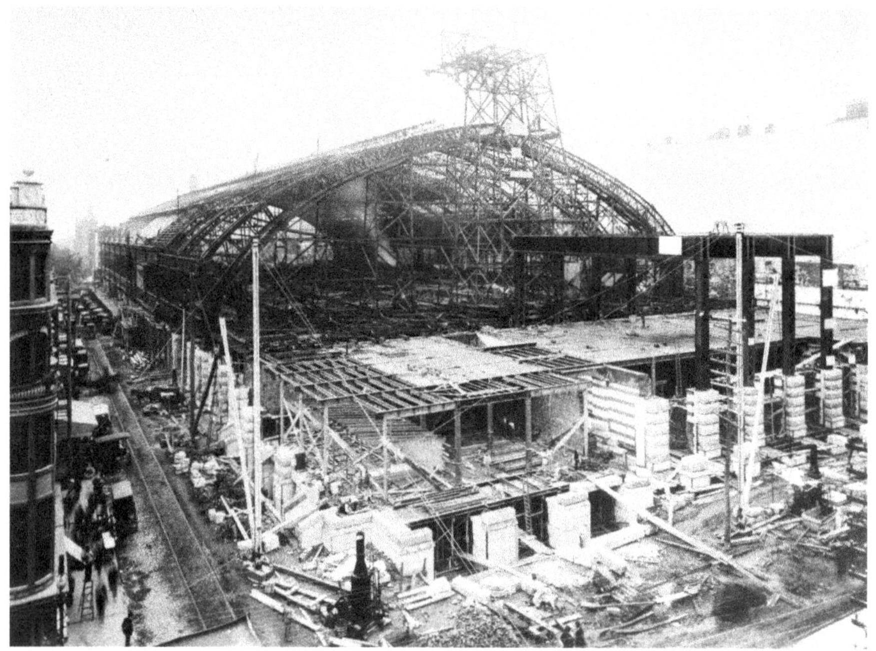

Reading Terminal is under construction in this period photograph. Covering thirteen tracks and eight platforms, the trainshed was designed by Wilson Brothers & Company, which had worked on the Pennsylvania Railroad's Broad Street Station years before. Reading Terminal's location was previously the site of two farmers' markets, which explains how Reading Terminal Market came to be under the shed. The celebrated marketplace still operates on the ground level. *Library of Congress.*

Farmers' Market Company) erected a brick marketplace on the north side of Market Street, east of 12th, as a replacement for the market stalls that had been removed by city ordinance from the center of Market Street in 1859. Another indoor emporium, the Twelfth Street Market Company (later the Franklin Market), was put up in the 1880s side by side with the Farmers' Market, touching 12th Street.

Then along came Reading Railroad in the early 1890s with plans to build a huge new passenger depot where the two bazaars stood. The markets joined forces to hold out for a price of more than $2 million for the properties, but the Reading refused and litigation ensued. The railroad then suggested a compromise: $1 million plus erection by the railroad of a new collective markethouse at ground level (under a great trainshed) to be managed as part of the Philadelphia & Reading conglomerate.

This was a truly artful solution to the dilemma at hand. While some three hundred merchants would sell their wares from individual market stalls below, Reading passenger trains would enter the station overhead, the floor supported by a grid of steel columns and protected from the weather by a tremendous trainshed over thirteen tracks. Meanwhile, the Pennsylvania Railroad mercilessly ridiculed the Reading for situating its downtown depot atop a market.

The ground-floor market operated for decades without a waterproof ceiling, causing incessant drips to plague the market stalls, given the station floor's porous nature. Some Philadelphians still recall when sawdust was scattered on the market's floor to absorb the ooze. (The sawdust also soaked up animal blood from the market stalls.)

A celebrated Philly attraction, Reading Terminal Market is a favorite with downtown residents and workers, not to mention tourists and conventioneers from the adjacent Pennsylvania Convention Center. Shopkeepers sell all types of fresh produce, choice meats, and ethnic foods. In years past, thousands of suburban housewives shopped each week in the trainshed's basement, often sending groceries home for free on Reading trains.

Beneath the stalls, Reading Market's basement contained the world's largest mechanical cold storage plant at the end of the 1800s. Aside from enabling Bassett's Ice Cream to make and sell ice cream on site, the ammoniated brine system could make twenty-eight tons of ice a day for market stores and nearby restaurants, breweries, hospitals, and flower shops. The Reading even offered tours of the facility, which were popular on hot summer days. Expensive to operate, the cold storage plant lasted until 1960. The basement has been utilized for general storage since then.

The Market Street–facing headhouse contained a ticket office, waiting rooms, baggage rooms, and the like, as well as general offices for the Philadelphia & Reading Railroad Company. The passenger lobby was 50 feet long and extended the width of the building. But the terminal's chief feature was the 267-foot-wide trainshed with its pointed arch roof rising 88 feet over the tracks. This remarkable engineering achievement became an esteemed landmark in Philadelphia.

Reading Terminal buzzed with activity night and day from the moment it opened on January 29, 1893. But ironically, the station's cost was partly blamed for the P&R going into receivership later that year. By the early twentieth century, stock control of the Reading was held by the New York Central and Baltimore & Ohio (B&O) Railroads, but the company was managed locally and had settled into its role as a regional railroad, mainly a carrier of anthracite coal and passengers.

As many as forty-five thousand riders passed through Reading Terminal daily during World War II. But decline set in at both Reading Terminal and the parent railroad after the war. In 1948, the station underwent a misguided "modernization," and much of the facility's winsome public areas were remade as dreary retail space by the 1950s. The headhouse's original granite cladding was removed to accommodate contemporary glass panels, six arches on the second floor along Market Street were bricked in, and a plain brick parapet replaced the ornamented balustrade and copper cornice. Reading Terminal had become a sad shadow of its prior grandeur as one of the East Coast's greatest railroad hubs.

Concurrently, the Reading's freight business withered as America turned away from coal as a fuel in the 1950s. The Reading Lines also experienced declining long-distance passenger service and only moderate commuter rail service. All this resulted in the railroad's fourth bankruptcy on November 23, 1971. In 1976 (on April Fool's Day, no less), the 143-year-old Reading Company ceased being a railroad. Most of its assets were transferred to Conrail, although SEPTA took over the Reading's lackluster commuter operations.

The last suburban train departed Reading Terminal on November 6, 1984. It was a nine-car SEPTA special to Lansdale made up of 1931 Reading multiple-unit commuter cars painted in blue and cream ("Blueliners").

The Reading Company emerged from insolvency on January 1, 1981, and redirected its efforts to real estate development, mostly of property it owned along its old right-of-ways. Nowadays, the old P&R is a Los Angeles–based entertainment and real estate firm named Reading International. It develops

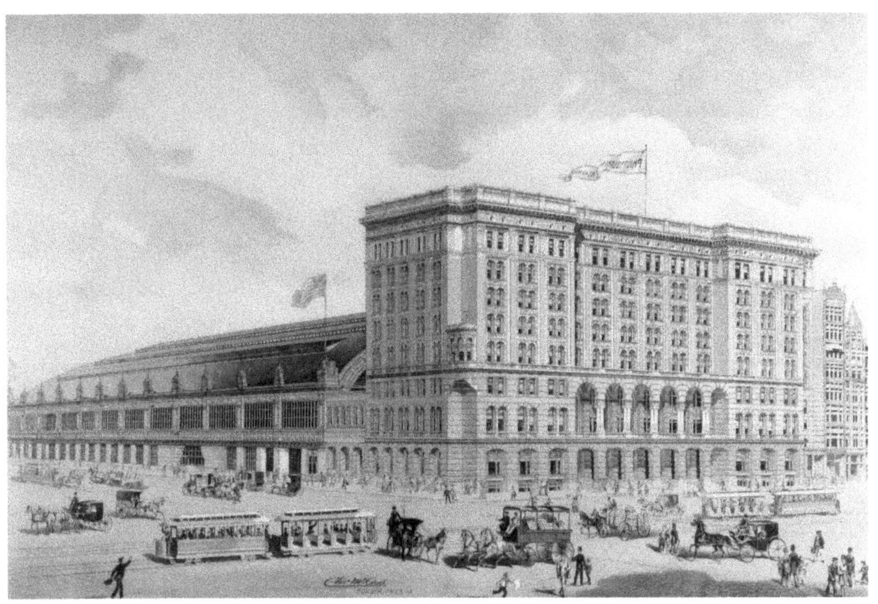

This handsome lithograph shows Reading Terminal at the building's opening in 1893. The station was instantly acclaimed not only for the richness of its Victorian architecture but also for the vast scale of its trainshed, the widest single-span shed in the world. Although superseded later by the trainshed of Broad Street Station, Reading Terminal regained its prime position when Broad Street Station's shed was destroyed by fire in 1923. *Library of Congress.*

and operates multiplex cinemas and retail and commercial properties in the United States, Australia, and New Zealand.

One Reading Center, built in 1984 beside Reading Terminal, was Reading International's first substantial real estate venture. The thirty-two-story skyscraper has been called Aramark Tower as world headquarters for Aramark Corporation until 2018. Its name will then change to Jefferson Tower, as the building has been leased as administrative offices by Thomas Jefferson University. The building is ultimately owned by the Stephen Girard estate.

The fate of Reading Terminal was in serious jeopardy after the Reading's final bankruptcy. Fortunately, it was located squarely within the Market Street East Redevelopment Area, a massive urban renewal development east of City Hall envisioned by city planner Edmund Bacon. The Philadelphia Redevelopment Authority purchased the historic terminal so that it could be incorporated into the Pennsylvania Convention Center. Before long, old and drab Reading Terminal was exchanged for new and shiny Market East Station (now Jefferson Station), part of the Commuter Rail Tunnel project.

Reading Terminal trainshed was masterfully rehabilitated and transformed into the Convention Center's Grand Hall ballroom. It is the oldest surviving single-span arched trainshed roof structure anywhere and the only one of its kind left in the United States. The shed was placed on the National Register of Historic Places in 1972 and was declared a National Historic Landmark in 1976. Moreover, by saving and reusing the trainshed, the oldest operational farmers' market in the nation was preserved.

The Italian Renaissance headhouse of Reading Terminal revealed itself to be quite handsome with its terra-cotta façade restored and cleaned of generations of dirt. The station's windows were replaced, and its exterior granite cladding and terra-cotta details were repaired. Interior renovations included the creation of a multi-level atrium that provides direct access to Market East (Jefferson) Station, the Gallery, the Convention Center's Grand Hall, Aramark Tower, and the city's underground pedestrian concourse network. A mural of historic Reading locomotives was added in the headhouse basement, and a Hard Rock Café opened on its ground floor. The rest of the historic structure is now part of the Philadelphia Marriott Hotel across 12th Street, connected by a footbridge over the street.

Commencing in 1990, work on the Pennsylvania Convention Center revitalized four derelict city blocks between Arch and Race from 11th to 13th. The facility was the largest public works project in state history, opening in 1993 and proving so successful that an extension west to Broad Street was finished by 2011.

The Convention Center is built over both 12th and 13th Streets. Cars and trucks go through two-block-long street-level passageways that assault passersby with the echoes of traffic and the exhaust of idling tour buses. Additionally, Filbert Street passes underneath Reading Terminal via a street-level tunnel. This once dank underpass has lately become a dynamic gateway to the Reading Terminal Market with LED lighting and art/music programming.

The Reading's other major station in Philadelphia was North Broad Street Station at 2601 North Broad. Designed by Horace Trumbauer, it was regarded as one of the country's most beautiful train stations when finished in 1929 because of its classical façade. North Broad served the Reading's former Philadelphia, Germantown & Norristown line—now SEPTA's mainline to and from Wayne Junction—as it curved to align with the elevated route above 9th Street (the Ninth Street Branch or Elevated). Located on the east side of Broad Street, the station appropriated the site of Reading's old Huntingdon Street Station, which had entered service in 1891.

Reading Railroad officials had planned to make North Broad Station the Quaker City's central train station of the Baltimore & Ohio Railroad (B&O), and they believed that the North Philadelphia district was ripe for apartment house development. Plus, it was positioned opposite the Baker Bowl—the Phillies' baseball park from 1887 to 1938—at the southwest corner of Broad and Lehigh. Reading tracks ran through a tunnel under the stadium, creating a hill ("the Hump") below center field. A tunnel provided direct access to the mezzanine level of the Broad Street Subway at Glenwood Avenue, but it was closed in the 1980s, having been described as a security nightmare.

North Broad catered to North Philadelphians for many years, but few people were using the unkempt station by the mid-1950s. Plans to make it the B&O's main station failed, the apartments never materialized, and the Baker Bowl was demolished in 1950. Reading Company shuttered the station ten years thereafter, auctioning it off in 1962. The building was a motel until suffering a fire in 1981. Listed on the National Register of Historic Places, it is now office and residential space for a nonprofit educational/correctional organization. SEPTA Regional Rail trains still stop at a lowly surrogate shelter nearby.

The ex-Reading/SEPTA tracks pass directly under Amtrak's North Philadelphia Station, only three blocks away at 2900 North Broad Street, on the opposite side of Broad. This intercity/commuter rail complex served Amtrak's Northeast Corridor mainline tracks, which in this vicinity are known to rail enthusiasts as the famous "Connecting Railroad" of the Pennsylvania Railroad. North Philadelphia Station was constructed in the 1890s, when the Pennsylvania Railroad elevated its tracks crossing at Broad Street and simultaneously replaced an inadequate 1870s depot.

Featured in the docudrama *Pride of the Marines* (1945), North Philadelphia opened in 1901 and became the only stop in the city for most long-distance national rail traffic by permitting trains to avoid a reverse move into Broad Street Station. The French Renaissance station had two platforms serving four tracks, accessed through a tunnel from the main waiting room. A separate tunnel connected to the mezzanine of the Broad Street Subway at Lehigh Avenue, but the frightening corridor was a setting for muggings and was sealed some time ago.

Much like the Reading's North Broad Station, North Philadelphia Station entered a period of deterioration in the mid-twentieth century. The Pennsylvania Railroad no longer operated the station complex by the 1970s, but SEPTA Regional Rail trains still stop there, and in 1991 Amtrak constructed a rectangular concrete and glass replacement station on the north side of the tracks. The original depot was entered on the National Register of Historic Places in 1999, the same year that it was remade for use as retail space. Nevertheless, Amtrak soon closed the old station's ticket booth, a reflection of the facility's diminished usage.

A $162 million proposal has been tendered to develop the parking lots and warehouses amid North Philadelphia Station into a mix of homes, offices, and work spaces. "North Station District" may even induce the restoration of the blocked passage to the Broad Street Subway.

Chapter 8

Philly's Commuter Rail Tunnel (the "Center City Commuter Connection")

In 1970, two years after the Pennsylvania Railroad merged with the New York Central, the Penn Central Railroad went bankrupt, and its freight, passenger, and commuter services were split. Its regional commuter service first went to Conrail and then to SEPTA by 1983.

The rival Reading Company had also gone bankrupt (in 1971), and SEPTA assumed its moribund commuter rail operations by 1976. With the longstanding competition between the Pennsylvania Railroad and the Reading Railroad eliminated by the failure of both companies, SEPTA could run its Regional Rail service over the two systems with no distinction.

The two electrified rail networks were not fully integrated until completion of the Commuter Rail Tunnel in 1984. Officially termed the Center City Commuter Connection (CCCC), the 1.7-mile-long tunnel essentially connected Reading Terminal and Suburban Station. Both of these older stations were inefficient stub-end terminals that had formerly competed for commuter traffic. The CCCC enabled the through-routing of commuter trains and eliminated operational difficulties imposed by dead-end terminals.

The project was first urged in 1958 by R. Damon Childs, a planner with the Philadelphia City Planning Commission. It would bring more people into Center City—which was then losing population and business activity—and would offer better access to struggling department stores on East Market Street from Philly's suburbs. His supervisor, Edmund Bacon, was doubtful about the tunnel at first, but he incorporated it into his 1960

Comprehensive Plan for the City of Philadelphia and encouraged it for the city's future development once he grasped that it would reinforce downtown Philadelphia as the region's transportation hub.

Yet the tunnel was reckoned for years to be a dream that would not come true. Funding issues, engineering challenges, and resistance from nearby businesses and residents delayed the onset of construction for years. Ground was finally broken on June 22, 1978, during Frank Rizzo's administration. Engineering and community-related problems continued for the maligned project throughout its construction. The $330 million scheme received 80 percent of its funding from the Urban Mass Transit Administration, now the Federal Transit Administration.

Design and construction of the CCCC were very challenging, as the tunnel weaves both above and below preexisting subway lines and through a good amount of downtown Philly. Intricate construction scheduling helped maintain pedestrian and vehicular traffic at street level, with timber beam decking atop Filbert Street on the north side of Center Square. There was also a monumental relocation of sewers, gas pipes, water mains, and electrical and telephone cables, all of which had to be kept in service without disruption. The same goes for the Broad Street Subway and the Broad Street Spur.

The Commuter Rail Tunnel is a steel-reinforced concrete box tunnel of cut-and-cover construction. To keep train noise and vibration from disturbing the occupants of downtown buildings (and to make for a more comfortable ride), the CCCC's tracks use continuous-welded rails on specially cushioned concrete ties. Track level insulation and acoustical panels between the four tracks further deaden noise. The concrete tunnel is also isolated from bordering structures by a two-inch layer of cork.

The tunnel lengthened the five-block subway to Suburban Station that the Pennsylvania Railroad built in the late 1920s, making the whole tunnel, from end to end, almost 2.5 miles long through the heart of Center City. It extended eastward four Suburban Station tracks that once ended at a concrete wall near 15th Street. The project also encompassed widening the station's platforms to double their previous width by replacing two of Suburban Station's original tracks with island platforms to serve the tunnel's through-tracks. Although the four through-tracks are on the south side, Suburban Station was originally designed so that its two northernmost tracks could be continued east toward a proposed tunnel under the Delaware River to connect to Pennsylvania Railroad lines out of Camden, New Jersey. This was never done.

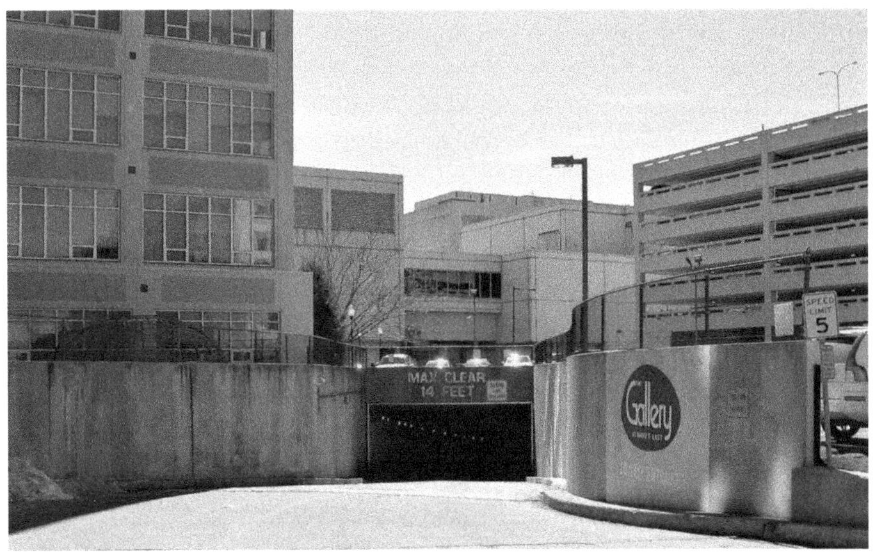

The entrance to the delivery vehicle tunnel that runs under the Gallery is on the south side of Arch Street, between 8th and 9th. It parallels the Commuter Rail Tunnel as it proceeds several blocks east–west under Filbert Street. The underground roadway was a part of the East Market Street Redevelopment Area, which remade Market Street east of City Hall in the 1980s. *Photograph by Harry Kyriakodis.*

The Municipal Services Building (MSB) is the first structure the tracks encounter as they head east underground. The MSB was designed by Philadelphia architect Vincent Kling and took the place of Reyburn Plaza in the early 1960s. (Named after Mayor John Reyburn, the plaza replaced a row of refined townhouses along Arch Street in 1915.) City departments requiring the most public access opened directly onto MSB's depressed plaza, which was integrated into the city's pedestrian concourse network. Even so, the half-indoors, half-outdoors MSB Plaza is an utterly unappealing place. A bronze sculpture titled *Benjamin Franklin, Craftsman* (1981) is near the subsurface plaza, showing a muscular young Franklin manipulating his manual printing press.

The tunnel then passes over the Broad Street Subway. Even though this transit line was designed to allow a future subway above it north of City Hall, clearances were barely adequate for the Commuter Rail Tunnel. A twenty-foot section of subway roof was reconstructed to support the tunnel, and a four-hundred-foot length of tunnel used by SEPTA's Subway-Surface trolleys was moved sixteen feet south. A new westbound 15th Street trolley stop was also built. Nearby, along the northern sidewalks of JFK Boulevard and Filbert Street, are large ventilation grates for the CCCC and the Broad Street Subway. At least one is painted yellow to identify it as an emergency exit and to warn that vehicles should not park over it.

The CCCC continues eastward under Filbert Street and City Hall Annex, a fourteen-story tower erected by the city in 1926. The structure required extensive underpinning treatment since one track of the tunnel box passes directly under its support columns along Filbert Street. A below-ground pedestrian mezzanine was built from City Hall Annex to the MSB, but the narrow zigzagging hallway is usually closed due to security concerns. City Hall Annex was refurbished in 1999 as the Marriott Courtyard Hotel.

The Masonic Temple, consummated in 1873, also necessitated special underpinning when cracks appeared in its ornate interior plaster. Designed by James H. Windrim, John Torrey Windrim's father, this serves as the Grand Lodge of Free and Accepted Masons of Pennsylvania. The Romanesque-style building is among the largest Freemason lodges in the world and is considered the preeminent Masonic temple of American Freemasonry. An old tunnel was supposed to have connected the Masonic Temple with City Hall, although the website of the Pennsylvania Masons claims that "there are no passable tunnels that connect [the Temple] to any other building," likely referring to City Hall. Maybe the tunnel is no longer "passable" because it was severed when the Commuter Rail Tunnel was built.

Farther east is Market East Station, a $75 million transportation center completed in 1984 along the tunnel right-of-way. Now called Jefferson Station (the naming rights having been purchased by Thomas Jefferson University in 2014 for $4 million), this rail facility is 120 feet wide and two blocks long between 10th and 12th, effectively replacing the function of Reading Terminal. The CCCC passes underneath the near center of the Reading Terminal trainshed, far below its elevation and perpendicular to it. SEPTA's Jefferson Station is also fully integrated with the pedestrian concourse connecting the Market Street Subway, Subway-Surface Lines, the Broad Street Subway, and SEPTA's Regional Rail System.

A huge atrium filters daylight down to the station's track level thirty-five feet below the street. There, a large abstract wall mural of a forest—fabricated with 250,000 ceramic tiles arranged by computer program—enlivens the tunnel walls. This was the world's largest mosaic mural in the 1980s. The objective was to bring some colorful above-ground scenery into the subterranean space. But the nine-hundred-foot-long mural was designed to be seen from a moving train, which does not occur at Jefferson Station, so the forest effect is hardly perceptible.

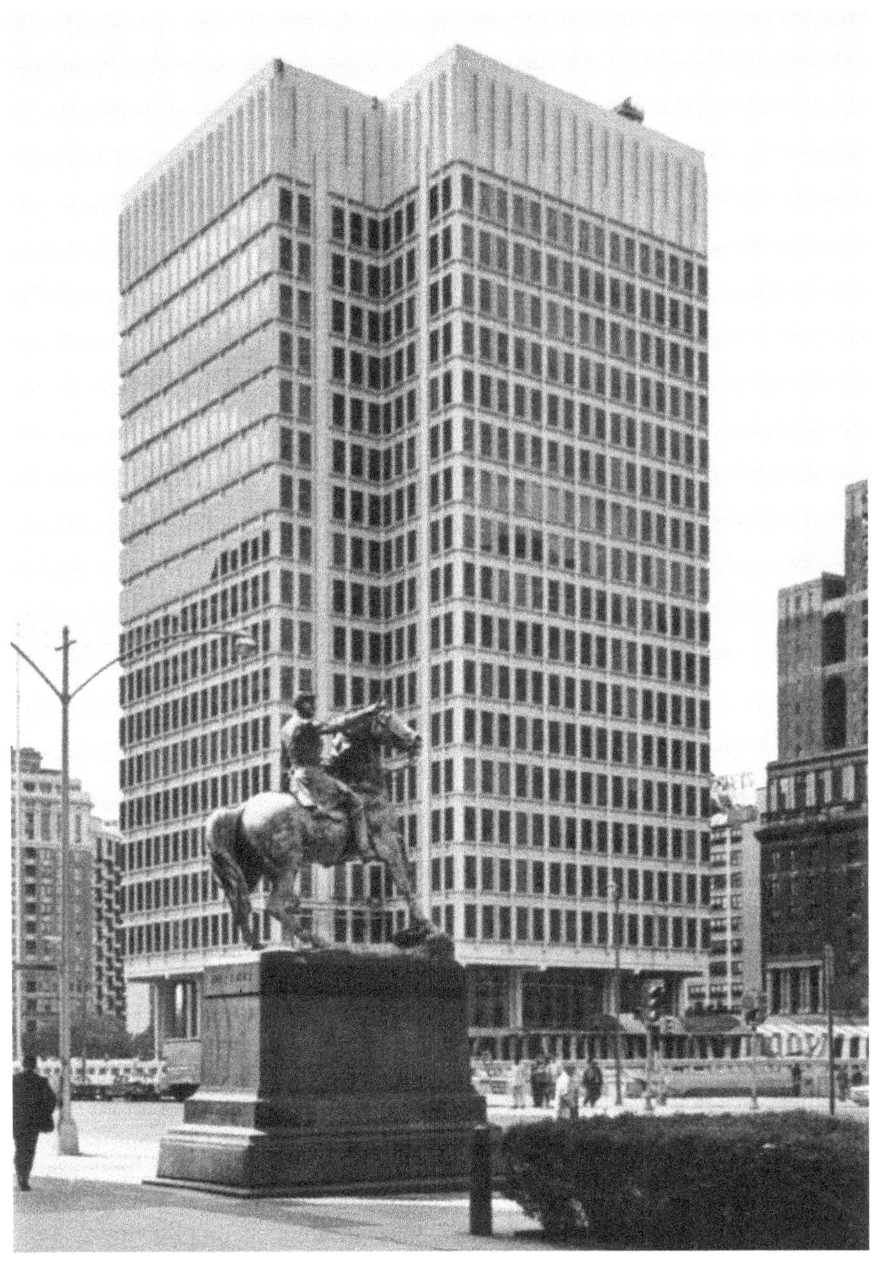

The Municipal Services Building (MSB) has a direct connection to the city's underground pedestrian concourse network at its basement level. The city's construction of the sixteen-story tower in the 1960s gave private developers confidence to build other modern office towers in the Penn Center zone near City Hall. A statue of Civil War major general John Reynolds is in the foreground. *Art Color Card Distributors; courtesy Gus Spector.*

Market East (Jefferson) Station is the centerpiece of the Market Street East Redevelopment Area. All nearby office, commercial, and hotel buildings constructed during and since its opening were designed for ready access into the station. Edmund Bacon had written of Market Street East's transit interconnectivity in a 1959 essay titled "Philadelphia in the Year 2009."

The redevelopment of east Market Street began with 1970s construction of the Gallery, a three-story-high, four-block-long complex of department stores, retail shops, and food courts meant to compete with suburban shopping malls. Bacon's idea was to transport the mall experience downtown, attracting both city dwellers and suburban shoppers.

Gallery I was the first inner-city shopping center built after World War II, completed in 1977. It was viewed as a positive return of retail shopping to Center City, as well as a disaster waiting to happen. But Gallery I was appraised as a success, so much so that it was soon expanded with Gallery II in 1983. Altogether, the Gallery became among the most successful urban shopping malls in the country and was also the nation's largest underground shopping mall in the 1980s. In effect, the marketplace became another kind of Chinese Wall along Market Street, this one east of City Hall. The Gallery mall has had its ups and downs since opening and is currently undergoing a sweeping makeover. It will soon be rechristened as "Fashion District Philadelphia," the largest cohesive retail project in downtown Philly.

As with Penn Center, the Gallery has a delivery vehicle tunnel. Running several blocks along/under Filbert Street, parallel to the Commuter Rail Tunnel, it was part and parcel of the 1980s redevelopment of East Market Street. The entrance to this obscure underground road is on the south side of Arch Street, between 8th and 9th.

The Gallery's basement level adjoins Jefferson Station's mezzanine and extends the city's pedestrian concourse all the way to 8th Street. It is thus possible to walk nonstop underground in Center City Philadelphia from 18th Street to 8th Street, along the line of JFK Boulevard and Filbert Streets, paralleling Market Street. The intersection of 8th and Market is a key transportation crux, with access to stations for the Market Street Subway, the Broad-Ridge Spur, and the PATCO Hi-Speedline (Chapters 11, 12, and 13).

What's more, the concourse connects to a pathway through the lower level of the Lit Brothers Building, so a walk underground can extend even farther east—to 7th Street. Lit Brothers Department Store closed in 1977, and the full-block building was vacant until the late 1980s. It was saved from demolition by civic outcry and has since become an office-retail complex called Mellon Independence Center. The basement level offers a lively food court these days.

Commuter Rail Tunnel construction upset Chinatown, under which the subway curves northward out of downtown. (A long line of vent grates and emergency exits are approximately above the bend, along the eastern sidewalk of 9th Street.) The city's engineers worked closely with local residents and business owners to solve noise, dust, and traffic flow problems. Parking lots were subsequently located above the tunnel heading north from Filbert to Vine, although the one-story Foot and Ankle Institute of Temple University's School of Podiatric Medicine was built atop the tunnel at Race Street. Formerly the Pennsylvania College of Podiatric Medicine, the school contains a shoe museum that displays hundreds of shoes in glass cases.

The 9th and Vine Station of the Broad-Ridge Spur lay directly in the CCCC's path and had to be demolished. A replacement station, designed in a Chinese motif, was built near 8th and Race as the spurline's new Chinatown stop. This station is the lowest point of the Commuter Rail Tunnel, about twenty feet below sea level.

The CCCC then passes underneath the subterranean slash of the Vine Street Expressway (I-676). This submerged freeway—discussed intermittently in this text—links the Schuylkill Expressway with Interstate 95, crossing over the Schuylkill River, passing through Center City along Vine Street, and connecting to both I-95 and the western terminus of the Benjamin Franklin Bridge. I-676 is a block wide (about eight lanes) and divides lower North Philadelphia from the city's core—at least psychologically.

The expressway took almost thirty-five years (1957–91) to build. The western part, from the Schuylkill River to 16th Street, was constructed first as a below-grade roadway. Farther east, I-676 was placed on the surface because of latent engineering problems—namely, getting the highway under Broad Street and the Broad Street Subway. The problems were solved in the 1980s (see Chapter 12), and the thoroughfare was continued as a lowered freeway eastward to 8th Street. The Vine Street Expressway's mile-long trench is mostly open to the sky as it passes thirty feet below street level from the Schuylkill to 8th Street. There, it rises to become an elevated roadway as it makes its way east toward I-95.

The Pennsylvania Department of Transportation (PennDOT) has recently finished rebuilding seven structurally deficient overpasses carrying city traffic and pedestrians over the I-676 west of Broad. (One of these, over 17th Street, sports a whimsical stainless steel bust of Ben Franklin.) The replacement bridges are single-span structures, with no center support piers, unlike the previous bridges.

Since the Chinatown, Callowhill and Logan Circle neighborhoods through which the highway passes have changed, the notion of capping I-676 has become a priority for city agencies. PennDOT's work included the covering of some sections of the freeway, creating more underpasses in that part of town. One cap is in front of the Free Library of Philadelphia (Central Branch), creating a new Shakespeare Park at Logan Circle with a dramatic courtyard that might someday be the setting for one of the Bard's plays.

It's just too bad that PennDOT did not hide more of the deep scar of I-676 across Philadelphia's midsection. The cost of a broader cover and the need for ventilation and fire suppression systems are reasons why the half-block-wide canyon was not fully concealed.

The Philadelphia Chinatown Development Corporation (PCDC) was organized in 1966 to save Holy Redeemer Chinese Church and School—a focal point of the Chinatown community—from demolition for the Vine Street Expressway. Neighborhood activism forced a highway redesign in those parts. In the 1990s, PCDC created a village of mixed-income residences over the Commuter Rail Tunnel from 8th to 9th Streets. This was a creative way to comply with regulations prohibiting heavy construction on land above an underground rail line.

The CCCC then dips below the Willow Street Sewer and passes alongside the Willow Street Steam Generation Plant as it proceeds north and rises on a steep 2.8 percent grade approaching the Green Street transition portal—the spot where the subway exits to the surface—and the Poplar neighborhood. A few blocks ahead, the tracks connect on a direct high-speed alignment to the old elevated Reading mainline—the Ninth Street Branch (or Elevated)—that used to take commuter trains into Reading Terminal. Now owned by SEPTA, the Ninth Street Branch brings SEPTA Regional Rail traffic through North Philadelphia into Center City.

The four-mile Philadelphia, Germantown & Norristown Railroad, dating back to 1832, was the earliest part of the Ninth Street Branch and used to operate on the surface of 9th Street. One of the oldest rail lines in America, it was one of about forty minor railroads that were amalgamated to form the Reading Railroad. In the early 1900s, the Reading raised the tracks off the street to eliminate some thirty grade crossings on the way to Reading Terminal. This was done to save lives and reduce train-related injuries—9th Street had been dubbed "Death Alley" in the papers. The project was achieved by 1913 with negligible interference to the five hundred or so daily train movements along 9th Street.

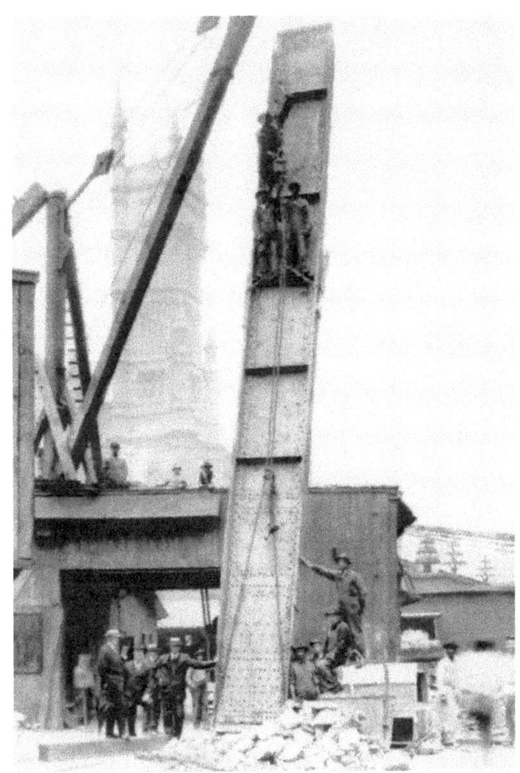

Dating to the late 1920s, this picture shows workers positioning a large steel girder for the Broad Street Subway at the northwestern apron of City Hall. The locale would see similar construction half a century later for the Commuter Rail Tunnel. In the background is the Masonic Temple of Philadelphia, among the world's largest Masonic lodges and one of the best examples of post–Civil War architecture in North America. Opened in 1873, it remains the nation's preeminent shrine of American Freemasonry. *Joel Spivak's collection.*

A few blocks from the Green Street Portal is a foreboding warehouse near Poplar Street by which the 9th Street Elevated passes. Built in 1918 for Strawbridge & Clothier, the hulking structure served as a storehouse and furniture showroom for the Philadelphia retailer. It was taken over by Quaker Storage Company in 1970, and other tenants used the building before it was abandoned in the 1990s. It has recently been approved for conversion into a 350-unit apartment complex. Nearby, the decades-vacant Spring Garden School at 12th and Ogden has been transformed into housing for homeless veterans and low-income seniors. The old K-8 school was designed in 1928 by Philadelphia architect Irwin T. Catherine.

The renovation of the storied Divine Lorraine Hotel into apartments, a long-awaited undertaking, was finally completed in 2017, adding to the Poplar neighborhood's redevelopment activity. If SEPTA were to ever rebuild the Ninth Street Elevated's old Girard Avenue Station for Regional Rail traffic, this vicinity may become the next big thing/place in Philadelphia. (Straddling Girard Avenue at 9th Street, that Reading passenger station was erected in 1913 and was gone by 1948.)

The Edgar Allan Poe National Historic Site is a block or so from the Green Street Portal. The Gothic author lived in the modest house at 530 North 7th Street when he wrote "The Raven," "The Bells," and "Annabel Lee" and when he published "The Gold Bug," "The Tell-Tale Heart," and "The Black Cat." Operated by the National Park Service, the 1842 home is the country's only nationally recognized site devoted to Poe and includes cellar space that was presumably inspiration for the entombment scenes in some of his stories.

The Commuter Rail Tunnel was originally slated for completion in 1981, but serious delays occurred in finishing connecting trackwork, interlocking, and signaling, as well as on the power supply (due to a City-Amtrak squabble over whether to use eleven or twenty-five kilovolts). The sparkling-new tunnel finally opened on November 10, 1984.

Then, six days later, a bridge at Columbia Avenue Station, near Temple University, was discovered to be on the brink of collapse, visibly sagging when trains passed. (Columbia Avenue is now Cecil B. Moore Avenue.) The once lavish ex–Reading Railroad station, built in 1909, was by then partly used as a community center, thus impeding routine bridge inspection and maintenance. The weakened span's condition forced the Ninth Street Elevated and the new Commuter Rail Tunnel to abruptly close. It was replaced in about a month's time in a daring 'round-the-clock effort.

This incident led to SEPTA's $354 million RailWorks project of 1992–93 in which twenty dilapidated Reading Railroad bridges on the Ninth Street Branch were replaced and five were rebuilt. Columbia Avenue Station was removed, and a new Temple University Station was built two blocks north. Plus, a buried conduit was added along the route to carry new signal and communications lines, and the overhead catenary system was renewed too. Continuous-welded rail was also swapped for the old bolted rails.

In 2017, SEPTA picked a Chinese company to build forty-five bi-level railcars for Philadelphia's Regional Rail System. (Will they fit through the CCCC?) The railcars will add six thousand seats to the system and will go a long way in augmenting and replacing SEPTA's fleet of aging Silverliner multiple-unit electric cars, generations of which have been in service since 1958.

The Commuter Rail Tunnel infinitely improved SEPTA's Regional Rail System by allowing the two original rail networks of Philly to work together—a first for an American city. Belonging to the City of Philadelphia, the tunnel was elected the Outstanding Civil Engineering Achievement for 1985 by the American Society of Civil Engineers. A plaque to that effect is on the southern wall of Jefferson Station's mezzanine near 12th Street.

Chapter 9

The Reading Viaduct, the City Subway Branch, the Pennsylvania Avenue Subway and Tunnel, and Fairmount Park Tunnel

The Reading Viaduct was part of Reading Railroad's Ninth Street Elevated (or Branch) as the line approached Center City and Reading Terminal. Last used in 1984, the above-grade route from Vine to Green Streets is an assortment of embankments, steel bridges, and arched masonry spans running ten blocks through the Chinatown North sector—next to and part of the Callowhill Loft District.

Impressive stone and brick arch tunnels convey city streets under Reading Viaduct in this locale. These underpasses are nerve-racking, as they have no lighting, are coated with graffiti, and have broken walkways. The underpasses for Carlton and Wood Streets are the longest and gloomiest. One for Nectarine Street has been closed for years and is shrouded by urban detritus, as is the passageway for tiny Shamokin Street. But the Pearl Street underpass has been enlivened in recent years by the Asian Arts Initiative with art installations and site-specific performances inspired by the narrow street and the wider neighborhood.

North of Callowhill Street, Reading Viaduct becomes a trestle carried on steel plate girders. It was initially a two-track structure before being expanded to four tracks in 1912. The original steel truss bridge at Spring Garden Street could not accommodate two additional tracks, so the Reading proposed building an exact duplicate of that truss span, paralleling the old one. But a graceful and sturdy three-arch bridge made of concrete was deemed a better solution. This 1913 overpass, though looking rather shabby, still carries the Reading Viaduct over Spring Garden Street.

The area around 9th and Spring Garden had been a transportation nexus since 1851, when the Philadelphia, Germantown & Norristown built its southern terminus next door at 9th and Green. The ground-level passenger/freight depot was considered in its time to be an architectural exemplar and was known along the Atlantic Seaboard. It was erected outside city limits because the railroad was heeding the municipal prohibition against steam locomotives entering the city. (Vine Street was Philly's northern boundary until 1854.)

After the Reading Railroad took over the line in 1870, the elegant 9th and Green Street Depot became the Reading's primary Philadelphia passenger station until Reading Terminal opened in 1893. In conjunction with that opening, the Reading built Spring Garden Station for passengers on the east side of the tracks at 9th and Spring Garden. The elevated station opened in 1893 and replaced the original 9th and Green Street Depot, by then used only as a freight station. The grand 1851 depot was taken down in 1909.

That year, the Reading began erecting a new freight station/warehouse on the west side of the 9th Street tracks. Finished by 1911, it served as the epicenter of cargo shipping in downtown Philadelphia for decades. The railroad auctioned off the five-story building in 1962, and it was successively converted into a textile factory, a printing house, and a warehouse. Now called "915 Spring Garden Street Studios," the old depot provided studio space to artists starting in 1981 and has lately been purchased for redevelopment as creative workspace.

A Reading commuter train plowed into the back of another one at Spring Garden Station in January 1963, injuring more than two hundred passengers. The trains had been packed due to a city transit strike then going on. Getting stretchers holding wounded riders down from the elevated line was difficult for rescuers, and seventeen-degree weather did not help matters. The collision was caused by faulty brakes on the rear train.

The 1893 passenger station at 9th and Spring Garden was forsaken in 1984 when the Center City Commuter Connection opened for traffic. Spring Garden Station still stands—in severely deteriorated condition. The Commuter Rail Tunnel comes up to the surface at nearby Green Street (through the transition portal) and connects there to the Ninth Street Elevated. The SEPTA line is then carried over many streets in North Philadelphia as it heads to the city's northern suburbs.

SEPTA discontinued service on the Reading Viaduct when the Commuter Rail Tunnel opened in 1984. Three blocks of the elevated structure, from Vine Street southward to the Pennsylvania Convention Center, were cleared away in the early 1990s as part of the Center's construction. The rest of the mile-long trestle was completely deserted by 1992 and was declared off-limits to public access. High above eye level, the viaduct yielded to rampant plant growth and illicit activity of all sorts.

Reminiscent of the Pennsylvania Railroad's long-gone Chinese Wall, the Reading Viaduct offers a window into the Quaker City's bygone railroad activity. This history has endeared the structure to urban explorers and generated clamor for its preservation. In addition, the viaduct offers splendid views of Philadelphia's skyline.

In 2003, the City of Philadelphia analyzed the cost of demolishing the viaduct compared to the cost of redeveloping it as a linear park. The estimated cost to raze the structure was ten times greater than the cost of environmental remediation to reclaim it as a park. The recent reuse of the Chelsea High Line in New York City has also helped in this movement. (New York's High Line is a portion of the former New York Central Railroad's West Side Line.) The High Line's success, in terms of economic development and as an urban recreational amenity, brought dreams of a similar elevated park for the City of Brotherly Love. The Promenade Planteé, a corresponding project in the City of Light, has likewise contributed to the rebirth of adjoining communities in Paris, France.

The Philadelphia scheme includes aboveground and underground segments and has gone by several names, including the Reading Viaduct Rail Park, ViaductGreene, and the Reading Viaduct Project. Many have propelled the effort, such as Paul vanMeter, founder of ViaductGreene, as well as artist Sarah McEneaney and John Struble, co-founders of the Reading Viaduct Project. Formed in 2003, the latter grass-roots campaign merged with Friends of the Rail Park, which then partnered with the Center City District, an economic improvement agency in the city. Paul vanMeter died in 2014 and is remembered for his dedication to ViaductGreene and for the tours he led to highlight his conception of a below-ground rail park for Philly.

Reading Viaduct Rail Park will traverse ten Philadelphia neighborhoods and will consist of three miles of greenway—all without crossing a city street at grade. Instead of being a blighted refuge for trespassers, this old industrial artery will feature pedestrian and bicycle paths, benches, landscaping, programming spaces, access staircases and ramps, and lighting. The viaduct's adaptive reuse will both preserve and rejuvenate the former industrial heart of Philadelphia and will be a catalyst for continued residential and commercial growth of peripheral neighborhoods. Even nearby Chinatown, which initially objected to the Rail Park, has come around.

Reading Viaduct's conversion into a linear park commenced in 2016. Grants from various sources have allowed construction crews to clean the discarded route of chemicals deposited by trains over decades and a staggering amount of wild vegetation. Old rails and ties had already been removed by the Reading Company, although the steel catenary structures still remain overhead and will be retained as a vestige of the past.

Evincing the Reading's wonderful masonry work, the viaduct splits in two directions near 11th and Callowhill: to the north for the Ninth Street Branch and to the west for the City Subway Branch. Phase I of the Rail Park undertaking began with the quarter-mile elevated portion of the City Branch route, the leg that ducks under Broad Street and heads west paralleling Callowhill Street. A hundred volunteers, including Sarah McEneaney and John Struble, planted 1,100 trees and shrubs along Phase I in 2017, providing a morsel of green space in an urban-industrial zone that had none.

A stairwell from 13th Street will provide one of three ways up to the elevated Rail Park. In the 1890s, 13th Street was lowered thirteen feet to enable City Branch tracks to pass above via a multi-track steel girder bridge. Noble Street still uses the same bridge, which has recently been limited to a three-ton weight limit due to deterioration. Nearby buildings were also affected by the 1890s work, with basement levels becoming main entrances.

Phase I, costing $10 million, was completed in 2018. The City of Philadelphia will take ownership of the two-block right-of-way, and the Center City District will manage this new urban amenity. Given the funds required for Reading Viaduct's overhaul, the Rail Park's completion will clearly be a step-by-step process.

The City Branch right-of-way stems back to 1792 with the inauguration of a canal project between the Schuylkill and Delaware Rivers. The Delaware & Schuylkill Canal Company chose this route because it was the narrowest corridor between the two waterways and thus a natural place to dig a trench to link the rivers. The channel might have converged with Pegg's Run (Cohoquinoque Creek) as it flowed eastward toward the Delaware River. The "Philadelphia Canal" was meant to become part of a chain of waterways between Philadelphia and the Susquehanna River that would collectively be designated the Union Canal. William Penn had proposed such a canal system back in 1690 to unite the western part of his colony with Philadelphia.

Sections of the Philadelphia Canal were hand-dug from behind where the Philadelphia Museum of Art is today to almost Broad Street. Other canal digging also occurred near where Spring Garden Street came to be, not far from Ridge Avenue. But work was suspended when investors lost faith in the venture and the canal company's assets plummeted. The Delaware & Schuylkill Canal Company went bankrupt in the mid-1790s, after spending $220,000. Some shoveling reportedly occurred as late as 1798.

The Philadelphia Canal's right-of-way, as authorized by the Commonwealth of Pennsylvania, was subsequently appropriated by the Philadelphia & Columbia Railroad, one of the earliest railroads in America and the first railroad in the world undertaken by a government (Pennsylvania) rather than by private enterprise. Started in 1828 and completed in 1834, the line extended westward from Philadelphia eighty-two miles to Columbia, Pennsylvania, on the Susquehanna River.

In the city, the Philadelphia & Columbia began at Broad Street and ran west on the surface of a street called Pennsylvania Avenue, paralleling Callowhill Street. Excavated portions of the Philadelphia Canal were filled in, and tracks were laid along the canal's towpath and within its deserted bed, a matter of convenience that worked out in the sparsely settled landscape of Philadelphia County.

The Philadelphia & Columbia became part of the Pennsylvania Railroad by 1857, except for this particular section in lower North Philadelphia, which went to the Reading Railroad. This right-of-way became the Reading's City Branch in the second half of the nineteenth century and remained as such for a hundred years. The line's tracks were on Pennsylvania Avenue west of Broad Street and continued northwestward out of the city, crossing several north–south streets at grade to almost the Schuylkill River. East of Broad, Pennsylvania Avenue proceeded eastward as Noble Street, and railroad tracks ran to port facilities along the Delaware River. Tracks were on the surface of Noble and then shifted to Willow Street on their way to the central waterfront.

Sixteen tracks of the Reading Railroad bisected Broad Street at grade immediately north of the intersection of Broad and Callowhill until the 1890s. A watchman lowered gates to halt city traffic on Broad Street each time a train used the City Branch. That such a major city artery was repeatedly blocked for trains to cross was especially irritating to Philadelphians.

The Reading Railroad and the City of Philadelphia together studied the concept of elevating Broad Street over Pennsylvania Avenue and the Reading's tracks. When it was pointed out that doing so would ruin the city's finest avenue (used for civic parades), both parties agreed to dig away Pennsylvania Avenue toward the west so that the City Branch could secure the entire right-of-way—*below grade*. The Reading and the city each paid $3 million for the

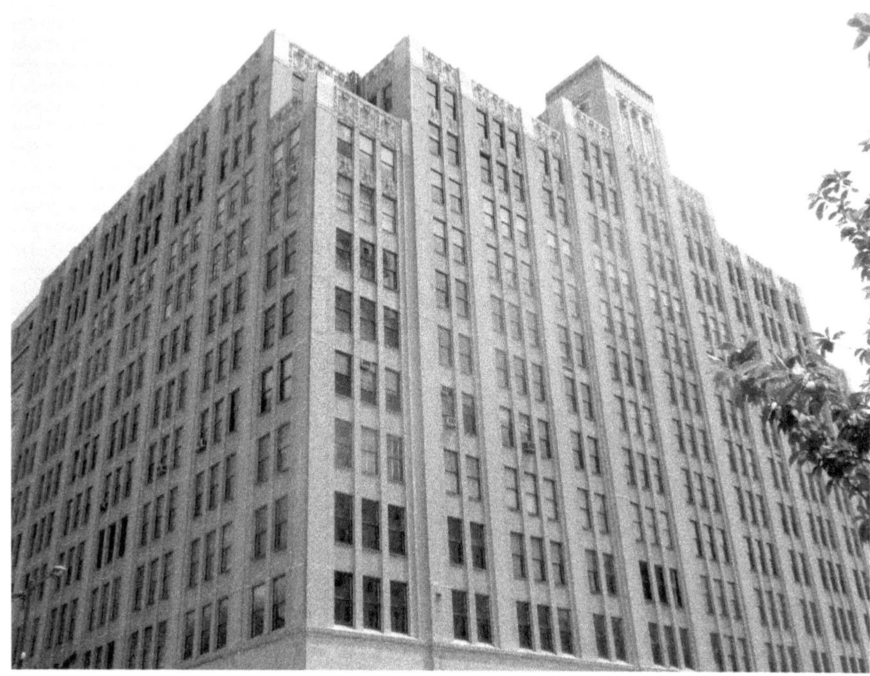

The immense and strangely handsome Terminal Commerce Building at Broad and Callowhill, built and formerly owned by the Reading Railroad Company, is on the former site of Reading freight stations, next to the City Branch tracks. The building has been repositioned as a "data carrier hotel" since the 1990s. Numerous air conditioning systems to cool high-tech telecommunications equipment can be heard on Terminal Commerce's ground floor, where trains once passed. It is said that a good chunk of the nation's East Coast Internet traffic goes through the building, similar to how the Verizon Building at 24th and South handles East Coast voice and data communications. Also a major junction for national optical fiber data routes, the carrier hotel further provides a direct connection to Europe through transatlantic submarine cable networks. Terminal Commerce is hiding the Lasher Printing Building on the same side of Broad Street, on the northern side of Noble Street and the City Branch tracks. Built in 1927, the Lasher Building also serves as a data carrier hotel. *Michael Bixler.*

joint undertaking, which was devised to eliminate traffic problems (and deaths and injuries) caused by the intersection of city streets with the railroad's tracks. (Note that the City "Subway" Branch is not a "subway," as in transit line, but a "sub-way," a right-of-way below ground level).

More than a million cubic yards of earth were scooped out to create the Pennsylvania Avenue Subway and Tunnel. A great amount of underpinning of factory buildings along the route was required, as was the laying of new sewers, electrical, and telephone conduits; gas lines; and water mains, not to mention reconstruction of railroad tracks, engine and freight houses, and coal facilities. Completed by 1899, the lowering work effectively eliminated Pennsylvania Avenue for almost two miles west of Broad Street, thus removing seventeen grade crossings. East of Broad, the right-of-way rose up (as it still does) at Noble Street and joined with the Ninth Street Viaduct toward Reading Terminal. The City Branch is called "the Cut" by Rail Park enthusiasts.

The Reading built a bridge to carry Broad Street over City Branch tracks in 1898. The span has since been hidden by buildings on either side of Broad. Thirty-some years later, the Broad Street Subway was threaded under the City Subway Branch, far below street level, at the point where Broad Street gently rises in front of Terminal Commerce Building. The ponderous Art Deco–style pile at 401 North Broad is one of the buildings obscuring the bridge over the City Branch.

Terminal Commerce Building may very well be the most imposing structure in Philadelphia. Totaling more than 1.3 million square feet, the office/warehouse complex was constructed by the Reading Company between 1929 and 1931. The railroad proclaimed that this was the nation's first warehouse with a freight station beneath it.

Ground on which the Commerce Building stands has been part of Philadelphia's transportation infrastructure since long before the City Branch route was submerged. The site first hosted the Philadelphia & Reading Railroad's Broad Street Depot, a cavernous structure erected in 1861. The Reading took that building down in the 1890s and set up the North Broad Street Freight Station, encompassing two warehouses and a seven-track railyard along the City Branch route. Terminal Commerce Building and its novel underground freight depot afterward replaced this freight station.

Note that the first main Reading terminal in Philadelphia was a large station built in 1839 on the southeast corner of Broad and Cherry. It was destroyed by fire in 1868 after having been used as a U.S. Army hospital during the American Civil War.

Reading sold the Commerce Building in 1955, whereupon it was renamed the North American Building. During the 1960s, many young men in the Philadelphia region took their physicals for military service at 401 North Broad. Miscellaneous businesses operated out of the building until the 1980s. Its size and strength account for the structure's current-day use as a telecommunications carrier hotel, housing Internet servers, routers, and data storage computers.

The old Reading Railroad dining car parked alongside the Commerce Building will soon be refurbished as a welcoming center for the Reading Viaduct Rail Park. Located at Broad and Noble alongside a future entrance to the park, car 1186 was built in 1922 and subsequently provided luxury dining accommodations on the Reading's Iron Horse Rambles (excursion trips). The railroad sold the car in the 1970s, and it has since rested (and rusted) there, used as a passport photo shop and also a luncheonette ("The Steak and Bagel Train"). Reading car 1186 is stranded at that spot since the tracks on which it stands no longer connect to active rail.

Across Broad Street from Terminal Commerce Building is the former Philadelphia Inquirer Building, also called the Elverson Building. The first issue of the *Inquirer* printed there came off the presses on July 13, 1925. At the time, the ivory edifice was touted as the most modern newspaper plant on Earth. With its 340-foot bell/clock tower, the "Tower of Truth" (as it has been called) is one of the tallest Philadelphia landmarks north of Market Street.

Like Terminal Commerce Building, the Elverson Building was built on pilings to allow City Branch tracks to pass beneath and to provide a rail sidings under the building. The courtly structure was built exceptionally strong so that the vibrations of unremitting train movements would not affect the printing presses on the second floor. The Elverson Building's heft is carried on 150 caissons reaching to bedrock.

The *Philadelphia Inquirer* built a large newspaper plant beside the Elverson Building in 1948, fronting Broad Street. This annex housed rotogravure presses used to print color sections of the Sunday *Inquirer* and other publications. The building has been center of operations for the School District of Philadelphia since 2005.

The *Inquirer* was a steady patron of the Reading Railroad for years, using the City Branch for the delivery of giant rolls of newsprint and other supplies. The line was last used for this purpose in 1992, by which time it was conducted by Conrail. SEPTA, seeing potential opportunity in the route's intersection with the Broad Street Subway, purchased the open-air trench. But nothing came of this.

The publishing operations of the *Philadelphia Inquirer* decamped to the historic Strawbridge & Clothier Building at 8th and Market in 2012. The Elverson Building, meanwhile, was purchased for conversion into a hotel-casino, but that plan foundered. Plans are now cooking to transform the pile into the new Police Administration Building. The Philadelphia Police Department will vacate its current command center, the four-story

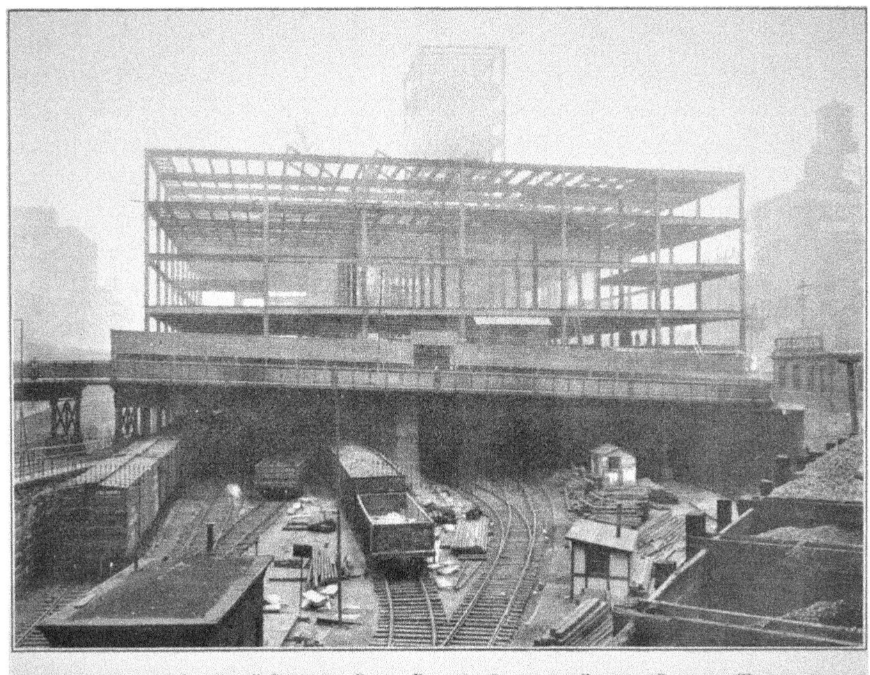

"PHILADELPHIA INQUIRER" BUILDING BEING ERECTED OVER THE READING RAILWAY TRACKS AT BROAD STREET, SHOWING HOW EVEN A "SKY SCRAPER" CAN BE BUILT OVER A RAILROAD.

The City Branch Line passes beneath the Philadelphia Inquirer Building, under construction (and on stilts) in this early 1920s photograph. The owner and publisher of the *Philadelphia Inquirer*, Colonel James Elverson Jr., and his wife resided on the twelfth and thirteenth floors with their extensive art collection. Elverson's father had purchased the *Inquirer* in 1879 and nurtured it into a major newspaper. The *Philadelphia Inquirer* was later owned by Walter Annenberg, who maintained a plush suite of offices on the twelfth floor that only a select few could visit unbidden. *From* The Redemption of the Lower Schuylkill *(1924), by John Frederick Lewis.*

Roundhouse at 750 Race Street, and move into the new headquarters by 2020. Renovations are expected to cost roughly $290 million.

In its heyday, the City Branch freight right-of-way catered to a handful of heavy manufacturing concerns, most related to railroading. In the 1890s, this collection of factories in lower North Philadelphia was noted as "the greatest center of gigantic and diversified railway industries in the world." The most important business in that primordial industrial park was Baldwin Locomotive Works of Philadelphia.

Inspired by the need for a domestic source of locomotive power, Matthias William Baldwin (1795–1866) designed and built a miniature demonstration railway in 1830 for Peale's American Museum. The success of this railway prompted the Philadelphia, Germantown & Norristown Railroad to hire him to fabricate a full-scale locomotive. This is how Matthias Baldwin came to construct Old Ironsides, the first commercial steam locomotive in America. It started service along 9th Street on November 23, 1832. Baldwin finished his second locomotive two years later, this time inventing a way to double steam pressure. In no time, his engines outperformed those imported from England.

In 1835–36, Baldwin erected a brick factory on the west side of Broad Street at Hamilton Street to house his locomotive manufactory. Many buildings were added to the complex until it filled most blocks between Callowhill and Spring Garden west of Broad. Baldwin Locomotive Works made its reputation building steam locomotives for the Pennsylvania Railroad and other North American railroads, as well as railways in England, France, India, Haiti, and Egypt. Philadelphia thus became the locomotive capital of America.

This appellation actually began with the Norris Locomotive Works, located two blocks away at 17th and Hamilton. The family-owned firm, founded in 1832, was the first American exporter of railroad locomotives; 30 percent of its production was shipped to foreign markets by 1840. Although Norris Locomotive was the largest maker of locomotives in the United States, if not the world, during the 1850s, the concern went out of business after the Civil War, a casualty of family indifference. The Baldwin company acquired and added much of the Norris site to its factory compound in 1873.

Baldwin Locomotive moved to Eddystone, Pennsylvania, in the late 1920s, and its vacant manufactories in Philadelphia were demolished in 1937 as a Federal Works Project. After lying fallow for many years, that locality has become the campus of the Community College of Philadelphia. The educational institution in 1971 procured the Third U.S. Mint Building—used from 1901 until 1969—at 1700 Spring Garden Street as its main building. The college is at the core of Franklintown, a neighborhood that has recovered from the post-industrial conditions of the last century.

The Reading Company Grain Elevator on 20th Street alongside the City Branch was raised on the footprint of a grain elevator that had been there since the Civil War and which was destroyed in 1925 due to a grain explosion. It is certainly different from the many deluxe condominiums being constructed throughout this erstwhile industrial zone. Even Matthias Baldwin Park, a welcomed expanse of green space atop a former manufacturing tract, skirts the City Branch.

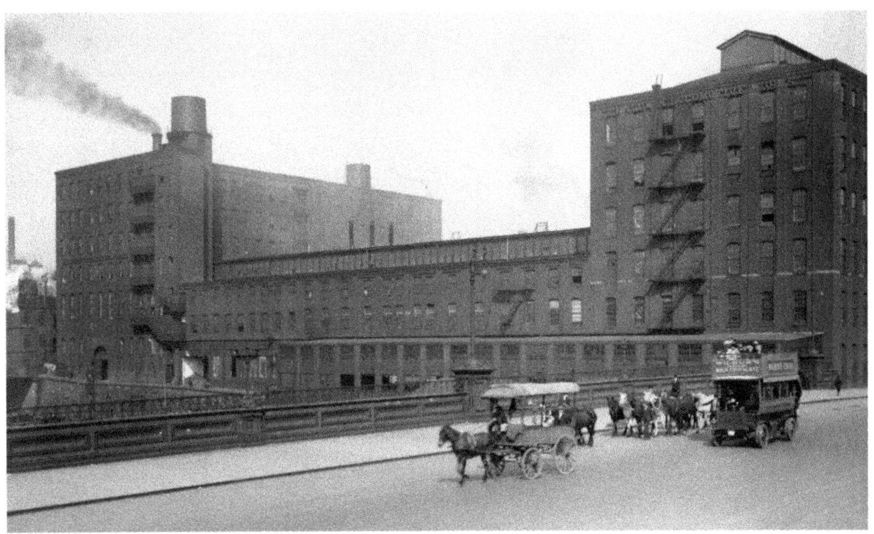

Baldwin Locomotive Works of Philadelphia faces Broad Street in this early twentieth-century image but would be supplanted in 1925 by the Philadelphia Inquirer Building. The bridge in the foreground carries Broad over the City Branch tracks of the Reading Railroad. By the late 1920s, the Broad Street Subway would be excavated under the street and bridge (and the perpendicular City Branch tracks). Built in 1898, the span is still there today, hidden by the Inquirer Building and the Terminal Commerce Building on either side of Broad. *Library of Congress.*

Tracks of the desolate City Branch have been removed, and nature has reclaimed much of the old right-of-way, as seen from several street bridges over the submerged route. The open subway curves northwest near 21st and Hamilton, behind the Rodin Museum, and continues as a covered subway tunnel under Pennsylvania Avenue. Steel ventilation grates mark the way.

Around the year 2000, there was chatter of SEPTA building a light-rail line to use the City Branch route, but the agency took no action to reactivate the line. The right-of-way was then incorporated into a $2 billion state plan to reintroduce commuter rail service between Philadelphia and Reading, Pennsylvania. But the Federal Transit Administration dismissed the concept in 2006. The most recent plan was to use the subway for bus routes that would run below street level to evade traffic.

However, it does seem assured that the Pennsylvania Avenue Tunnel will become a subterranean park to be completed after Reading Viaduct park is done. The ambitious endeavor has already attracted grants to offset a price tag ranging from $30 million to $80 million.

A portion of the Pennsylvania Avenue Tunnel is still actively utilized by CSX Railroad's East Side Line, which carries freight trains alongside the eastern bank of the Schuylkill River. The use of this route is a point of contention with many Center City inhabitants, since CSX trains are routinely left on the tracks, often with their locomotives idling for hours. Beyond blocking access to the river, many of these CSX trains are filled with garbage, making them smelly and unsightly as they wait by the Schuylkill. Other trains carry dangerous cargo, such as crude oil and toxic chemicals.

Over and above this danger, the CSX tracks lessen the allure of the Schuylkill's east bank for recreational activity. "Schuylkill Banks" is the name of the narrow strip of river frontage that the city has been making a full-fledged park for downtowners in recent years. An at-grade pedestrian/bicycle crossing with automatic gates was added to the East Side Line at Race Street in the early 2000s, but this is still a risky place. For instance, a woman collecting unburned coal along the tracks in 1907 was struck by a train and beheaded along this stretch. Another gated crosswalk is at Locust Street. Both junctions are unique in the United States and were added to make Schuylkill Banks more user-friendly. Administered by Philadelphia Parks & Recreation, Schuylkill Banks is part of the Schuylkill River Trail, the multipurpose pathway along the river.

South of Locust, Schuylkill Banks Boardwalk extends the River Trail to South Street *on top of* the river via a two-thousand-foot esplanade installed in 2014. About fifty feet out from the shore at its furthest, the fifteen-foot-wide footpath includes a pedestrian/bicycle ramp up to South Street together with scenic overlooks for excellent views of Center City. Depending on the tide (the Schuylkill River is tidal up to Fairmount Dam), the curvaceous concrete causeway is five to ten feet above the water. Schuylkill Banks Boardwalk was necessary because CSX tracks are too close to the Schuylkill's edge at that point, making it impossible to accommodate a riverside trail. Various improvements to the Schuylkill's eastern bank (like this) have taken almost a century to plan and execute.

The Baltimore & Ohio Railroad built the East Side Line in 1883 and operated it as a subsidiary, the Schuylkill River East Side Railroad. The four-mile route was part of the railroad's Philadelphia-Baltimore mainline and handled all B&O freight and passenger traffic to and from New York City.

Coming into the city from the south, the CSX tracks pass through the Grays Ferry Tunnel, situated under the busy junction of Grays Ferry Avenue and 34th Street. This rail passageway was originally two 835-foot-long

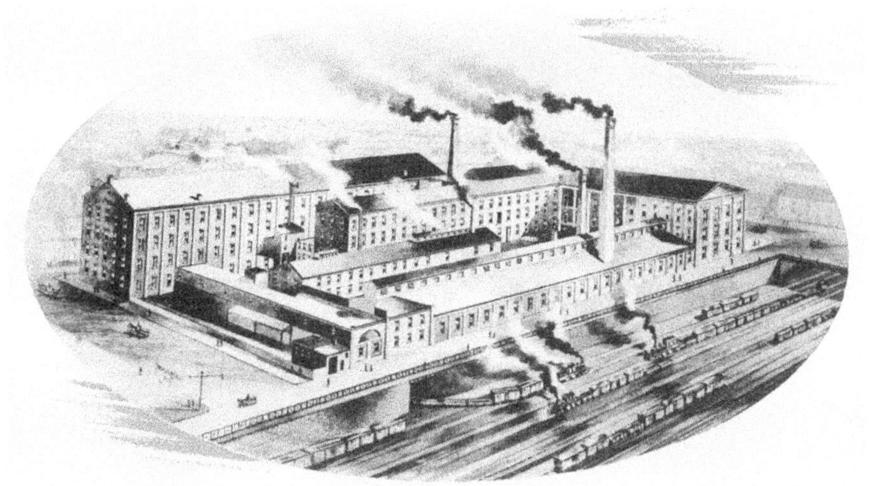

Besides Baldwin Locomotive Works, the City Branch provided rail service to the factories of William Sellers Machine Tool Works, Asa Whitney & Sons Car-Wheel Works, and Bement & Miles Machine Works, among others. The firms were makers of sundry tools and equipment for railroads, steel plants, and shipbuilders. Even the federal government's third Philadelphia Mint—the world's largest coin-making factory in the early twentieth century—chose the neighborhood in 1901 for the engineering expertise and skilled workforce available in the vicinity. This image shows the Union Malleable Iron Works (aka the Stanley Flagg Company) at 19th and Hamilton, alongside the submerged City Branch. The foundry was the first to manufacture malleable iron-threaded pipe fittings, enabling gas, steam, and water pipes to be easily joined. This location is now the site of the Tivoli condominium complex. *From* One Hundred Years of Leadership, 1854–1954: Stanley G. Flagg Co. *(1954).*

tunnels side by side that opened on November 11, 1886. Increased use of the East Side Line required the B&O to add an additional tunnel in 1918. Pennsylvania Railroad tracks that were once on the surface of Grays Ferry Avenue used to pass over the B&O's tracks via this structure.

The CSX tracks skirt the Schuylkill River's east bank as they proceed past the onetime site of Philadelphia's B&O Station. Known also as both the 24th Street Station and Chestnut Street Station, this was the main passenger terminal for the Baltimore & Ohio Railroad in Philadelphia. The B&O built this terminal when it decided to extend service to New York by utilizing the Reading Railroad's routes between Philadelphia and Jersey City, New Jersey (opposite New York City).

The B&O Station was designed by Frank Furness and was completed by 1888 in the Flemish Revival style. Like 30th Street Station and the Main Post Office (erected later on the Schuylkill's opposing bank), the brawny B&O

Station was basically built on stilts. The main entrance on Chestnut Street was thirty feet above ground level, practically on the Chestnut Street Bridge over the Schuylkill River.

A trainshed and railyard bordered the station and the B&O tracks that ran along the Schuylkill's east bank. This was not a favored station complex on the Baltimore & Ohio system, as the place would flood whenever the river overflowed. The station saw its last scheduled passenger train on April 27, 1958, when the B&O Railroad discontinued passenger service north of Baltimore. It was destroyed by fire in 1963 and soon after razed. A residential complex, 2400 Chestnut Apartments, is on the site nowadays. Schuylkill Banks sponsors film showings and other events along the river in that locale.

The CSX right-of-way advances north and passes under bridges used by Market Street, JFK Boulevard, and SEPTA Regional Rail. The riverbank route crosses over the Market Street Tunnel (Chapters 10 and 11) as well. Two sets of CSX tracks merge into a single set and enter the half-mile-long Fairmount Park Tunnel at a point edging Franklin's Paine Skatepark. The tracks proceed beneath Eakins Oval and Spring Garden Street Tunnel (Chapter 15) before joining and paralleling the Reading's City Branch tracks inside the Pennsylvania Avenue Tunnel, under Pennsylvania Avenue. The City Subway Branch's tracks were removed decades ago, but the CSX tracks endure and are still in use. They continue northward to exit Fairmount Park Tunnel at 27th Street. From there, they split, with one branch heading northwest along the Schuylkill and the other heading east through the city to the Port Richmond Yards and to the north.

Considered an engineering marvel of its day, the 1880s Fairmount Park Tunnel encircles the southeastern half of the Philadelphia Museum of Art and is the busiest freight tunnel in Philadelphia at present. It was built to allow the B&O Railroad to access the Reading's tracks farther north while preserving East Fairmount Park. Before 1921, the tunnel began under Callowhill Street, which at one time passed through where Franklin's Paine Skatepark is today. It then proceeded north under 25th Street—an avenue previously in front of the Fairmount Reservoirs.

Work on Fairmount Park Tunnel commenced in the mid-1880s, making it Philadelphia's earliest underground railway project (after the Thirty-Second Street Tunnel, explored in Chapter 6). An open cut was excavated through rock varying from twelve to thirty feet deep. The tunnel was then built as a brick arch supported on stone walls thirty feet apart. Water mains and sewers had to be rerouted, and large buildings were raised up to eleven feet

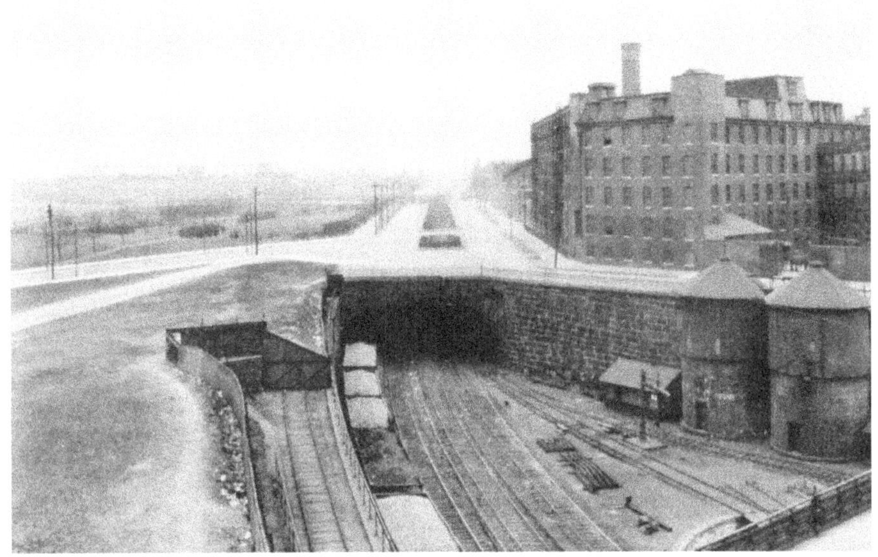

The Philadelphia Museum of Art is under construction on the horizon of this 1923 photograph of Pennsylvania Avenue and the Pennsylvania Avenue Subway. The rail route was excavated in the 1890s by the City of Philadelphia and the Reading Railroad to remove train traffic from surface streets in the city's northwestern sector. The subway, now partly abandoned, is a component of the Reading's City Branch line. *From* The Redemption of the Lower Schuylkill *(1924), by John Frederick Lewis.*

to the new grade of the reinstated surrounding streets. The tunnel opened for rail traffic in December 1886.

Fairmount Park Tunnel was reconfigured and enlarged in 1921—a year that appears in concrete above the southern portal adjacent to Franklin's Paine Skatepark. The tunnel was uncovered, and its walls and supporting arches were reconstructed of concrete. A three-inch layer of asphalt was deposited over the roof structure to waterproof the revamped tunnel, which was elongated to 2,540 feet in length.

Today, only a few ventilation grills on Pennsylvania Avenue reveal the extent of rail infrastructure beneath the surface near the Philadelphia Museum of Art. Fairmount Park Tunnel is a main reason why the museum has not installed a passageway under Kelly Drive and Pennsylvania Avenue to connect to the Perelman Building at Fairmount Avenue. The museum renovated this building as new gallery space in 2007.

Mile-long CSX trains transporting crude oil periodically move through Fairmount Park Tunnel. There is fear of a potential explosion inside the passage, a prospect that worries the Philadelphia Museum of Art most of all.

In fact, the tunnel has already experienced a calamity involving oil tankers. Around midnight on the evening of May 11, 1900, several tankers carrying oil and naphtha exploded when a Reading freight train smashed into a stalled B&O train inside the tunnel, about five hundred feet south of the tunnel's northern portal. The Reading's engineer and fireman died upon impact, and according to vague newspaper reports, five tramps stealing a ride also perished. Flames and smoke shooting out of both portals hampered firefighting efforts, and attempts to reach the blaze by blasting holes down through Fairmount Avenue were unsuccessful. Thirty city firemen were overcome by smoky oil fumes while battling the underground inferno as the wreckage burned for two days.

An investigation disclosed that B&O telegraph operator William Lantell failed to switch the white "all clear" light to red (so as to stop oncoming trains), in violation of company rules, because he fell asleep at his post. He disappeared after the collision, thereafter giving himself up to authorities, saying, "I am ready to stand the censure and take what comes to me. I have no excuse to offer." Lantell was charged with voluntary manslaughter but was ultimately exonerated when the court concluded that sleeping on the job was not negligence for which he could be found culpable!

While these tunnels are within East Fairmount Park, the park's western sector also contains several rail tunnels. The Fairmount Park Transportation Company operated the Fairmount Park Trolley to Woodside Amusement Park in West Philadelphia from 1897 until 1946. The scenic route through West Fairmount Park included Strawberry Mansion Bridge, a steel arch truss span across the Schuylkill River built in 1896–97 and still standing for the use of pedestrians and motor vehicles. The bridge displays two sections of re-created trolley tracks and catenary poles as a commemoration of the beloved old line, which went out of business due to declining ridership. The Fairmount Park Conservancy's new "Trolley Trail" is a five-mile loop for bicyclists and joggers along the Fairmount Park Trolley's right-of-way and through its 1896-era tunnels.

Chapter 10

PRT, PTC, SEPTA, and the Subway-Surface Routes (Green Lines)

Philadelphia inventor Eleazer A. Gardner patented plans for the first *cable* streetcar (trolley) system in 1858. It was composed of a sequence of pulleys and buried conduits containing a steel cable between the tracks. Trolleys rolling on iron rails were moved by a clutch that gripped the cable with a jaw-like device. The cables actually crossed over one another several times along Market Street. While Gardner's system was not embraced in Philly, it was essentially the design instituted in San Francisco starting in 1873.

A cable car system was finally installed in Philadelphia in 1883. On April 7, rails in the bed of Columbia Avenue allowed for service to the entrance of East Fairmount Park via 23rd Street. Designed to accommodate summertime travelers, this line was managed by transit entrepreneur Peter Widener through the Philadelphia Traction Company. Within a few years, the rails ran to 7th and Master and, from there, all the way to Locust Street (southbound on 7th; northbound on 9th). Another cable car route began service along Market Street on January 26, 1885.

These lines were ultimately unsuccessful. The steel cables wore out quickly, and weak cable conduits squeezed shut when the ground froze. The cable cars were also disparaged for the annoying lurches that marked their violent starts and stops. By 1895, the routes had been switched over to electric trolley car service.

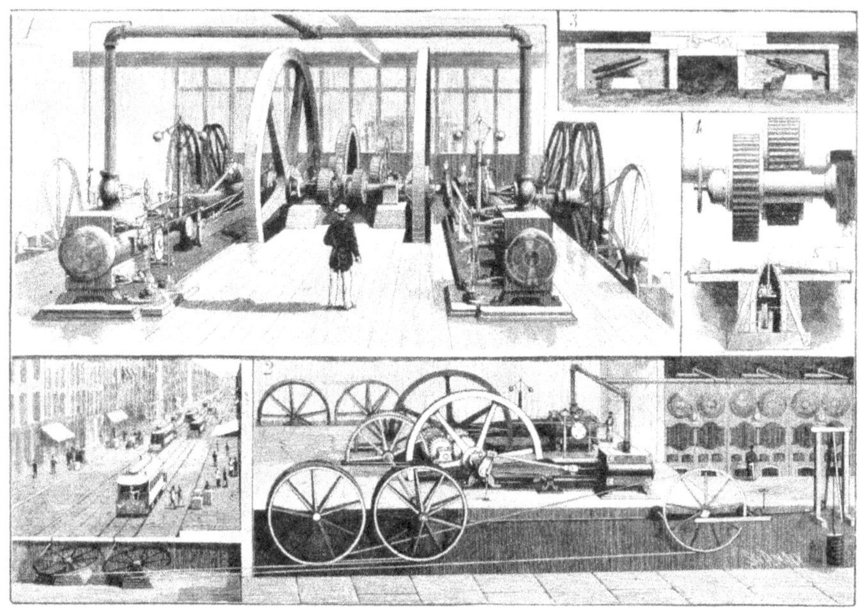

THE MOTIVE POWER OF THE PHILADELPHIA CABLE RAILWAY.

The Philadelphia Traction Company's cable car line on Market Street ran from 41st and Haverford Avenue eastward to an engine house and station on the south side of Market between 19th and 20th. It then continued eastward on Market Street to serve the ferries along Delaware Avenue. Steel cables ran in wrought-iron conduits placed between the trolley gauge and a complex system of pulleys routed the cables across town. *From "The Motive Power of the Philadelphia Cable Railway,"* Scientific American *(February 21, 1885).*

Horses were the motive power of Philly's streetcar routes since the first horsecar lines started in 1858. One aberrant aspect of the city's trolley operation was a result of an 1857 ordinance that mandated that space between the rails was to be just over five feet, two inches (aka Philadelphia Broad Gauge) and not four feet, eight and a half inches, as was standard for most railroads.

The first *electric* trolley route in the city began operation on December 15, 1892. Managed by the Philadelphia Traction Company, the Catherine and Bainbridge Streets Railway Company ran its trolleys from a depot at 36th and Grays Ferry Avenue east to Front Street by way of Bainbridge Street and then returned west to the depot via Catherine Street and Grays Ferry Avenue. The line was an unqualified success, and Philadelphia soon became the nation's trailblazer in electric streetcar service. Indeed, Philadelphia was one of the country's first cities to abolish the horsecar—so abruptly that the last horse-drawn car vanished within five years after electric trolley service began.

One of the largest manufacturers of trolleys and interurban railcars was based in Philadelphia. The J.G. Brill Company of West Philadelphia began as a horsecar maker in 1868 and fabricated streetcars, interurbans, and buses for almost a hundred years. John A. Brill (1852–1908), son of the founder, was responsible for many of the firm's innovations and traveled tirelessly around the world selling Philadelphia-made vehicles. Although Brill ceased production in 1954, some of its interurban cars served the Philadelphia area until the 1980s.

Transit magnates Peter Widener and William Elkins in 1895 formed the Union Traction Company, which soon controlled nearly all trolley lines in Philadelphia. Union Traction managed the city's trolley system with little competition until 1901. Then, an independent attempt was made to aggregate the 286 miles of trolley tracks that were operated by dozens of independent trolley companies. The goal was to establish a large syndicate to administer trolleys and elevated railroads in Philadelphia.

To remove this threat of competition, Union Traction investors reorganized the business into the Philadelphia Rapid Transit Company (PRT) in 1902. The revised firm proceeded to absorb the competing conglomerated company. By 1911, PRT owned and operated about four thousand streetcars, the largest working fleet of trolleys in the United States. Just about every major street in Philadelphia maintained a trolley line, almost all controlled by PRT.

Owing to trolley congestion in the downtown area, Philadelphia Rapid Transit undertook construction of both the Market Street Subway (in downtown Philadelphia) and the Market Street Elevated Passenger Railway (in West Philadelphia), joining the two to create the Market Street Line (see Chapter 11).

The Great Depression's lingering effects and the expense of leasing routes from antecedent companies caused Philadelphia Rapid Transit Company to become insolvent in 1939. The PRT was then reconstituted as Philadelphia Transportation Company (PTC), which came to manage the city's network of subways, elevated trains, trolley lines, and bus routes by 1940. Among the PTC's first actions was to replace PRT's decrepit vehicle fleet. The company placed orders for 130 President's Conference Committee (PCC) streetcars, 50 electric trackless trolleybuses, and 153 buses. Some of this new equipment was made in Philadelphia by the Brill Company.

National City Lines (NCL) acquired PTC in 1955, converting many trolley routes to bus operation or abandoning them entirely. NCL was a Chicago company partly owned by General Motors, Firestone Tire, Standard Oil, and Phillips Petroleum for the express purpose of acquiring local transit systems throughout the country.

In an era when Philly had more PCC streetcars running to more destinations and with greater frequency than any other city in the country, NCL cast aside scores of Philadelphia streetcar lines or converted them to diesel bus operation. Over 1,000 of Philadelphia's stalwart trolley cars were scrapped in the 1950s, and much of the trolley network has since been paved over. Even so, Philadelphia had the second-largest fleet of streetcars (about 385) in the Western Hemisphere as recent as the mid-1970s. Today, SEPTA's sixty-eight miles of trolley tracks constitute the largest streetcar network in the United States.

The Southeastern Pennsylvania Transportation Authority (SEPTA) was created in 1964 by the Pennsylvania legislature as a corporate body to subsidize most suburban (i.e., commuter) transit rail lines operated by the Pennsylvania and Reading Railroads. Financial support to help keep the commuter lines running in the face of growing losses had started in the late 1950s. SEPTA entered into operating contracts that furnished funds in return for fare concessions and service enhancements. It subsequently owned and operated the lines outright.

On September 30, 1968, SEPTA assumed all of Philadelphia Transportation Company's transit functions. These days, SEPTA manages three divisions within its five-county service area:

- The City Transit Division: providing heavy-rail rapid transit (subway), light-rail (trolley), trackless trolley, and bus service chiefly within Philly. The City of Philadelphia owns most of the infrastructure and rolling stock, as well as some light-rail and trackless trolley infrastructure, and has a leasehold interest in the balance of the system.
- The Suburban Transit Division: providing light-rail and bus service within the suburban counties of Bucks, Chester, Delaware, and Montgomery, with a few routes extending into Philadelphia.
- The Regional Rail Division: providing commuter railroad service on thirteen lines within the five-county Philly area. SEPTA's Regional Rail System is the progeny of six commuter lines of the Pennsylvania Railroad and six commuter lines of the Reading Company, along with the seven-mile Airport Line, constructed by the City of Philadelphia by 1985.

One may ask: How does SEPTA do it? Its three divisions manage five separate railroad and trolley lines (none with interchangeable rolling stock), a number of trackless trolley routes, and a comprehensive diesel bus system. SEPTA observed its fiftieth anniversary in 2014, and its 2016–17 budget was $1.4 billion. In 2012, the American Public Transportation Association named SEPTA the best large transit agency in North America. Not bad for an organization that critics sometimes call "SCHLEPTA" and "INEPTA."

The SEPTA Transit Museum is located in the lower level of SEPTA Headquarters at 1234 Market Street. Display cases contain archival photographs depicting the history of public transit in the Philadelphia region, and the museum store carries a variety of railroad books and gifts. A rebuilt PCC trolley car is also displayed on the basement level, visible from the bordering pedestrian concourse and from windows at street level.

Collectively referred to as the Green Line (or Lines), Subway-Surface trolley routes are differentiated from regular trolley routes that (used to)

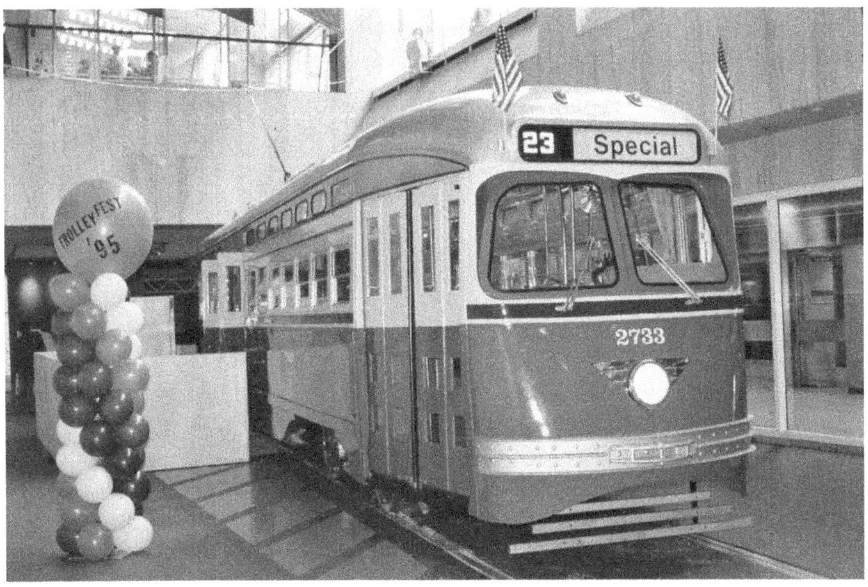

In September 1995, a lovingly restored PCC trolley car was moved into the basement level of the SEPTA Headquarters building to become centerpiece of the SEPTA Transit Museum. Car 2733 was brought to 1234 Market Street by truck, eased through the building's façade, and then carefully lowered to its permanent subsurface exhibition space. The move of the fifteen-ton trolley cost $100,000. Visible through the bordering pedestrian concourse from passing Market Street Subway trains, the vintage 1947 car can also be seen by looking down through windows at street level (as is being done by a passerby in this image). *Russ Jackson.*

run only on the surface of streets. PRT and city officials came up with the "subway-surface trolley" form of public transit as a way to reduce street-level traffic after studying Boston's Green Line. Service began in 1905. Today, half of SEPTA's ten most-used routes are Subway-Surface lines; almost eighty thousand people use city streetcars each workday.

Routes 10, 11, 13, 34, and 36 run on the two outermost tracks of the east–west Market Street Tunnel in Center City. The *Tunnel* is the passageway through which both Subway-Surface trolleys and the Market Street *Subway* operate. (A four-tracked transit tunnel is a rarity anywhere in the world.) The Subway-Surface routes survived in large part because the Market Street Tunnel allows trolleys to bypass downtown congestion. Tracks proceed through the tunnel into West Philadelphia and surface at two transition portals before continuing on city streets to western neighborhoods and suburbs of Philadelphia. All five SEPTA lines stop at underground stations at 13th, 15th, 19th, 22nd, 30th, and 33rd Streets.

Near City Hall, Subway-Surface routes come together as a single-tracked right-of-way approaching and departing Center City. A trolley loop around City Hall connects inbound and outbound tracks at 13th Street. This loop dips below the Market Street Subway and crosses above the Broad Street Subway. The original routing had two tracks in separate tunnels girdling City Hall, with the outer tracks for streetcars and the inner set for rapid transit trains of the Market Street Subway. The reason for this protracted way around City Hall was the expense that tunneling under the enormous building would have entailed.

By the mid-1930s, though, the Market Street Tunnel was routed straight under City Hall during the Broad Street Subway's construction. (The original passage can still be seen from trolleys passing by.) Two pedestrian concourse hallways were also built alongside the lengthened Market Street Tunnel, running east–west beneath City Hall. The 1930s mezzanines connect to preexisting concourses on the north and south sides of Market Street east of City Hall.

Thirteenth Street Station, formerly Juniper Street Station, is the beginning and end point for all five Green Line routes. Japanese-built Kawasaki Light Rail Vehicles (LRVs) operate in the same direction on a single track as they travel inbound past City Hall and turn parallel with Juniper Street to discharge passengers on the southernmost portion of the stop's platform. The long platform is located two stories below ground level, perpendicular to and directly under the Market Street Subway (and Market Street).

LRVs then proceed a few feet farther north to pick up passengers at either Berth 1 (Routes 10, 11, and 13) or Berth 2 (Routes 34 and 36). Stairs, escalators, and an elevator provide access to the eastbound and westbound sides of the Market Street Subway's 13th Street Station. Years ago, the Delaware River Port Authority called for extending SEPTA's Subway-Surface Lines from 13th Street east to the Delaware River frontage. But it's unlikely that this will ever happen, as the expense of relocating city infrastructure along East Market Street would be astronomical.

SEPTA LRVs curve to the west along the trolley loop beneath City Hall, passing a short spur tunnel under Juniper Street that is sometimes used to park stranded trolleys. They then head outbound toward the westbound 15th Street Station of the Green Line routes, where they make a direct connection to the Market Street Subway's 15th Street Station, along with a four-hundred-foot length of track. The Green Line station was moved sixteen feet south in the late 1970s as a result of Commuter Rail Tunnel construction. Subway-Surface LRVs share the Market Street Tunnel with the Market Street Subway to West Philadelphia from this point.

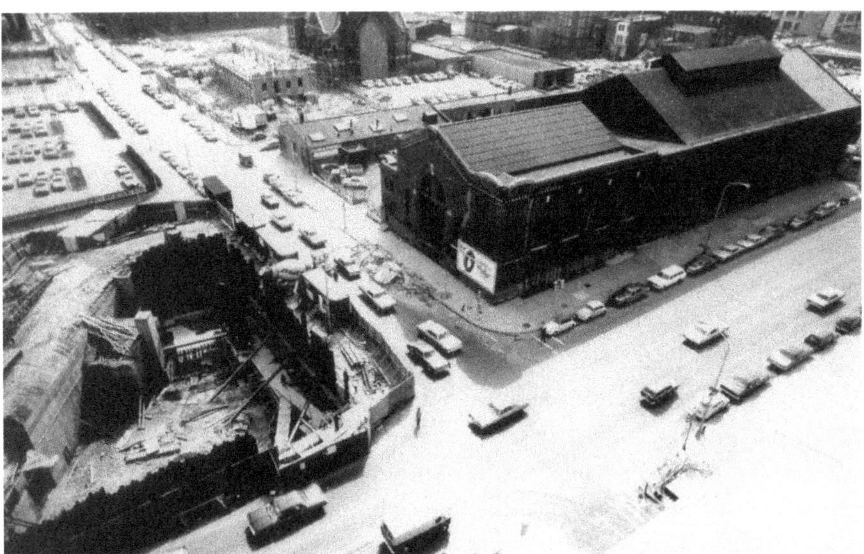

This early 1970s photo shows construction of an underground substation at the southeast corner of 33rd and Market, flanking the 33rd Street Station of the Subway-Surface Green Line. The SEPTA-built substation replaced the large brick building on the southwest corner (*at right*), which was a substation of the Philadelphia Traction Company, opened in 1894 to power electric trolleys on Market Street. Rebuilt in 1907–8 for use in the Market Street Tunnel, it lasted shortly after this picture was taken. Drexel University's Hagerty Library is now on the site. *Joel Spivak's collection.*

Builders of the Market Street Tunnel were very concerned with providing riders with enough air. Four ventilation shafts originally came up to the sidewalk beside the Pennsylvania Railroad's Chinese Wall between 15th and 18th, and two larger air chambers rose through the pavement at 19th Street. Passing trains kept the air moving. And at 22nd Street, an embellished ventilation tower arose sixty feet above street level to permit a natural air draft. All these openings have been replaced by a series of sidewalk grates along Market Street since the Chinese Wall's demolition.

The 19th Street Green Line stop features the old-style design of the original Market Street Tunnel. This was the tunnel's first station. Ornate cast-iron railings, ceiling columns, and tile walls date to 1907; an upper level has been closed off for decades. Nineteenth Street Station and the next one atone for the dearth of Market Street Subway stops in Center City's western ward.

The next trolley stop is at 22nd Street. Reflecting a dull 1950s style of design, the station replaced a little-used trolley stop on the surface at 24th Street by the Schuylkill River's east bank. The old stop was convenient for accessing the B&O Railroad Station a block away and was immediately west of the western transition portal where the Market Street Tunnel originally broke through the surface to cross over the B&O East Side tracks and the Schuylkill River. Twenty-Fourth Street Station was eliminated when the subway was extended westward in 1955. Until that time, trolleys had continued on surface streets into West Philadelphia after crossing over the PRT's Schuylkill River Bridge.

Dipping noticeably under the Schuylkill River, LRVs proceed west and reach SEPTA's 30th Street Station, where there is another interchange with the Market Street Subway. After passing beneath the Thirty-Second Street Tunnel (of the Pennsylvania Railroad; now SEPTA Regional Rail), trolleys enter the campuses of Drexel University and the University of Pennsylvania. While still underground, they first rise *above* the Market Street Subway's tracks and are sandwiched into their own alignment for a short distance. They then curve left (southward) toward 33rd Street Station and then right (westward) under Ludlow Street to the 36th Street Portal. At this point, SEPTA Route 10 cars exit the subway via an incline to 36th and Ludlow and head to Philly's Overbrook neighborhood on surface streets.

Other streetcars sidestep around the incline, swing sharply left (southward), and continue several blocks underground to 36th Street Station (aka Sansom Common Station). Past this stop, trolleys advance beneath the Penn campus to the station at 37th and Spruce. Offset to bestraddle the angle of Woodland Walk (formerly Woodland Avenue) on the surface, 37th Street Station is divided into two sections (eastbound and westbound). In 2006, Penn's class of 1956 donated a replica of a Peter Witt streetcar as a new entrance for the station's eastbound side. (Peter Witt trolleys were introduced in the mid-1920s by the Cleveland Railway commissioner with that name.) PRT owned 525 Witts, most made in Philadelphia by the Brill Company. Many served the Penn campus into the 1950s.

LRVs then make their way to the transition portal at 40th and Woodland Avenue. SEPTA Routes 11, 13, and 36 cars proceed to the left (southwestward) to the communities of Darby, Yeadon, and Eastwick (respectively), while Route 34 turns right (northwestward) to Philadelphia's Angora neighborhood. The 40th Street Portal, once a barren concrete setting, has been recently remade into a park-like place called "Trolley Portal Gardens," complete with a café and outdoor seating.

The 36th Street and 40th Street transition portals both entered service in 1955 when the trolley lines were moved underground. In past decades, motorists would occasionally drive their cars into these tunnel openings, usually at night. City papers would report such instances, typically in a gleeful, mocking tone. SEPTA has taken steps through the years to prevent these mishaps.

Across from the 40th Street Portal is The Woodlands, a National Historic Landmark District on the Schuylkill River's west bank that was the country estate of prestigious Philadelphia lawyer Andrew Hamilton. His grandson, William, put up an Adamesque mansion—one of the nation's earliest examples of Federal architecture—around the time of the American Revolution. The garden landscape was transformed in 1840 into a still-active Victorian cemetery. "Grave Gardeners" at The Woodlands Cemetery tend cradle graves through the growing season. A cradle grave is a planter-like grave site that would have been seeded and cared for by loved ones during the Victorian era.

Route 36 trolleys continue toward Bartram's Garden, located farther south along the lower Schuylkill River. John Bartram (1699–1777), the "Father of American Botany," was a Quaker horticulturist and explorer who spent his life collecting native American flora and fauna and was named the Royal Botanist for North America in 1765. In 1728, he began creating the foremost plant nursery in the American colonies, a rustic homestead surrounded by majestic trees, wildflower meadows, and scenic wetlands. Located near 54th and Lindbergh Boulevard, the forty-four-acre haven is America's oldest living botanical garden.

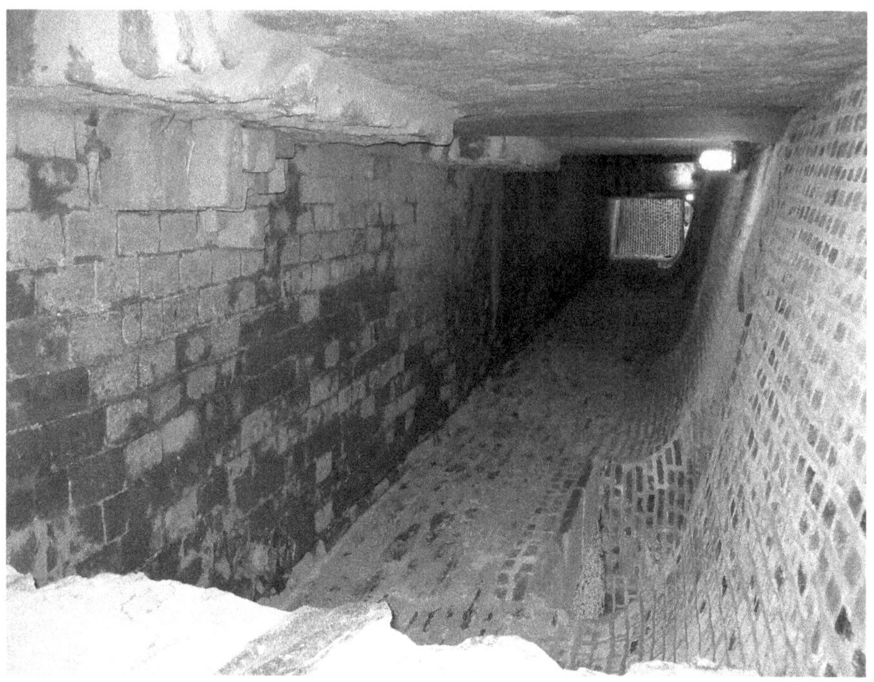

The Woodlands Mansion contains a cryptoporticus—a clandestine semi-subterranean room with a vaulted ceiling supporting the front portico and connected to a network of service tunnels beneath the house. The passageways guided servants to different points in the manor via its basement. In recent years, Woodlands' cryptoporticus has undergone a major structural restoration with the help of a million-dollar state grant. In addition, co-located Woodlands Cemetery has an underground icehouse that used to store bodies until they could be buried. The entrance is hard to find and has not been opened in recent memory. *Photograph by Harry Kyriakodis.*

John Bartram was also a skilled stone carver. Besides erecting his farmhouse of stone, he carved a cider press into some Wissahickon schist jutting up on the Schuylkill's embankment. A large wooden wheel attached to a center post crushed apples placed into a circular groove about twenty feet in circumference. The wheel was moved by either horsepower or manpower, and a cleft at the groove's bottom enabled apple pomace and juice to drain into a stone basin. The age-old cider press is still there today, as is a contiguous outcropping of Wissahickon schist by the river that has doubled as a boundary marker since the 1600s.

The Woodlands and Bartram's Garden are not the only bygone homesteads along the Schuylkill River with subterraneous connections. The Solitude was the country house of John Penn, grandson of William Penn, and was the last property of the Penn family in North America. Completed on the river's west bank in 1784, the mansion is noted for its exquisite plaster ceilings, the first of their kind in America.

John Penn returned to England in 1788, leaving the place uninhabited—except as a summer rental. The Solitude became part of Fairmount Park by 1867 and was soon enveloped by the Philadelphia Zoological Gardens. Having served as the zoo's reptile house and then its administration building, the dwelling has been restored and is now open for tours. Not on a tour, though, is the forty-five-foot-long tunnel that runs under the main house to a kitchen outbuilding and which is allegedly haunted.

The Philadelphia Zoo itself is catacombed by an underground crawlway system. M. Night Shyamalan's 2016 thriller *Split* includes pivotal scenes in a dungeon beneath zoo grounds. What's more, SEPTA commuter trains head through intricate sub-ways as they navigate around the zoo to and from 30th Street Station. The "duck-under" tunnels were built by the Pennsylvania Railroad in 1910 to prevent the obstruction of north–south traffic—today, Amtrak's Northeast Corridor—by trains traveling to western destinations. The longest underpass around the zoo is called the "New York–Pittsburgh Subway" and is well-known among rail enthusiasts. It allowed Pennsylvania Railroad trains to skip a time-consuming stop and reversal of direction at 30th Street Station, enabling faster service between New York and Harrisburg. (Passengers for Philadelphia used North Philadelphia Station instead of 30th Street Station.)

This trackage is all part of Zoo Junction, by all accounts the busiest and most complex interlocking rail junction in the United States. Built in stages from 1885 until 1935 and orchestrated by Zoo Tower, the marvelous maze of switches and signals directs some four hundred Amtrak trains a day in three different directions: north toward New York, south toward Washington, D.C., and west toward Harrisburg and beyond.

Other early Philadelphia villas stand along the banks of the Schuylkill and are now part of Fairmount Park. Laurel Hill Mansion, for example, was put up in the 1760s by Francis and Rebecca Rawle. Rebecca married Philadelphia mayor Samuel Shoemaker after Francis died. The Pennsylvania legislature confiscated the house during the American Revolution because of Shoemaker's purported Loyalist sympathies, leasing it to the minister to France. In 1782, a dog belonging to the minister's cook sniffed out and dug up truffles on the grounds of Laurel Hill. This was where the delicate mushrooms were first discovered in America. After anti-British feelings waned, Rebecca Rawle Shoemaker bought back her house from Pennsylvania in 1784. The house was purchased by the City of Philadelphia in 1869.

Laurel Hill Mansion should not be confused with Laurel Hill Cemetery, a mile to the north. Both received their names from the laurel shrubs that proliferated on the east bank of the Schuylkill River. The renowned cemetery is the final resting place of many illustrious names of Philadelphia and the nation, from a signer of the Declaration of Independence to fictional character Adrian Balboa of the *Rocky* movies. (Adrian's gravestone appeared in 2006's *Rocky Balboa*; the marker of her brother, Paulie, joined hers in the 2015 film *Creed*.) Laurel Hill also contains numerous family crypts amid headstones undermined by groundhog dens. Some of its mausoleums even have glass covers that offer glimpses into the underworld.

A vehicular tunnel cuts through (and under) the center of Laurel Hill Cemetery itself, allowing Hunting Park Avenue to connect with Kelly Drive while avoiding Ridge Avenue. The two-lane underpass was built in 1948–49 when the existing surface road, Nicetown Lane, was moved underground to eliminate traffic bottlenecks at Ridge Avenue.

Turning from tasty morsels and buried bodies in the ground back to transit matters, the Girard Avenue Line (Route 15) is another Philadelphia streetcar route, although it is not a constituent of SEPTA's Subway-Surface (Green) Lines. Running from the Delaware River through the city, over the Schuylkill via the Girard Avenue Bridge, and past the Philadelphia Zoo into West Philadelphia, Route 15 began as a horsecar line in 1859 and became electrified to use powered trolleys in 1895. Almost a hundred years later (1992), diesel buses replaced trolleys on Girard Avenue.

But on September 4, 2005, a fleet of reconditioned PCC streetcars reintroduced trolley service on the route. Originally assembled in 1947, these rebuilt trolleys have added air conditioning, regenerative braking, and a wheelchair lift for ADA compliance. They are still soldiering on today. When not rolling along Girard Avenue, their abode is Callowhill Depot, a historic bus and trolley barn in West Philadelphia that was built in 1913 by PRT and later operated by the PTC before being taken over by SEPTA.

And speaking of Girard Avenue, Stephen Girard bequeathed the city $2 million to establish Girard College, the world's first residential school for orphaned children. This was the largest act of philanthropy during the country's younger days. As of today, 90 percent of the school's funding is still supported by revenue generated by the Girard estate's investment, real estate, and mining activity. Girard College's 1848 opening in lower North Philadelphia inspired the naming of Girard Avenue about that time.

A surface or elevated street through Girard College, or a tunnel beneath the campus, was repeatedly suggested and scrutinized in the late nineteenth and early twentieth centuries. The two-block-long shortcut would have gone along the line of 22nd Street and was seen as vital for improving traffic flow between North College and South College Avenues. No such pathway ever came to fruition. Not only would it have split the boarding school in half, but it clearly would also have run afoul of Girard's will.

After his death in 1831, Stephen Girard's home on Water Street, near Market, was torn down and replaced by warehouses in the mid-nineteenth century. Workmen exposed imported wine and beer bottles from the cellar, probably buried there for a century. Interstate 95 has covered the forgotten site of Girard's house since the 1970s.

Girard was buried in a vault at Holy Trinity Catholic cemetery at 6th and Spruce. In 1851, his mortal remains were reinterred in the vestibule of Founder's Hall at Girard College.

Holy Trinity's graveyard contains an area in which many Acadians repose. About 1,400 of these descendants of French colonists came to Philadelphia from Nova Scotia and New Brunswick in 1755 when the British seized French Canada. Called "the French Neutrals," they were housed in an encampment at 6th and Pine while waiting for transportation to Louisiana. Holy Trinity cemetery is "the little Catholic churchyard in the heart of the city" in which the Acadian lovers of Henry Longfellow's epic poem "Evangeline" (1847) are said to be buried.

Another man of influence with an unusual burial circumstance along Girard Avenue is John Nepomucene Neumann (1811–1860). The fourth bishop of Philadelphia, Neumann was the first male saint in America and the third American citizen to be canonized. Upon his sudden death at age forty-eight, Bishop Neumann was entombed in the basement of St. Peter's Church at the southeast corner of 5th and Girard. He often preached at the Baroque church built in 1843.

The bishop's body lies in repose within a glass altar in the National Shrine of Saint John Neumann, in St. Peter's lower level. Countless worshipers have visited to seek the holy man's intercession. While numerous Philadelphia churches have remains of the departed under their floorboards, the story of Saint John Neumann is exceptional—in both his life and afterlife.

Lastly, SEPTA has announced a billion-dollar trolley modernization plan that will introduce 120 new trolleys for the Subway-Surface routes and Route 15 by 2024. The cars will be wheelchair accessible and will hold about twice as many people as existing Kawasaki LRVs, which are years past their operational expectancy. A new electrical system would be installed, replacing the single electric trolley pole with pantographs. And updated stops will feature platforms raised above street level in this transformational infrastructure project.

CHAPTER 11

THE EL

Market-Frankford Elevated (Blue Line)

Originally named High Street, Philadelphia's east–west Market Street is the city's chief commercial and retail corridor. "High Street" was derived from two things: 1) High Street was the familiar name of the principal street in English towns, a custom dating to Roman times; 2) The foot of High Street began at the highest point of the Delaware River's western bank when the Quaker City was founded.

Covered market sheds (stalls) were positioned in the middle of High Street from the city's earliest days, starting at Front Street and proceeding west to 8th Street and later from 15th to 17th Streets. High Street began to be called Market Street around 1800 because of this. Market Street's name was made official by ordinance in 1858, a year before the stalls were ordered removed. It has since been branded "the most historic highway in America" for its association with events of the founding of the United States.

A double-tracked branch of the "City Railroad" ran on the surface of Market Street east from Broad Street (see also Chapter 12). These railroad tracks had been installed by the city as far back as 1837. The freight and passenger line became a single track (skirting the market sheds) on the *northern edge* of Market Street, between 8th and 3rd. At 3rd Street, the tracks turned south and made their way toward Dock Street and then to a freight depot on Front Street, alongside the Delaware River. Railcars were pulled by teams of oxen and horses. Horse-drawn streetcars shared Market Street with the railroad too.

By 1850, the Pennsylvania Railroad had taken over the City Railroad right-of-way and added tracks on Market Street west of Broad Street, heading west over the Schuylkill River and out of Philly. Mid-nineteenth-century Philadelphians normally embarked on trips to western Pennsylvania and beyond by using the City Railroad. The Pennsylvania Railroad successfully lobbied for the removal of the Market Street sheds because it wanted an unhindered route down the *center* of the street toward the Delaware River. The railroad further added tracks on 2nd Street nearing Dock Street so as to curtail railroad activity on congested 3rd Street.

All these railroad tracks were eliminated by 1870 or so. The tracks had to be taken up because City Hall was on the drawing board for Center Square.

As for the *subway* on Market Street, the thirteen-mile Market-Frankford Line—or Blue Line—is the city's most heavily used rapid transit (heavy-rail) route. Popularly called "the El," the workhorse line is an intrinsic metropolitan artery and a key component of Philadelphia's character. It consists of two sections:

- the Market Street Subway, an east–west route that operates within the Market Street Tunnel (along with Subway-Surface trolley cars), coupled with the Market Street Elevated Passenger Railway (atop Market Street to 69th Street Transportation Center in West Philadelphia)
- the Frankford Elevated Line, a upraised right-of-way from Old City to Frankford Terminal in the Frankford section of Northeast Philadelphia

Until the Market Street Tunnel entered service, electric trolley cars had rolled on Market Street since 1895, having replaced the cable car route discussed in the previous chapter. It could be said that the Blue Line hearkens back to 1892 when the Quaker City Elevated Railroad was authorized to build and operate an elevated railroad atop Market Street in the downtown area. Public furor over such a structure on Philadelphia's main business thoroughfare halted construction after the first pillar's emplacement. It seems that retailers did not want an elevated structure in front of their stores. A court case settled the matter against the railroad.

The Pennsylvania legislature in 1901 passed an act permitting construction of both elevated and underground railroads in cities throughout the state. Two years afterward, Philadelphia City Councils authorized construction of elevated lines over Market Street into West Philadelphia, and the

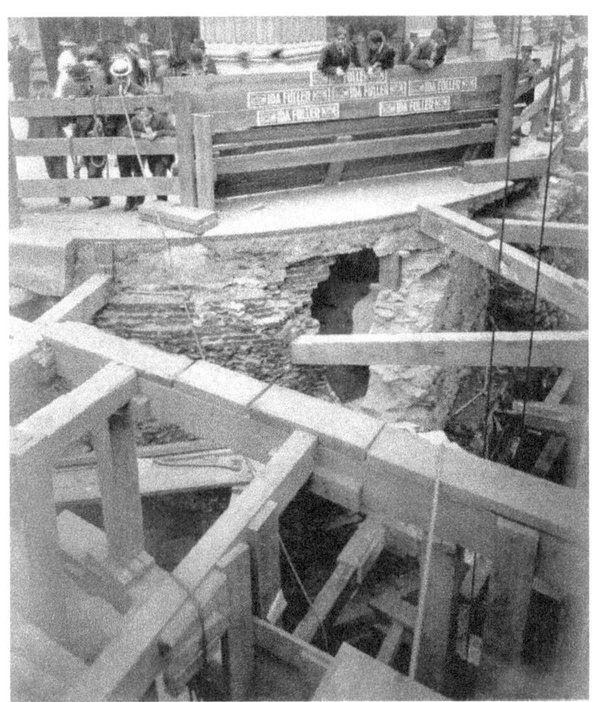

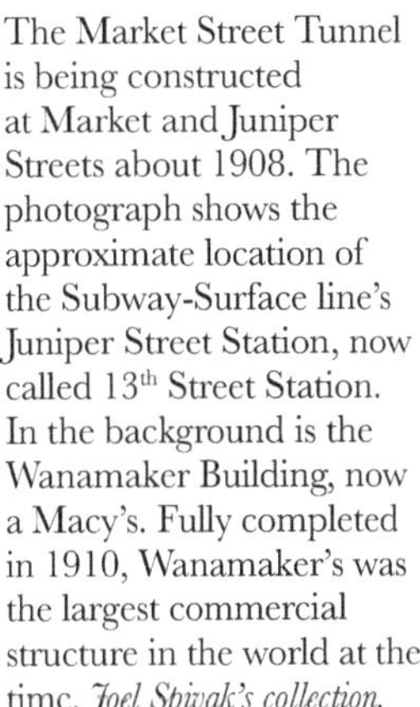

The Market Street Tunnel is being constructed at Market and Juniper Streets about 1908. The photograph shows the approximate location of the Subway-Surface line's Juniper Street Station, now called 13th Street Station. In the background is the Wanamaker Building, now a Macy's. Fully completed in 1910, Wanamaker's was the largest commercial structure in the world at the time. *Joel Spivak's collection.*

Philadelphia Rapid Transit Company (PRT) immediately began erecting a truss bridge over the Schuylkill. The Schuylkill River Bridge was a local landmark for more than fifty years.

In 1904, PRT began work on support piers for an elevated structure above Market Street through West Philadelphia. Test trains between 15th Street (in the subway portion) and 69th Street ran in January 1907; regular service between these points was formally scheduled on March 4. The subway's soft opening was applauded in the papers, although countless pickpockets who turned out that day were not so lauded. (It cost riders five cents each way to make the trip.)

The entire Market Street Subway opened on Monday, August 3, 1908, providing through-service between 2nd and 69th Streets. More than 100,000 cheering passengers took the subway that day. Some made opening day a family outing to West Philadelphia, a part of town they had never visited before.

Philadelphia thus became home of the third-oldest subway system in North America (after Boston and New York) and the ninth oldest in the world. The heavy-rail line is further distinct in that it is a subway, an elevated railway, and a surface railroad (approaching 69th Street).

Tracks of the Market Street Subway initially split upon reaching Center (Penn) Square, with eastbound tracks breaking south to go around City Hall and westbound tracks taking a northern route around the municipal building. The tracks were realigned to pass directly under City Hall in 1936 during construction of the Broad Street Subway (see the next chapter). Entry to that line and Subway-Surface Lines can be made at the Market–Frankford Line's 15th Street Station.

The Blue Line's twin pedestrian concourses run east–west along both the north and south sides of the Market Street Tunnel. Dating from 1907–8, the two tunnels ranging from 11th to 13th Streets offer links to SEPTA's modern-day Jefferson (formerly Market East) Station. (The northern passage initially reached 8th Street, but this portion was eliminated when the city decided to reroute pedestrian traffic through the Gallery mall in the 1970s.) The tunnels were both extended westward in the 1930s to pass below City Hall, with both extensions connecting to the Broad Street Subway's mezzanine. The lengthened passageways also offer access to SEPTA's Regional Rail System at Suburban Station farther west.

The matching 1907–8-era pedestrian concourses under Market Street were the genesis of Center City's expansive underground concourse network, although the derivation of both tunnels had more to do with commerce than with keeping transit riders dry in wet weather. Department store owners—John Wanamaker, the Gimbel family, the Lit brothers, the Snellenburg family, and the Strawbridge & Clothier clan—were the Quaker City's movers and shakers in the early twentieth century. Their stores were located along the largest retail corridor in the United States, if not the world: both sides of Market Street between Broad and 8th Streets. Even today, the Gallery mall calls that vicinity home.

The imperious merchants requested (more like demanded) that a subway stop be placed adjacent to each of their department stores. This accounts for the incipient pedestrian mezzanines and for why El stops east of City Hall are so annoyingly close to one another (those stops make a ride on the Blue Line that much longer). Since there were no department stores west of City Hall, this accounts for the scarcity of subway stops along that stretch of the route (excepting 15th Street Station). Stores forsook this portion of Market Street because the Pennsylvania Railroad's Chinese Wall made that section of downtown undesirable. Contemporary workers in Philly's tallest office buildings—clustered between 15th and 20th Streets where the Chinese Wall used to be—still bemoan this happenstance.

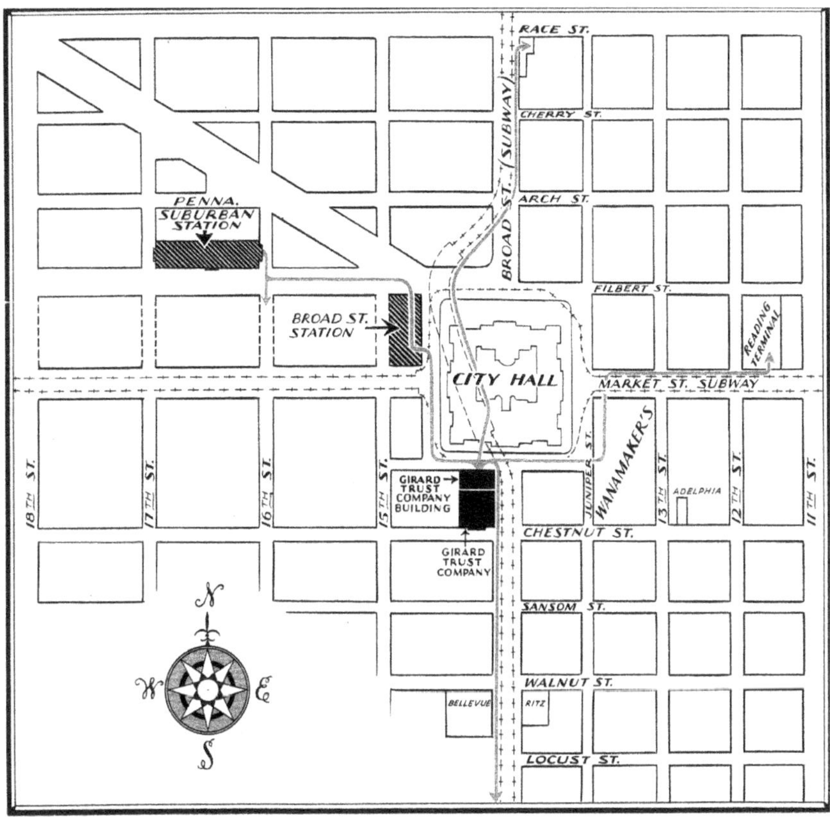

Facing South Penn Square, the Ritz-Carlton Hotel used to be the Girard Trust Company Building. Since opening in the 1930s, the tower has had an entrance from the pedestrian concourse network that the public could use to enter the adjacent Girard Trust Bank (at Broad and Chestnut). The underground passage was on the same level as vaults in the bank's basement. Today, this subsurface space contains the Ritz-Carlton's Grand Ballroom, and hotel employees can access the hotel's basement via the concourse entryway. Looking up through a large crystal chandelier, there is an oculus that opens to the top of the lobby rotunda. Another oculus above gives a view of the sky. This drawing, from a real estate promotional brochure for the Girard Trust Building, indicates how easily the concourses connected to office buildings, subway lines, and train stations in downtown Philadelphia. *Harry Kyriakodis's collection.*

Department stores altered their basement levels into shopping space for working-class Philadelphians. Shoppers from West Philadelphia would use the Market Street Line to get to Center City and then walk from subway trains straight into the stores. This was a convenient and safe way to avoid the weather and downtown street traffic. There was hardly any reason to visit a store's upper level.

This development correlates to the rise of "bargain basements" at these department stores. The first bargain basement was created by Gimbels in 1902, some years in advance of the subway. The emporium would later make a big deal of its "Gimbels Subway Store," proclaiming Tuesdays as "Subway Store Days" and advertising special sales into the 1960s. Strawbridge & Clothier's named its bargain center the "Fashion Basement," which is akin to the reinvigorated Gallery's new name, "Fashion District Philadelphia."

Department stores took advantage of the mezzanines in front of the basement levels of their stores by fashioning display windows to show off clothing for sale inside. The stores spent their own capital for these window storefronts, many of which were quite lavish. Snellenburg's, for example, had window displays and entrances with plaster detailing, mosaic tile, and terrazzo floors.

Snellenburg's went out of business in 1963 after ninety years on Market Street, directly across Reading Terminal. The upper floors of the Snellenburg's building were then taken down, and a string of drab retail shops moved into the remaining ground level. The site is currently under redevelopment as a sweeping retail and residential project dubbed "East Market." A future underground pedestrian connector between East Market and 11th Street Station is possible.

The property—a city block from Market to Chestnut and from 11th to 12th—was once owned by Stephen Girard and still owned by the Girard estate. (It was originally intended to be the site of Girard College.) Joseph Bonaparte, the king of Spain and elder brother of Napoleon, wanted to purchase the square from Girard. He offered to pay a fair price for it, to which Girard asked, "What do you consider a fair price?" Bonaparte replied that he would cover the block with silver half dollars. The clever Girard responded, "Yes, Monsieur, if you will stand them up edgeways." No sale occurred.

Wanamaker's (now Macy's) Department Store at 13th and Market debuted its entrance on the subway level in 1908, when the Market Street Line opened. At the time, the store there was Wanamaker's Grand Depot, covered in other chapters. Three years later, John Wanamaker opened a new store at the same location and advertised its subway store as a "New Kind of Clothing Store" and a "Store Within a Store." He also upgraded the south-side Market Street mezzanine with brass window frames and marble walls along the storefront to display clothes. Worried about ventilation in his store's subbasement, Wanamaker ensured that air would be completely recirculated every six minutes.

The fancy display windows are still there, albeit no longer showing any garments. Plus, a large brass directional compass, installed by Wanamaker's and now partially covered by an elevator, is laid in the floor in front of 13th Street Station. An ancient stairwell with wooden handrails still brings subway riders up to the store's street-level entrances (a Macy's today). It once provided access to service center—with a branch post office, a dry cleaner, a travel bureau, and even an optometrist's office—halfway between levels. These all departed long ago when the bargain basement level was converted into a parking garage.

The Market Street Tunnel's south-side pedestrian concourse provides an entrance to SEPTA's Headquarters (1234 Market Street) at 13th Street Station. A connecting tunnel between the concourses on either side of Market Street was once accessible from the basement of SEPTA's building. Hard as it may be to believe, this passageway took pedestrians *under* the tracks of the Market Street Subway. It was built with federal funds in 1979 together with the elongation of 13th Street Station's eastbound platform as part of work for the Market Street East Redevelopment project. Edmund Bacon had commended plans for this deep tunnel in his book *Design of Cities* because it would allow pedestrians to walk from 1234 Market to a bank across the street without encountering surface traffic. The risky underpass did not last long; it has been sealed since the early 1980s on account of crime concerns.

An Art Deco sign in the ceiling of the southern concourse draws attention to a bricked-up entrance into the architecturally famous PSFS Building, now a Loews Hotel. This stretch of both the north and south concourses is lined with glass blocks, although the reason for this aesthetic treatment is not apparent. And at 11th Street, near where the subway concourse network reaches its easternmost point, is a pedestrian crossover original to the Market Street Tunnel of 1908. Crammed into the constricted space beneath Market Street and sporting 1970s stainless steel cladding, the crossing looks like a scene from *Star Wars* or *Dr. Who*.

The city purchased the underground concourse network in 1968 when SEPTA acquired the Philadelphia Transportation Company. The agency could not then afford to purchase the tunnel system, but SEPTA gained control of the mezzanines in recent years by entering into a lease agreement with the City of Philadelphia.

SEPTA has launched a $164 million repair and improvement program with the adding of modern escalators, elevators, and other embellishments. New trash and recycling cans, brighter lighting, and updated signage are also elements of SEPTA's Center City Concourse Program, as is an earmarking of the whole concourse network. It will soon be labeled "Downtown Link." The addition of retail stores, public artwork, and event programming for more prominent corners of the concourses are also being examined for implementation by 2021.

The City Planning Commission has employed GIS (Geographic Information System, used to capture, analyze, and present spatial or geographic data) and robotics to map the underground spaces in this expanse to better understand the area's public infrastructure. Collected data is relevant for planning and preparedness purposes in relation to public transit and public safety, providing the city with an accurate glimpse of how its subsurface infrastructure connects to buildings and roads above.

A passageway connecting the Market Street Subway to the concourse under South Broad Street (next chapter) is being rehabilitated as part of this undertaking. This passage once contained an entrance to One Meridian Plaza, an office tower in which three firemen died when it caught fire in 1991. The thirty-eight-story high-rise was demolished in 1999, years after its fire-damaged exterior was featured in the opening scenes of the film *Philadelphia* (1993).

Recent repairs and enhancements to the concourse system were initiated about the time that Dilworth Plaza was rebuilt. Named after Mayor Richardson Dilworth, the sunken courtyard on the west side of City Hall was initially assembled in the 1970s of stone and unyielding concrete on the northern footprint of Broad Street Station's headhouse. (A direct below-grade passage connecting the headhouse with the Fifteenth Street Station of the Market Street Subway once existed in this vicinity.) Secluded gardens and fountains intimated that Dilworth Plaza would be a valued downtown attraction following its eleven-year, $21 million construction, but the place wound up altogether disheartening as either a public commons or a transit hub. In fact, director Terry Gilliam turned it into a post-apocalyptic wasteland in his movie *12 Monkeys* (1995).

Dilworth Plaza's $55 million face-lift of 2012–14 transformed it into more functional public space, while offering safer and more cheerful access to subway and trolley crossing lines below. Trees, a lawn, and an interactive fountain that converts to a seasonal ice skating rink were also added, as were a café and two large sloped glass canopies leading down to transit lines beneath City Hall. The multi-level courtyard is now a city showpiece, providing a venue for all manner of festivals, film screenings, and live entertainment. It is said that the place is now called

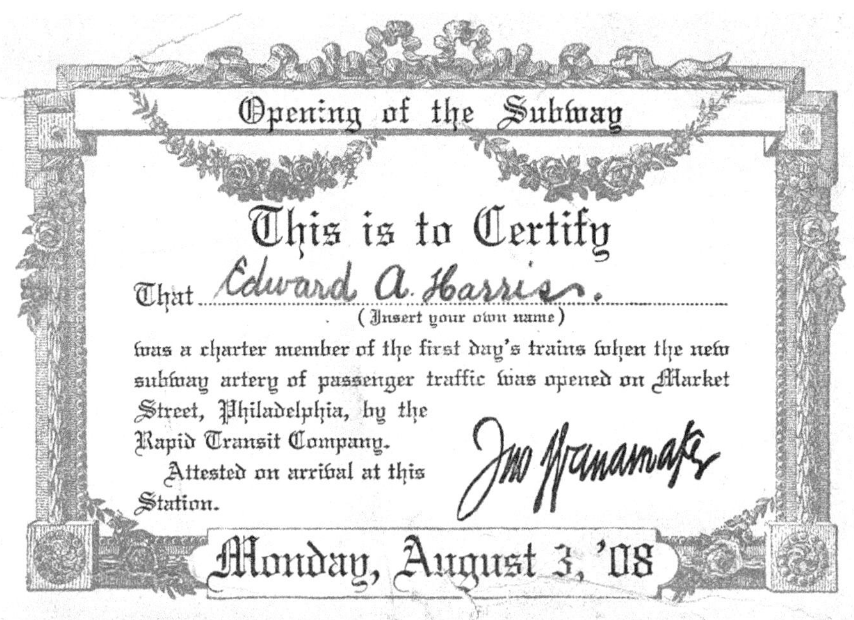

Opening of the Subway

This is to Certify

That Edward A. Harris.
(Insert your own name)

was a charter member of the first day's trains when the new subway artery of passenger traffic was opened on Market Street, Philadelphia, by the Rapid Transit Company.

Attested on arrival at this Station.

Jno Wanamaker

Monday, August 3, '08

This souvenir ticket was issued on Monday, August 3, 1908, on the first day of through-service on the Market Street Line. Bearing a facsimile of John Wanamaker's iconic signature (known throughout Philadelphia), it was handed out at 13th Street Station, where the Wanamaker Band performed in the concourse in front of the Wanamaker department store. *Joel Spivak's collection.*

Dilworth Park because city regulations can prohibit smoking in a "park" but not a "plaza."

Returning to the Market Street Tunnel, 400,000 cubic yards of earth were excavated by hand (pick and shovel) to create the Market Street Subway, since existing infrastructure prohibited the use of excavating machines. Some 13 million pounds of steel and 67,000 cubic yards of concrete were used in the tunnel's cut-and-cover construction, creating walls sixteen inches thick. Timber planks on Market Street for a temporary roof allowed weighty surface traffic, including PRT streetcars, to travel unimpeded. And the foundations of many building had to be underpinned.

Elongation of the tube (meaning tunnel) westward from 22nd Street under the Schuylkill River to 32nd Street was completed in 1932–33. The underwater tunnel is seventy-four feet below street level and approximately thirty feet below the depths of the Schuylkill, with the river being about eighteen feet deep above. In a unique bit of engineering, the tunnel was built integrally with the piers of the 1932 Market Street Bridge over the Schuylkill.

A naval cannon from the Revolutionary War was uncovered forty feet below Market Street west of the river during the digging of the tunnel extension in 1932. The relic had a three-inch bore and was spiked (i.e., incapacitated), like other American field guns that were discarded when the British occupied Philadelphia in 1777–78. Exhibited outside the former Philadelphia Main Post Office for years, it was moved to Fort Mifflin on the Delaware River in 1970, where it remains on display today.

The lengthened passage under the Schuylkill did not receive any tracks during the 1930s and was sealed at each end with concrete plugs. This is because clearance problems arose inside the bore and capital ran out during the Depression. It would be twenty years before the tunnel under the river would finally enter service.

A tunnel beneath the Schuylkill River had been proffered as far back as 1836 to augment bridges across the channel. Richard A. Gilpin, a British-born engineer for the Croton Aqueduct in New York, made the proposal and stressed that his design for a toll tunnel at either Race, Callowhill, or Spruce Streets would be simple to accomplish and would facilitate the city's growth. Gilpin's proposal did not get far since it was ahead of its time by about a hundred years.

As mentioned before, the Market Street Line crossed into West Philadelphia via the PRT's Schuylkill River Bridge and ran as an elevated abreast of the Pennsylvania Railroad's 30th Street Station from 1907 until the 1950s. There were earnest plans to integrate the Market Street Line with the railroad terminal: a transit station would have attached to the south side of 30th Street Station, similar to how 30th Street Station's Regional Rail station is attached on the north side. But this idea was dropped when the City of Philadelphia announced in the late 1920s that it would one day extend the Market Street Tunnel west to 44th Street. And so there is no direct connection today between SEPTA's 30th Street Station and Amtrak's 30th Street Station. The underground passageway that used to link the two facilities was discussed in Chapter 6.

In 1947, construction resumed on the Market Street Tunnel from 32nd to 44th in West Philadelphia. The new tube connected to the prior-built tunnel under the Schuylkill by 1953, and underground service on the augmented Market Street Subway began on October 31, 1955. The raised structure from 45th Street to the PRT's Schuylkill River Bridge was completely dismantled by June 20, 1956, and the fifty-three-year-old bridge itself was soon to follow.

The city also shifted the line's original elevated 32nd Street stop to a large underground station at 30th Street—the Market Street Line's 30th Street Station, with its very bland concourse. (SEPTA has started a long-term upgrade of the stop, which will include improvements for the headhouse and replacement elevators.) Furthermore, the originally elevated 36th Street and 40th Street stations were moved below ground. The City of Philadelphia paid $50 million for this work.

In 2017, the 40th Street Improvement Project added fresh stairways, lighting, signage, surface canopies with artwork, and elevators for ADA accessibility. The project was part of SEPTA's "Rebuilding for the Future" campaign to modernize the entire transit system.

There was talk in the 1950s of pushing the extended Market Street Tunnel farther west to the western city limit and perhaps even to Broomall, Pennsylvania, but engineers could not figure out how to build the subway past the Mill Creek Sewer, among other problems. (The sewer bisects Market Street at 46th Street.) A short underground stub where this never-completed westward extension would have connected to the tunnel is just prior to the western transition portal, west of 40th Street Station and best seen from the front of westbound trains as they begin the incline out of the subway.

The line then continues through West Philadelphia on what was originally called the Market Street Elevated Passenger Railway, atop Market Street. SEPTA rebuilt this elevated line in the early twenty-first century, demolishing the hundred-year-old guideway, with its dual columns straddling Market Street, and substituting it with a single-column design to improve traffic flow on the street. New sections of guideway, including the track structure, were assembled elsewhere and transported by truck to be set into place. Before this rebuild, a short stub atop Market Street stopped in midair at 45th Street. This stub previously connected to the rest of the elevated line (removed in the 1950s), as it proceeded above the street toward Center City.

Also rebuilt were the stations at 46th, 52nd, 56th, 60th, and 63rd Streets. The replacement transit stops are colorful, brightly lit, and comply with modern ADA accessibility standards. The multi-year reconstruction caused much havoc in West Philadelphia, with many businesses along Market Street closing during the project due to the loss of business. To counteract this, commercial artist Stephen Powers in 2009 created a grouping of fifty rooftop murals from 45th through 63rd Streets that could be seen from Market-Frankford El trains. Sponsored by Philadelphia's Mural Arts Program, the singular art installation, collectively titled *Love Letter*, has garnered national and international notoriety for its size, scope, and appeal, besides drawing positive attention to West Philadelphia.

Millbourne Station and 69th Street Transportation Center (formerly 69th Street Terminal) are located in Delaware County, outside the city of Philadelphia. The Market Street Line's Millbourne Station owes its existence to a legal quirk: the Borough of Millbourne required that any train operating through the municipality must stop there.

On the east side of City Hall, the subway proceeded—as it still does—eastward with stations at 13th (offering a direct link to Subway-Surface Lines), 11th (in front of Reading Terminal), 8th (a major transit hub), 5th (scheduled for refurbishment), and 2nd (remodeled in the 1970s with federal money).

Just after 2nd Street, El trains used to make a tremendous squeal as they navigated the sharp northward curve out of Old City, passing directly under a house at the northwest corner of Front and Market. (The building was supported by the subway's roof.) Trains then emerged from the original eastern transition portal between Front and Water Streets, just south of Arch Street. About three hundred feet long and enclosing part of the incline to the surface (actually, to an elevated; see below), the portal structure was used as a freight station for PTC trolleys that ran on both Market and Front Streets. The station was a lively spot in the days when freight trolleys delivered milk, newspapers, and other time-critical items.

Older Philadelphians may remember the dazzling strobe light effect that subway trains experienced on sunny mornings upon entering or exiting the eastern portal. The flashing was caused by sunlight shining through the portal's east-facing ventilation openings as trains rolled by. This bit of daily excitement lasted until the portal structure was demolished in the mid-1970s.

By the way, the intersection of Front and Arch really once sported an arch. Arch Street was at first christened Holme Street, after William Penn's chief surveyor Thomas Holme, and then it became Mulberry Street. In 1690, the lane was dug down (i.e., lowered) east of 2nd Street to make it level with the Delaware shoreline. A stone-arched bridge was constructed to carry Front Street over the depressed road. Henceforth, Philadelphians began to refer to Mulberry as "the arch street." The archway was taken away in 1721 after falling into disrepair, but the name stuck.

As originally built, the Market Street Line exited the eastern transition portal and continued up a steel incline before turning 180 degrees in hairpin fashion over Arch Street to reach Delaware Avenue. It then proceeded southward over the avenue's southbound lanes as an elevated structure and

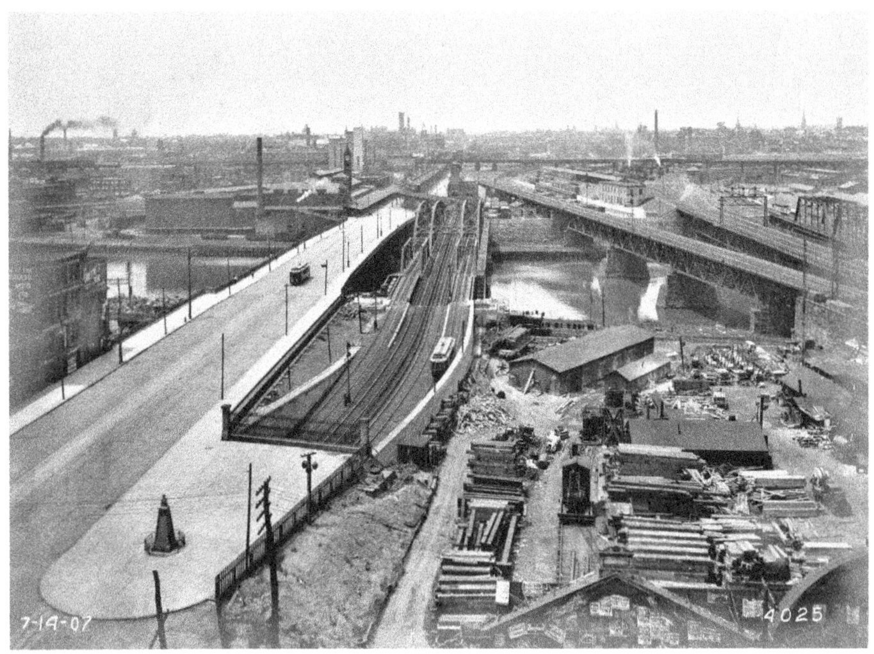

This 1907 photograph shows the original western transition portal of the Market Street Tunnel—the point where the subway and subway-surface lines exited to the surface. At center, paralleling the previous Market Street Bridge, is the Philadelphia Rapid Transit Company's Schuylkill River Bridge, a multi-arch, two-level bridge that carried both subway trains and trolleys cars into West Philadelphia. Crossing over three bridges on the right are tracks leading to Broad Street Station via the Chinese Wall. The foreground, around 23rd and Market, was property of the Market Street Gas Works; the photograph must have been taken from atop a gas-holder on the grounds. The Philadelphia Electric Company's "Tower of Light" building now stands at this site. The far side of the river shows where 30th Street Station would come to be, in place of the West Philadelphia Stockyard Company, partly visible at the upper right. The West Philadelphia Elevated Branch—the "High Line"—appears in the distance. *Joel Spivak's collection.*

ended abruptly at a stub-end station three-quarters of a mile away at South Street. Completed in 1908, this part of the route was formally known as the Delaware Avenue Elevated but was commonly called the Ferry Branch or the Ferry Line since its stops serviced the many ferries to New Jersey along Delaware Avenue. There were two stops: one between Market and Chestnut Streets and the other at South Street.

In 1922, the Frankford Elevated connected to the Market Street Subway at Front and Arch, where the Market Street Line turned toward the Ferry Branch. The 5.25-mile Frankford El entered from Philadelphia's Frankford precinct, running southward atop Frankford Avenue,

Kensington Avenue, and Front Street. The route was built by the city, not by the PRT, and its seven years of construction and exorbitant price tag (at more than $15 million, twice the original estimate) were attributed to the effects of World War I. Service began on November 5, 1922. The city expected to extend the line to Rhawn Street in Holmesburg, but the Great Depression shelved that scheme.

The Frankford El and the Ferry Branch alternated service to 69th Street Terminal via the Market Street Line until 1937. The Ferry line gradually lost passengers as ferry traffic diminished after the Delaware River (Ben Franklin) Bridge opened in 1926. Most ferries ceased operating by 1938, and the Ferry Branch stopped running the next year, replaced by bus service. Just over thirty years after being erected, the elevated structure atop Delaware Avenue was dismantled, and the steel was sold to the Empire of Japan—immediately before World War II. Not even the shadow of a trace of the Ferry Branch remains along Delaware Avenue (Columbus Boulevard) nowadays.

A station for the Frankford Elevated was supposed to have been included *inside* the Philadelphia Anchorage of the Benjamin Franklin Bridge at Race Street and Columbus Boulevard. The El was to have passed next to the bridge-support structure (on its west side), much as it does today, though higher. A large station inside would have provided a handy interchange between the Frankford El and streetcars running across the bridge—although these trolley lines were never realized. The Philadelphia Anchorage even had elevators inside to bring people up from the street level to trolley level and, presumably, to the El's level. These elevators were installed but never used, and neither was the colossal interchange chamber, since the direct integration of the El and the Ben Franklin Bridge's proposed streetcar lines never came to be. The unused elevators are still there. (See Chapters 11, 13, and 15 for more about the bridge.)

The Market Street Subway's Second Street Station in Old City was modernized during the 1970s when Interstate 95 was built through the Quaker City's waterfront. The subway tube was restructured north of 2nd Street Station to reduce the wheel-squealing curve to a more manageable bend. Between Front and Second, ventilation grates and an access door to the remade tunnel can be seen on SEPTA property under the Market Street Viaduct to Penn's Landing. The tunnel then continues for two-tenths of a mile *beneath* the southbound lanes of I-95—where Water Street used to be—to a new eastern transition portal between Arch and Race Streets. The replacement subway portal is located on the inside of the highway median.

I-95's construction also removed the El's overhead structure on Front Street for more than a mile north of Arch Street. That stretch of Front had not seen the light of day in half a century. The only indications of the El having ever been over Front Street in that locale are concrete patches on either side of the road between Vine and Spring Garden Streets. These patches are scars of the El's old foundation supports that straddled Front Street. Construction of Interstate 95 also exchanged the El's Fairmount Station with the current Spring Garden Station, also within the I-95 median.

SEPTA rebuilt the Frankford Elevated in the early 1990s, replacing the original steel elevated guideway with single and dual columns supporting the tracks overhead. Costing $140 million, the project included supplanting Frankford Terminal with the larger Frankford Transportation Center, as well as a pedestrian bridge over Bridge Street.

Regarding Interstate 95, a proposal was put forth in 1965 to mitigate the harm foreseen in the throughway's pending construction along the city's central waterfront (i.e., Penn's Landing). An alternate design was submitted that would have laid a concrete roof over the superhighway from Arch to Pine Streets, with parkland and buildings placed on this lid. All major east–west streets from Race to Pine would have continued to Delaware Avenue via overpasses.

Prodded by this recommendation, the State of Pennsylvania produced plans for an eight-lane expressway submerged below the level of Front Street, along with a deck over the highway from Arch to Pine. Vice President Hubert Humphrey formed a committee to assess the design in 1967. This working group ordered the federal government to accept a below-grade design, but only from Market to Lombard. It rejected the six-block tunnel owing to the $25,235,500 additional expense of building and ventilating such a long passage.

The state and federal governments eventually (grudgingly) built covers over two short segments of the freeway: Chestnut to Sansom and Dock to Delancey. These concrete decks produce two tunnels totaling one thousand feet. Fifteen lanes of traffic—for mainline I-95, entrance ramps and shoulders—pass through them. The Pennsylvania Department of Transportation designed retaining walls between these two sections with the intent that a middle cap would be added thereafter. A park is on the shorter northern cover, while Foglietta Plaza and the Philadelphia Vietnam Veterans Memorial is on the longer southern cover.

The Center City section of Interstate 95 opened over Labor Day weekend in 1979, and the freeway was barreled through all of Philadelphia by the end of 1985. Running along the western side of the Delaware River for 19.2 miles in the city, this was one of the most expensive roads built until that time. Costs rose to $17 million per mile at Penn's Landing by virtue of the expense of the tunnels and the fourteen-foot-thick concrete pad that counteracted the upward thrust ("hydrostatic pressure") of the bordering Delaware. Philadelphia Rapid Transit had avoided this obstacle for the Ferry Branch by constructing the line *over* Delaware Avenue instead of continuing the Market Street Subway *under* the riverside boulevard.

The sunken superhighway became, in effect, a new Chinese Wall in Philly, a debacle the city has been trying to resolve since the 1970s. The Delaware River Waterfront Corporation is studying ways to ameliorate the problem of I-95 at Penn's Landing by covering the expressway and building park-space between Walnut and Chestnut Streets, connecting to the Delaware from Front Street.

Mayor Jim Kenney, Pennsylvania governor Tom Wolf, and the William Penn Foundation announced in 2017 a commitment to capping I-95 and creating a new civic space at Penn's Landing. A four-acre green-covered roof over I-95 and Columbus Boulevard, coupled with a lush eight-acre commons between Walnut and Chestnut, will slope down toward the Delaware, reconnecting Center City with the river—beside which Quaker settlers once lived in caves. In addition to tying Penn's Landing to the city's street grid, the project will inject a bit of Fairmount Park into the Old City/Society Hill area.

Estimated at $225 million, work on the plan will likely commence in 2020. While it falls short of displacing I-95 from the central Philadelphia embarcadero, the work will induce private real estate investment along the Delaware, generating an estimated $1.6 billion in tax revenue. Two ungainly vehicular ramps (the "scissor ramps") leading from Columbus Boulevard up to Market Street and from Chestnut Street down to Columbus Boulevard have already been removed as a preliminary step.

In related matters, I-95 was closed for weeks in the city's Port Richmond neighborhood in 1996 after an arson tire-dump fire under the elevated roadway damaged it. And on March 17, 2008, a concrete support pillar was found crumbling beneath this same zone of interstate, forcing a two-day closure for emergency repairs. These mini-debacles became widely publicized examples of Philadelphia's creaking infrastructure.

The worst disaster in SEPTA's history took place inside the Market Street Tunnel on March 7, 1990. A freak accident occurred when a traction motor on the rear truck of the third car of a westbound train partially fell off the car between the line's 15th and 30th Street Stations. The dragged motor engaged an interlocking crossover switch upon leaving 30th Street Station, causing the rear truck of the fourth car to take the diverging tracks—while the front truck stayed on the proper tracks. The fourth car was consequently sheared open and almost severed by steel pillars supporting the tunnel roof. Hundreds of first responders sprang into action in what was one of the biggest rescue operations ever in Philadelphia—4 people died and 162 were injured; the fatalities and most injuries were those trapped in the mangled fourth car.

Along with Subway-Surface trolleys, the Market Street Line runs on Philadelphia Broad Gauge tracks (five feet, two inches or so). Tracks in the tube have been swapped with continuous-welded rail for a smoother and quieter ride underground. A third rail supplies six hundred volts DC to trains.

Since most subway tunnels in the Quaker City are below the water table, the Market-Frankford Line has pump rooms to keep groundwater and storm runoff under control. Diverting water to city sewers, the pumps forestall washouts on the subway lines and keep water from contacting the third rail. A high-water alarm in each pump's catch basin triggers the pumps. This goes for other transit tunnels in the city, especially the Broad Street Line as it passes through the bygone marshland of South Philadelphia.

Emergency exits are incorporated into ventilation openings midway between stations. Grates over these exits are hinged and counterweighted so that they may open easily. This also goes for PATCO and other SEPTA transit tunnels in Philly.

The current batch of cars used on the Blue Line were manufactured by Adtranz (now Bombardier Transportation), a Canadian firm. They were delivered between 1997 and 1999, replacing a fleet of stainless steel subway cars that had been in service since the 1960s. Made in Philadelphia by Budd Company, those cars were nicknamed "Almond Joys" for the distinctive shape of their roofs.

Chapter 12

The Broad Street Subway and the Broad-Ridge Spur (Orange Lines)

Broad Street is the north–south counterpart to Philadelphia's Market Street. Like Market, Broad is 113 feet wide, but its length is more exceptional. Broad Street was once the longest *paved street* in the world and is still the longest straight *urban boulevard* in America. And like Market Street, it became the route of a subway line. Although not as popular as the Market-Frankford El, SEPTA's heavy-rail Broad Street Subway—or Orange Line—serves as the backbone of the Quaker City as it passes nine miles under Broad Street for almost the entire length of Philly.

Through the middle of the nineteenth century, Broad Street was home to a string of coal yards, lumberyards, and warehouses, since the city's developed area did not yet reach Broad. A city-owned railroad referred to as the "City Railroad" was built on the surface of Broad Street, spurred by tradesmen operating those businesses who desired easy access to the state-owned Philadelphia & Columbia Railroad that terminated at Broad and Vine.

Anybody who had at least one private railcar, toll money, and a contract for its use could use the City Railroad. Freight and passenger cars could be pulled by oxen and horses at no more than four miles per hour. Steam locomotives took the place of animal power in 1852. The mile-long railroad operated between Vine and South Streets from 1834 until 1870, and its tracks passed straight through Center Square—now Penn Square—where Benjamin Henry Latrobe's Pepper-Box pumphouse used to stand and where City Hall rises these days.

Surveyor Thomas Holme believed that he had situated Center Square where the Delaware and Schuylkill watersheds meet, but his calculations were off by a few blocks because he had been hampered by dense woodlands. Part of this mistake also designated 12th Street as the original Broad Street—that is, the main street atop the rough boundary between the two watersheds. Officials subsequently corrected Holme's errors and moved Broad Street and Center Square to where they are today. The Pennsylvania Convention Center now occupies the initial square's site.

The short-line Southwark Railroad extended the City Railroad southward on Broad Street, from South Street to Prime Street (future Washington Avenue), in 1835. The Southwark line ran west from the Delaware River and connected to the Philadelphia, Wilmington & Baltimore Railroad (PW&B) on Prime Street, later merging with that route. PW&B built the first rail line to the American South from Philadelphia, extending westward on Prime Street, then along Grays Ferry Avenue and crossing the Schuylkill River southward over the Newkirk Viaduct. PW&B came under the Pennsylvania Railroad's control in 1881.

A rope-drawn ferry had crossed the Schuylkill at that point starting in the 1670s, named after George Gray (1725–1800), a wealthy politician and landowner who would ultimately own the enterprise. Gray also ran a popular resort called Gray's Garden on the river's western bank by which all traffic to and from the South passed. Apart from being a pleasure trip destination for townspeople, Gray's Garden became a propitious spot to welcome visitors into Philadelphia. George Washington often received civilities at what may be called the Quaker City's original southern gateway. So did delegates to the Constitutional Convention.

The Newkirk Viaduct was one of several pontoon bridges and four permanent spans that have spread over the Schuylkill at the site of Grays Ferry. Completed in 1838, the truss bridge was the first bona fide structure over the river, named for the PW&B's president, Matthew Newkirk. Locomotives were not allowed to pass until 1852, so railroad cars were initially pulled by horses over the bridge and northward along three miles of track into town. The span also carried the first telecommunications link between New York and Washington, a telegraph line that had been installed partly along PW&B's right-of-way in 1846. The bridge was replaced in 1901.

The Newkirk Viaduct Monument memorializes the first bridge's completion. Erected in 1839 within what was once George Gray's resort property, the white marble monument was almost certainly the first marker in Philadelphia to commemorate infrastructure of any sort. The seven-foot-tall obelisk atop a five-foot base is also one of the earliest pieces of public art in the city. It has been positioned three times in its history, the latest move occurring in November 2016 after the monument had gained notoriety for the sorry place it had last been set—a neglected spot along Amtrak's Northeast Corridor. Restored, the venerable Newkirk Monument now stands commandingly along the Bartram's Mile segment of the Schuylkill River Trail.

PW&B had a freight station at the northwest corner of Broad and Washington since the 1840s. The old depot had been a marshalling post for Union troops heading south during the Civil War and was the arrival point for Abraham Lincoln's funeral cortege in Philadelphia. In 1876, PW&B erected a replacement depot at more or less the same place. The PW&B Freight Station was a Gothic Revival structure with an ornamented headhouse fronting Broad Street and a block or two of railyards stretching to the west behind it. The headhouse was removed in the 1960s, but the freight station's historic trainshed remained standing at 15th and Carpenter, surrounded by parking lots and serving until recent times as a food warehouse. Soon to become an organic grocery store, the station is a preservation victory now at the crux of a $100 million redevelopment of that block to be called Lincoln Square.

With respect to the City Railroad, its tracks on Broad Street were pulled up by 1870 in accordance with plans to develop the street as the Quaker City's major civic thoroughfare. (It would be another hundred years before tracks on Washington Avenue were removed.)

Talk of a *subway* under Broad Street dates to the early twentieth century. The Market Street Subway's success was the impetus for creating a Philadelphia Department of City Transit and for the evaluation of additional subway routes in Philadelphia. Along with what is now called the Broad-Ridge Spur, the Broad Street Line was among the subway lines suggested, although World War I caused a lengthy delay.

The Broad Street Subway was finally authorized in 1923. The City of Philadelphia constructed the north–south line, and the Philadelphia Rapid Transit Company was to operate it. The subway was built employing the cut-and-cover method, with wooden decks covering Broad Street during construction. Water, gas, steam, and sewer pipes were displaced along with innumerable electrical and telephone conduits. Much of the excavated dirt wound up as soil fill in South Philadelphia for the Sesqui-Centennial Exposition of 1926. Excavation under Philadelphia City Hall began the project.

The largest and most elaborate municipal building in the nation, City Hall is the chief symbol of Philadelphia, prominently featured in motion pictures and television shows of the city. The then-named "Public Buildings" can be regarded as the pinnacle of conventional masonry construction, designed in the French Second Empire style by architects John McArthur and Thomas U. Walter. While this architectural style was outmoded even before the structure's completion in 1901, City Hall is the best and biggest example of Second Empire construction in America. In spite of proposals to tear it down in the 1920s and '50s, the splendid marble and granite edifice has managed to survive—and flourish as of late.

City Hall Tower soars 548 feet and is the hub of downtown Philadelphia. Workers poured a slab of concrete 100 feet square and 8 feet thick 23 feet below ground for the monumental tower's base, and the largest block laid

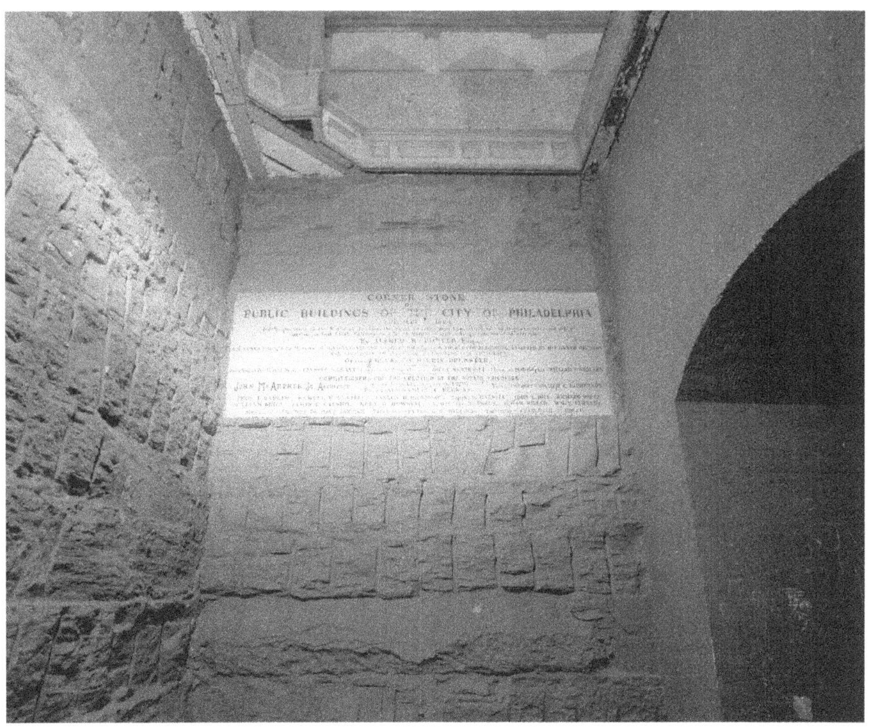

The cornerstone of Philadelphia City Hall as seen in its basement level niche. The eight-ton block was laid with great pageantry on July 4, 1874, and is visible from above by the north entrance. City Hall is reputed to be one of the safest structures on the planet, with its colossal stone construction making it an almost-impregnable fortress. The building took thirty years to build, complete with the usual charges of graft and corruption that large undertakings in the Quaker City have often generated. *Bradley Maule.*

on top was thirty-six tons in weight. The tower is topped by a mammoth statue of William Penn designed by Alexander Milne Calder, father of the sculptor of Swann Memorial Fountain. The 37-foot bronze statue is purportedly the highest and largest atop any building in the world. The center of the building contains a pedestrian courtyard (City Hall Courtyard) connecting Broad and Market Streets.

Ground was broken for the Public Buildings on August 10, 1871. That first scoop of dirt began an excavation that involved the removal of some 141,500 cubic yards of dirt and stone, practically by hand. The cost of the excavation was a mere $359,668, astonishingly low given the building's projected $24 million price tag.

Home to a hodgepodge of wires, pipes, and passages leading off in all directions, the arched basement of City Hall doubles as both foundation for the hulking masonry building above and roof of subway lines passing below. The ceiling is supported by ornate Victorian-style beams and columns and contains a series of prisms set in embellished frames. Installed to bring natural light into the subterranean space, the prisms of these early skylights were painted over at some point—possibly during World War II as part of blackout procedures.

Alexander Milne Calder was the first occupant of City Hall, using the basement as a studio in 1875. Aside from the statue of William Penn, Calder and his apprentices worked on more than 250 sculptures and carvings that would adorn City Hall's exterior. These works of art were sculpted and cast in plaster in the Public Buildings' underground workshop before being rendered in marble by stone carvers.

A stone-lined tunnel, roughly five feet in height, passes into the north basement from beneath the intersection of Broad and JFK Boulevard. This passage was designed to carry phone, electrical, and fire alarm cables for City Hall. From this point, shafts and conduits carried wires to every floor in the building, including what was once claimed to be the nation's largest municipal telephone exchange on the sixth floor.

The first electric lights were lit at City Hall in 1881, but plans to wire the building were not drawn up until 1888, requiring the chiseling of channels into marble interior walls to accommodate conduits throughout completed portions of the building. Electricians also used existing gas pipes as conduits for electrical wiring.

The underpinning of City Hall for the Broad Street Line, performed in the early 1920s, was until then the largest such procedure in the world. The building was transferred first from its original inadequate rubble footings to sturdier foundations of concrete and brick. Then, new foundations were incorporated in (and supported by) the subway roof, which, in turn, was upheld by concrete walls carried to bedrock by steel piles. One-fourth of City Hall's mass, 100,000 tons, was shifted with only a quarter inch of settlement. This stretch of subway cost $3 million, making it the world's most expensive subway construction until then.

City Hall Station was part of the work. This seven-hundred-foot-long station passes diagonally underneath the building and is somewhat cramped, with all too many bulky walls and columns between the tracks and on the platforms. These all support the foundations of City Hall above, as well as the Market Street Subway, which crosses over the Broad Street Line precisely below the Public Buildings. (Additional tunneling work was done in the 1930s to redirect the Market Street Subway straight under City Hall, along with the addition of more pedestrian concourses.) Altogether, this engineering work was done so well that subway trains traveling at high speed beneath the building cause no discernible vibration in City Hall itself.

Six Art Deco–style subway entrances—some now sealed—are located around City Hall and date from the Broad Street Subway's construction. They represent the myriad entrances installed over time to access the subway on both sides of Broad Street. Two cast-iron entrances on City Hall's east side retain their original lamp standards, with original "Subway" signs on each. Two others, located within City Hall Courtyard, housed escalator exits; the escalators stopped working long ago. Many historic subway entrances along Broad Street have been altered or replaced in their entirety in recent times. For both the Broad Street Subway and the Market Street Subway, entries have often been incorporated into building fronts. In 2018, remaining entrances along Broad Street were used as platforms atop which diehard football fans rooted for the Philadelphia Eagles.

The Broad Street Subway's tracks shift to the west at Arch Street to avoid the massive foundations of City Hall Tower. This is the only appreciable deviation of the Broad Street Subway's straight-as-an-arrow route through Philadelphia. The shift around the tower is known for the piercing screech that subway cars make as they navigate the curves. With its ungainly westward positioning, City Hall Station was also planned for use with a subway under the Ben Franklin Parkway that was never built (Chapter 14).

SEPTA is in the process of rehabilitating City Hall Station at a cost of $164 million by 2021. The complex will be made ADA accessible (more than a dozen elevators will be added), lighting will be augmented, and bottlenecks

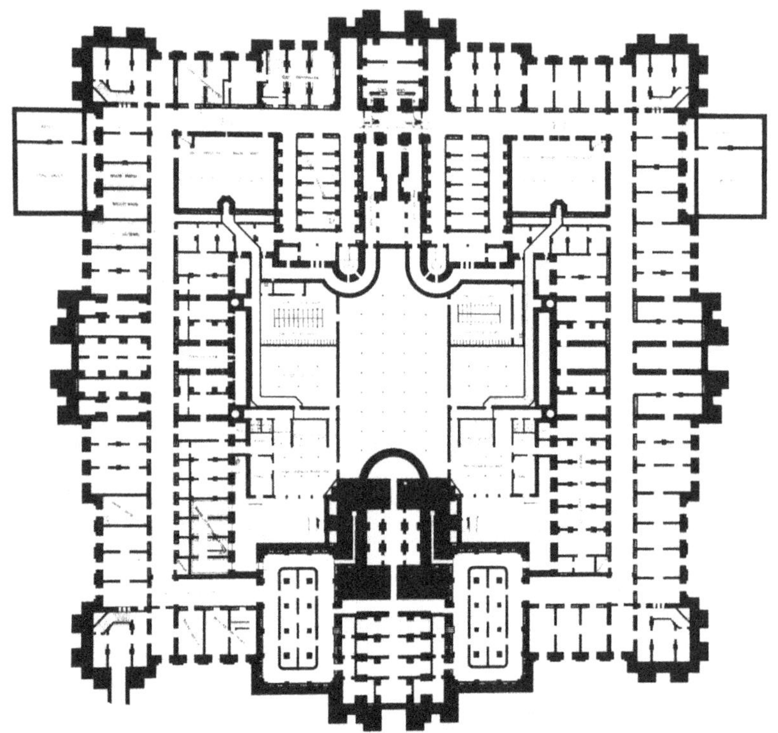

Plan of the subbasement of Philadelphia City Hall, showing office space, toilet rooms, engine rooms, boiler rooms, coal and ash vaults, fresh air shafts, elevators, and the massive foundations of City Hall Tower. Compressors and boilers for heat and hot water fill some rooms, and even a now-unused dynamo room is part of the building's subterranean crypt. Different chambers stored old wills and testimonials, and City Archives and Criminal Court records were stashed there until the 1950s; some inventory ledgers still remain. Ornate Victorian-style pillars and beams support the basement roof. *Library of Congress.*

will be eliminated. This work will surely make the station less claustrophobic. Much of the project's expense has to do with the identical engineering challenges that were faced a hundred years ago. A major enhancement will be the widening of the station's confined platforms, to which SEPTA is considering adding suicide prevention barriers with automatic glass doors to separate the platforms from the tracks.

City Hall Station is integrated with downtown's concourse network, allowing pedestrian access to the Market-Frankford El and Subway-Surface Lines.

The South Broad Street Concourse is a major module of Center City's concourse system, running above the subway and below the street surface from City Hall to Spruce Street. Steel grates on the concourse floor permit a view down to the Broad Street Subway's tracks and even the roofs of trains as they screech to and from City Hall Station. The concourse intersects with the Locust Street Subway mezzanine, since the Broad Street Line crosses perpendicularly over the PATCO Hi-Speedline (Chapter 13) at Broad and Locust.

South Broad Concourse, completed at intervals from 1928 until 1934, is rather frightening in its enormity. The green-and-white-tiled place is longer than three football fields and as wide as Broad Street (and its sidewalks) above. A forest of hundreds of steel pillars support the inexorable number of ceiling arches of its cut-and-cover construction. Back in 1941, several young women were attacked and robbed in the mezzanine, which only became more dangerous as the years passed. Police in the 1960s had problems using two-way portable radios in the lonely tunnel. Coupled with the din of subway trains careening below, the overall effect is surreal.

The cavernous concourse can be explained by remembering that it was meant to serve several planned transit lines both under and perpendicular to Broad Street—most that went unrealized. Moreover, the business center of Philadelphia was located along South Broad in the 1920s and '30s, and the street was home to scores of law firms, financial institutions, hotels, and theaters. South Broad Concourse offered underground entryways into many office buildings along the street, thus making it convenient for businessmen to dodge the weather after disembarking commuter trains at Suburban Station and Reading Terminal. Surface street congestion was also reduced through the use of this and other underground walkways. Access to the concourse network was considered a selling point for leasing space in buildings along both Broad and Market Streets.

Many edifices had shops in their basements that opened into South Broad Concourse, much as department stores had inlets along the Market Street Subway. One building had a drugstore, another a newsstand, another a coffee shop, and so on; there was an entrance to a bustling Horn & Hardart at Locust Street and a barbershop at Walnut, on the basement level of the Bellevue-Stratford Hotel. Under the Philadelphia Transportation Company's supervision, these outfits enjoyed robust business until the construction of Penn Center in the 1960s drove many to close shop.

Penn Center also moved Philadelphia's business district to the western part of Center City. Many large tenants deserted older office buildings on Broad Street for new quarters at Penn Center. Plus, some local banks were purchased by larger financial institutions, and their main offices left Philadelphia. Underground entries to many buildings were sealed, and the concourse was utilized less and less. The dearth of policing and maintenance have made this and other concourses quite dreadful, and their piecemeal construction over the years adds to the unsavory aura. SEPTA and the city are actively trying to remedy this state of affairs.

The city-owned South Broad Concourse has been the scene of curious happenings and unusual ideas throughout its existence. In the 1930s, the relatively cool space (about seventy degrees on average) granted people a haven during heat spells, and the mezzanine was declared an overnight air raid shelter during World War II. Even before the United States entered the war, at the time when London's Underground was used as an aerial shelter, the whole Philly concourse system was calculated to hold 200,000 Philadelphians in refuge.

One winter's day in 1975, during an event called "Lunch in the Subway," a picnic meal was doled out to passersby of the South Broad Concourse to highlight the space's possible use as a year-round mall and crafts center. Ten years later, there was a notion to use it as a five-hundred-car parking lot for theaters along Broad Street. Moving tenants of Reading Terminal Market there was proposed, as was making the space a subterraneous skateboard park in the 1990s. The Academy of Music even contemplated using South Broad Concourse as an underground antechamber, where food and drink could be sold to concertgoers. Nothing came of any of these and other ideas.

The Academy of Music's concept is not as far-fetched as it sounds, since the building has a basement level facing Broad Street that contained a restaurant when the Academy opened in 1857. There, ladies sipped sherry and gentlemen smoked cigars under crystal chandeliers. Conductor Leopold Stokowski in the 1930s had Bell Laboratories set up a recording studio in the subterranean space for the Philadelphia Orchestra. The restaurant became the "Stage Door Canteen" during World War II, serving refreshments and featuring appearances by stars of stage, screen, and radio (Abbott and Costello, Duke Ellington, and Frank Sinatra, to name a few). Furthermore, a great well for acoustic purposes is in the Academy's subbasement directly below the auditorium's dome.

The concourse's squalid space gained an even scarier reputation for its use as a nighttime homeless encampment starting in the late 1980s. Mayor Edward Rendell ordered nocturnal sweeps of this and other concourses and had them locked nightly by 1993. The situation has further improved

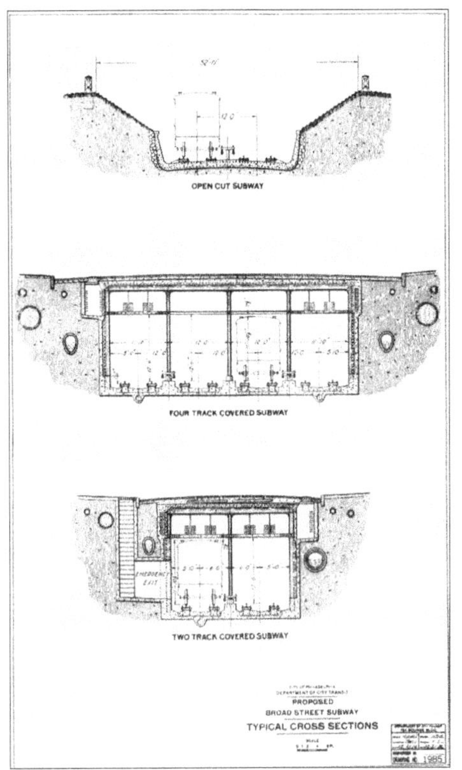

These cross-sectional drawings of the Broad Street Subway show methods of tunnel construction expected to be used in creating the subway when it was proposed before World War I: an open cut (cut-and-cover) subway; a four-track covered subway; and a two-track covered subway. All three techniques were used, but it took more than twenty years for the work to be completed. *From* Annual Report of the Department of City Transit of the City of Philadelphia for the Year Ending December 31, 1914 *(1915).*

ever since the Center City District began shouldering responsibility for maintaining the city's underground mezzanines.

At the turn of the twentieth century, long before South Broad Concourse was built, some buildings along South Broad had rathskellers in their basements. One of these below-street level restaurants was Soula's Rathskeller in the cellar of the Betz Building at the southeast corner of Broad and South Penn Square. Soula's became the premiere social spot for politicians, businessmen, and old-money millionaires and garnered national fame as the subject of a 1901 painting by John Sloan titled *Rathskeller*, today housed in the Cleveland Museum of Art. (The Betz Building was razed in 1926.) The most notable surviving contemporary rathskeller in Philadelphia is in the cellar of the Racquet Club at 215 South 16th Street.

Several electrical substations for the Broad Street Subway are positioned alongside the subway's route through Philadelphia. Filled with electrical switches and transformers, these 1920s substations house electrical equipment that converts high-voltage power from PECO into 630 volts of direct current to power the subway trains and to light the stations.

One Orange Line substation in Center City is at 402 South Juniper, a half mile south of City Hall. This palatial substation was built in 1930 for $453,000 and, not surprisingly, is directly across the street from Philadelphia Electric Company's Waverly Substation. Twin feeder cables under Juniper Street carry raw power from the electric company substation to the subway substation. Another downtown Orange Line substation is located at the intersection of Watts and Mount Vernon Streets just under a mile north of City Hall.

After thirteen years of construction, the Broad Street Line entered regular service from City Hall north to Olney Avenue on September 1, 1928. The southern portion from City Hall to South Street opened on April 20, 1930. Extending the tube south to Snyder Avenue was done by 1933, but with no tracks or finished stations since resources had languished during the Depression. After finances recovered, the Broad Street Subway tunnel was finished in 1937, and trains began running over the whole line by the next year.

The southern part of the Broad Street Line is two-tracked, while the remaining tube—from Walnut-Locust to the Fern Rock Transportation Center in North Philadelphia—is four-tracked. What was said about the Market Street Tunnel can also be said about the tunnel under Broad Street: a four-tracked transit subway is truly uncommon.

The Orange Line initially operated on two tracks to the north and had flying junctions at Erie and Olney Avenues for future extensions. These branch routes were not achieved. (See Chapter 14 for more about Erie Junction and the proposed line that was to have gone under the central median of Roosevelt Boulevard.) A never-completed junction was also built for an offshoot into Southwest Philadelphia; it remains an odd indentation in the tracks north of Snyder Station. A spurline down Passyunk Avenue was to have branched off from the Broad Street trunk too.

The Broad Street Subway was extended north from Olney Avenue to Fern Rock in 1956 and south to Pattison Avenue by 1973. Pattison Station was built with upper and lower platform levels to handle large crowds from Philadelphia's sport stadium compound. In 2010, AT&T signed a naming agreement with SEPTA; Pattison Station has been termed "AT&T Station" since then.

The challenge of making the new business center at the Philadelphia Navy Yard more accessible to commuters has stimulated proposals to lengthen the Broad Street Line beyond AT&T Station to the navy yard. The old naval facility, dating to 1876 at that site, closed on September 27, 1996, and has been redeveloped as a business center. A southern prolongation of the

Broad Street Subway would help foster plans to make the repurposed navy yard a genuine live-work-play environment. Pennsylvania lawmakers have endorsed such a project and federal funding for a feasibility study has been approved. The estimated price is in the range of $400 million.

There is also a proposition to extend the Broad Street Line even farther south under the Delaware River to southern New Jersey. This expensive endeavor, first proposed in 1991, will be pending for a very long time. If ever completed, the Orange Line would end at National Park, New Jersey.

As it happens, there was once a plan to construct a *vehicular* tunnel under the Delaware in this vicinity. The short-lived Delaware River Tunnel Corporation in the mid-1930s received legislative approval to build a $17 million tunnel between South Philadelphia and Gloucester, New Jersey. Political infighting and World War II hampered anything from happening, but there was no denying the need for another crossing since the Delaware River (Ben Franklin) Bridge was approaching traffic capacity. By the late 1940s, the Schuylkill Expressway's initial designs called for a tunnel to have been constructed from Paulsboro, New Jersey, to Essington, just below Philadelphia. Anticipated expansion of Philadelphia International Airport annulled these plans. So, a bridge was decided as the way to enable vehicle traffic to cross the Delaware. The Walt Whitman Bridge opened in 1957.

As with South Broad Concourse, a pedestrian concourse is underneath North Broad Street, formerly linking City Hall Station and Race-Vine Station. The passage was a discreet way to get to Arch Street to see the peep shows in that seedy part of town during the 1960s and '70s. North Broad Concourse is still more or less intact, although certain sections are totally closed to the outside world. Rooms adjoining the forsaken esplanade were used to store food, water, medicine, and other civil defense stockpiles in the 1960s and could take care of about a hundred people as a fallout shelter.

The section from Arch to Race had a drainage problem ever since new. An underground lake emerged on rainy days, making the subsurface walkway almost impassible—and those were days it would have been most useful to pedestrians. One newspaper article lamented that "a stream not quite as deep as the Wissahickon meanders down the concourse." During humid weather, drippings from the ceiling and walls formed a succession of pools around which to maneuver. And a dense fog would form in early spring as warm moist air came into contact with cool underground surfaces, giving the mezzanine a ghostly look.

North Broad Concourse was deemed a stench-ridden slum and a subject of universal derision by the 1960s, despite repairs made in 1961. A string

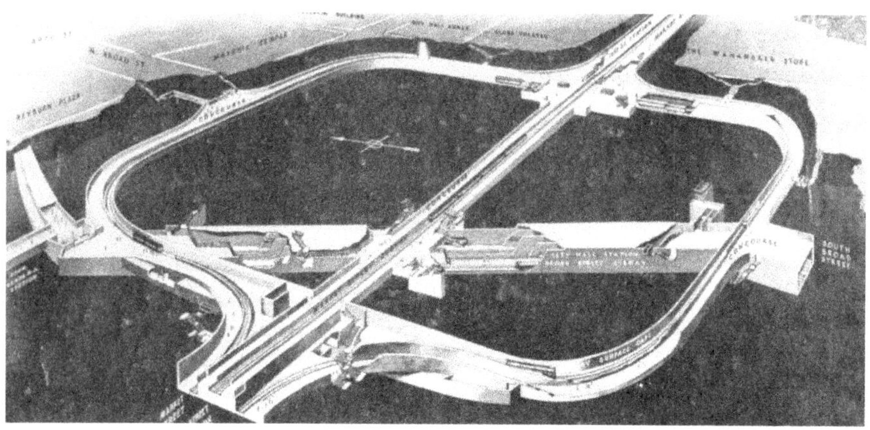

This undated and unidentifiable drawing shows the Market Street Subway and the Broad Street Subway under City Hall, as well as Subway-Surface routes around the municipal building. Pedestrian concourses associated with these lines are also illustrated. Since the Market Street Subway is shown going straight under City Hall—rather than around the building, as originally built—this illustration depicts a scene from after 1936, but it may have been drawn in the late 1920s. *Harry Kyriakodis's collection.*

of fires and other mishaps transpired in this part of the subway during the 1970s, and a blaze at Erie Station in 1979 resulted in 178 people getting injured in a panicked stampede to escape the train. In 1970, a fatally wounded man was discovered at Race-Vine Station after a probable mugging. The victim was a founder of the American Newspaper Guild, so his ensuing death was reported in papers across the country. Ten years later, a rape was committed on the concourse above Race-Vine Station and received much media attention. (The North Broad Concourse might revive if Broad Street continues to redevelop in North Philadelphia.)

The Commuter Rail Tunnel bisected the portion nearest City Hall in the mid-1980s, about which time the entire concourse was shuttered. A stairwell from the meager mezzanine of the Municipal Services Building once provided access to the abandoned passageway, but it was sealed long ago. On the north apron of City Hall, behind the statue of Matthias Baldwin, is a locked entrance leading to both the concourse and the north end of City Hall Station. A secured plywood door at Race-Vine Station is another way into disused North Broad Concourse.

The Vine Street Expressway runs *over* the Broad Street Subway and *under* Broad Street. Because the subway tunnel could not support the weight of the highway over it, the crossing is simultaneously an underpass and a cable-stayed bridge over the subway. Load-bearing cables are embedded in the side walls of the submerged expressway, which also obliterated much of Race-Vine Station in 1987.

SEPTA's Broad-Ridge Spur, also known as the Ridge Avenue Subway, is part of the Orange Line(s) and runs diagonally under eastern Ridge Avenue in the northeast quadrant of Center City. It then turns north to Fern Rock Transportation Center under Broad Street as a component of the Broad Street Subway. The Spur was designed to bring shoppers from North Philadelphia to what was once the nation's busiest retail avenue (Market Street, concentrated at 8th Street) without a change of trains. In other words, traffic would not need to transfer to a Market Street train once getting to City Hall via the Broad Street Subway. The Spur entered service on December 21, 1932, along with the Eighth Street Subway. These routes were related to plans for a Center City subway delivery loop (Chapter 14).

Through-service to Camden, New Jersey, from Girard Avenue by way of the Broad Street Line and the Broad-Ridge Spur began when the Philadelphia-Camden Bridge Line (Chapter 13) opened in 1936. After the Locust Street Subway was finally completed and connected to the Eighth Street Subway in 1953, this enabled the Philadelphia Transportation Company to offer through-service via those right-of-ways together with the Spur to Camden. This service ended in 1968 when much of the line was routed into New Jersey with the new PATCO Hi-Speedline the following year.

From its 8th and Market Terminal heading north, the Broad-Ridge Spur runs under 8th Street, on top of the PATCO Line's tracks. (The Eighth Street Subway is a portion of this right-of-way.) Spur trains—only two cars long—use a newer stub platform, once a pedestrian area, above the original 8th and Market Station now used by PATCO. The two routes split at (under) Race Street: the Broad-Ridge Spur curves northwest toward Ridge Avenue and the PATCO Line turns east toward New Jersey via the Benjamin Franklin Bridge.

The Spur's 9th and Vine Station had to be demolished in the early 1980s because it lay in the path of the Commuter Rail Tunnel. A substitute station was built near 8th and Race as the present Chinatown stop. This is the least-used station on SEPTA's rapid transit network. The station's grade rises and falls as the spurline passes over the Commuter Rail Tunnel. The Vine Street Expressway then goes over the subway near this spot.

Broad-Ridge Spur trains then roll by the forlorn Spring Garden Station, the only true discarded stop on SEPTA's transit system. SEPTA cited both low ridership and safety considerations when it sealed the entrances with galvanized metal in 1989. The station had by then become a hangout for drug users and pushers and has since become a graffiti mecca, with every inch of its walls obscured with graffiti tags. There are no plans to reopen it. Note that this is a different station than the Broad Street Line's Spring Garden Station (two blocks west) or the Market-Frankford El's Spring Garden Station—or, for that matter, the Reading Railroad's long-closed Spring Garden Station.

Southwest of Wallace Street, a pedestrian concourse once ran under Ridge Avenue, lined with stores that have long since closed, as has the mezzanine itself. Under this concourse is the Broad-Ridge Spur's unsettling Fairmount Station, the platform of which has been shortened to half its original length. This was done many years after 1956, when a couple was found dead in the dim station after a murder-suicide stemming from a lovers' quarrel.

The spurline's Fairmount Station connects directly to the northbound platform of the Broad Street Line's Fairmount Station via stairs; the southbound platform cannot be reached from the Spur without exiting the system. The Spur's southbound tracks plunge under the Broad Street Subway's tracks as they join those tracks and head north employing the line's express tracks. This subway-under-subway point is the lowest spot of all of Philadelphia's subways, besides being the most perilous and exhilarating.

Philadelphia became the second city in the nation with subway express trackage when express service was introduced on the Broad Street Line in 1959. Twin express tracks between Walnut-Locust Station and Erie Station were installed, extending out to Olney Station by 1991. Express trains reversed direction just south of Walnut-Locust Station, as they do today. Because of the lack of usable cars, express service was discontinued on November 19, 1979, and Spur trains operated only to Girard Avenue Station. But following SEPTA's purchase of new Kawasaki subway cars three years later, full service on both routes resumed. The same Japanese-built cars are still rolling on the Orange Lines.

The Broad Street Line and the Broad-Ridge Spur are reminiscent of a New York subway in look and feel. Trains run on standard-gauge track (four feet, eight and a half inches) with overrunning third rail. Since the Broad Street Lines do not share the same track gauge with the Blue Line or trolleys of the Green Line, these transit lines will always be segregated. The Orange Lines see the light of day only at Fern Rock Transportation Center in North Philadelphia.

Lastly, SEPTA is installing sensors in its subway tunnels to allow cellular modems to work below ground on the Blue and Orange Lines. This will enable riders with smartphones and computers to track subway trains. SEPTA buses, trolleys, and Regional Rail cars have already been equipped with cellular modems.

Chapter 13

The PATCO Hi-Speedline and the Eighth Street and Locust Street Tunnels

PATCO, a subsidiary of the Delaware River Port Authority (DRPA), operates the 14.2-mile rapid transit line between Center City Philadelphia and Lindenwold, New Jersey. The PATCO Hi-Speedline currently has nine stations in New Jersey and four in Philadelphia.

The first incarnation of a commuter rail line across the Delaware was commenced in 1926 with the construction of the Delaware River Bridge—thereafter renamed Benjamin Franklin Bridge—by the Delaware River Bridge Commission. The commission was reorganized in 1931 as the Delaware River Joint Commission (DRJC) and was given the go-ahead to construct a high-speed transit line between Philadelphia and Camden.

On June 7, 1936, the Philadelphia-Camden Bridge Line (aka Delaware River Bridge Line) opened from a stub-end terminal at 8th and Market en route to Broadway Station (now the Walter Rand Transportation Center) in downtown Camden. The line's fleet of Philadelphia-made Brill railcars, dubbed "Flash Gordons" because of their Art Deco styling, ran on tracks attached to both outward sides of the bridge, as PATCO trains still do.

The Bridge Line was seen as progress, as it supplanted the many competing ferries that crossed the Delaware River since the time of William Penn. By the 1920s, these ferries carried an endless stream of people, cars, trucks, and buses between Pennsylvania and New Jersey. More than 100,000 passengers were transported daily at the height of ferry business in 1925. The cessation of ferry service happened rather quickly after the bridge's opening in 1926 and the onset of Bridge Line service ten years later. (As previously mentioned, this was the decease of the Market Street Line's Ferry Branch too.)

The last Philadelphia-Camden ferry to regularly operate was the Pennsylvania Railroad's Philadelphia and Camden Ferry, which held out until 1952. The four-slip terminal headhouse at the base of Market Street was an elaborate Victorian structure with a four-sided, clock-equipped cupola. It became a food market in the 1950s and was later removed for the construction of Penn's Landing. The RiverLink Ferry, a lone tourist-oriented ferryboat between Penn's Landing and the Camden waterfront, is a small connection to the past.

Philadelphia Rapid Transit administered the Bridge Line on behalf of the DRJC until the Philadelphia Transportation Company took it over in 1940. The transit line offered workers and shoppers from Camden fast and easy access into the City of Brotherly Love.

Soon, community groups in New Jersey began agitating for a more integrated line linking the New Jersey suburbs with the metropolis. With that in mind, Pennsylvania and New Jersey authorized the Delaware River Port Authority in 1951 to construct a more comprehensive transit route. Consultants studied tunneling under the Delaware River for a new line into the Quaker City but instead decided to use the extant Bridge Line because doing so was less costly.

When the DRPA took over the line, it extended the New Jersey part of the route from Broadway Station southeast to Ashland, New Jersey, and then to Lindenwold. The Philadelphia Transportation Company operated the Bridge Line until 1968, one year before DRPA created the Port Authority Transit Corporation (PATCO). On January 4, 1969, the Hi-Speedline began operating between Lindenwold and Camden. Service reached Philadelphia on February 15. It featured air-conditioned cars and computer-run trains.

The PATCO Line encompasses the Locust Street Subway and the Eighth Street Subway in Philadelphia. These connected sub-ways were related to plans for a Center City subway loop (to be discussed in the next chapter). The city first started excavating a three-block tube under Locust Street around 1918, but work was mothballed during World War I. Digging resumed in 1931 after the city determined that the old sub-way was too small in diameter for 1930s subway cars; the tunnel had to be re-bored along the same right-of-way. Later that year, the widened tube was finally completed to 18th Street—the eastern edge of Rittenhouse Square. The redone tunnel cost $5 million, but it too was abandoned since money to finish the line had dwindled during the Depression.

The Locust Street Subway was at length completed and connected to the Eighth Street Subway by 1953. After thirty-five years of intermittent work, the tunnel under Locust was belittled as "the hole in the ground." The completed route was touted as a handy way for Rittenhouse Square residents to get to the shopping district at 8th and Market. The Philadelphia Transportation Company was then able to offer through-service to Camden via the Philadelphia-Camden Bridge Line. But ridership was minimal, and cashiers in the Locust Street Subway spent much of their time reading magazines. (They were derided as the world's best-read cashiers.) Bridge Line service ended in 1968 when the route became part of the PATCO Line. The revised line offered suburban New Jerseyans access to job opportunities in Center City and shopping opportunities at Market Street department stores.

A pedestrian concourse runs above the Locust Street Subway's 9th–10th Street Station. A separate concourse runs from 12th–13th Street Station to 15th–16th Street Station and at Broad and Locust bisects the Broad Street

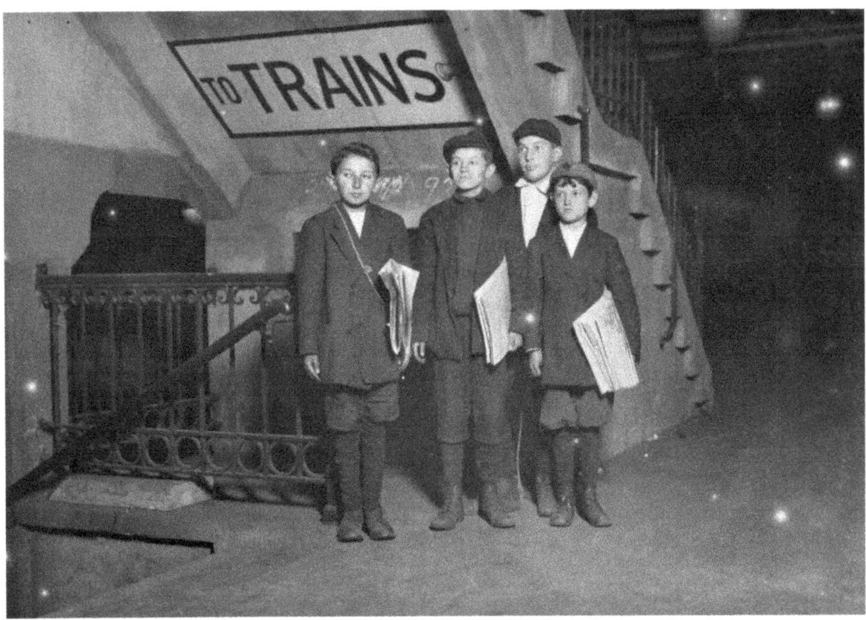

This oft-reproduced photograph by American sociologist and photographer Lewis Wickes Hine shows four newsboys who sold newspapers day and night inside Philadelphia's subway system, earning twenty-five cents a day. As this picture was taken in 1909, these newsies would have to be working somewhere within the Market Street Tunnel, probably on a concourse near City Hall. *Library of Congress.*

Subway's enormous southern mezzanine, making it an integral part of the city's pedestrian concourse network. The Locust Street Tunnel crosses perpendicularly under the Broad Street Subway some forty feet below the surface at that spot.

Early on during its control of the line, PATCO contemplated lengthening the Locust Street Subway to 30th Street Station, which was considered a desired place for PATCO to serve. The line under Locust Street was even proposed to have continued to Darby, Pennsylvania. Needless to say, these extensions were never completed.

The Eighth Street Subway was completed after several years of excavation in late 1932 and united the Locust Street Subway with the Broad-Ridge Spur. The subway beneath 8th Street crosses under the Market Street Subway at Market Street and began using the Spur's former station at 8th and Market. (In 2017, a wayward raccoon was caught at PATCO's 8th and Market Station, startling passengers; it was released at the end of the line in New Jersey.)

When the Eighth Street Subway was built in the 1930s, a pedestrian concourse was installed above the subway and underneath 8th Street from Chestnut to Market. Still widely used today, it was meant to provide sheltered access to the Broad-Ridge Spur, the Market-Frankford El, and the Locust Street Subway (i.e., PATCO trains today).

The Philadelphia Parking Authority's "Parkade on 8th" was constructed over 8th Street between Filbert and Arch in 1964. The block-long tunnel carrying a parking garage has lately been equipped with decorative LED lights that illuminate a once forgotten strip of retail stores. The garage, an eyesore for decades, was also revamped and beautified.

The PATCO Line runs *under* the Broad-Ridge Spur tracks along 8th Street until the two lines go their separate ways at 8th and Race. PATCO's westbound tube crosses beneath the Eighth Street Subway, an alignment made in the 1950s when the Bridge Line connected to that subway.

From 8th and Race, the Hi-Speedline turns east, running under Franklin Square toward the Ben Franklin Bridge. It crosses over the Market-Frankford Elevated near the Philadelphia waterfront as it heads on the bridge over the Delaware.

The City of Philadelphia owns the 8th Street and the Locust Street sections of the PATCO Line and receives millions of dollars in annual rental payments from the DRPA. As with the Broad Street Subway and the Broad-Ridge Spur, PATCO trains run on standard-gauge track with overrunning third rail.

There were proposals in the 1920s and '30s for carrying the Locust Street Subway across the Schuylkill River to 49th Street in West Philadelphia, but the idea died due to lack of funds. In the 1970s, a $90 million plan to continue the PATCO Line from 16th and Locust west to the old Philadelphia Civic Center (demolished in 2004–7) was bandied about. The Delaware River Port Authority recommended this project as a way to strengthen its service into Philadelphia.

The planned extension would have gone under Rittenhouse Square and the Schuylkill River and would have included stations along Locust Street at 19th or 24th. It would have connected to a new SEPTA high-speed line from Suburban Station to Philadelphia International Airport. (SEPTA subsequently completed a distinct Airport Line as a constituent of the Regional Rail System.)

A station for the extended line at Rittenhouse Square was on the drawing board, but it was rejected by Philadelphia's City Planning Commission after spirited community opposition. The thought of disturbing fashionable Rittenhouse Square with a noisy construction project was too much for the square's inhabitants. Still, the Locust Street Tunnel and tracks do reach a bit beneath Rittenhouse Square, and this stretch is utilized as a "turnback" for PATCO trains.

The same opposition probably put an end to notions of extending the PATCO Hi-Speedline at all. Moreover, the cost was judged to be too high, even though the federal government was to cover 80 percent of construction expenses. Then again, federal allocations for projects like this had evaporated by the 1980s. The Commuter Rail Tunnel was the last major federally funded infrastructure project completed in Philadelphia.

Another threat had befallen Rittenhouse Square back in 1950 when a gigantic below-ground parking garage was seriously deliberated for the site. The 1,400-car garage was proffered by Underground Garages Inc., a company formed to meet the demands of motorists in the automobile-crazy post–World War II era. Underground Garages would have leased Rittenhouse Square for fifty years, paying the city a nominal ground rent each year before relinquishing the garage to the city.

The $4 million plan was universally denounced as "sheer vandalism" and "desecration of a shrine." Opponents pointed out that vehicular congestion around Rittenhouse Square would increase dramatically. Plus, since the historic square's layout—devised by Paul Crét—would have to be obliterated, the park's lovely plantings and trees would not and could not be restored in a natural way. This opposition helped galvanize the nascent Center City Residents Association.

Other large underground parking garages were proposed for downtown Philadelphia after World War II. In 1946, Mayor Bernard Samuel asked the Department of City Transit to prepare designs for a nine-hundred-car parking facility under Reyburn Plaza, opposite City Hall. As it turns out, the property was put to better use when the Municipal Services Building replaced Reyburn Plaza in 1962–63. But could the 1946 proposal have been the genesis of the multi-level parking garage built under adjacent JFK (Love) Park twenty years later?

As horrible as these garages sound, the same year (1946) saw a plan to place a five-hundred-car parking garage beneath Independence Square, right behind Independence Hall. The Commonwealth of Pennsylvania allocated $4 million for the project, and Mayor Samuel directed city engineers to draw blueprints. This would-be sacrilege was studied for years with no action.

On the other hand, a three-level 680-car parking garage *was* approved by 1962 for Independence Mall, two blocks north of Independence Square. In 1977, revelers who had just witnessed Fourth of July fireworks started their cars en masse in the packed Independence Mall Garage, sending carbon monoxide fumes throughout the facility. People stumbled to the surface needing oxygen, and scores were carried away on stretchers to be treated at area hospitals. Making national headlines, the near catastrophe came about when both exits were blocked by disabled cars and high humidity overwhelmed the garage's ventilation system. Managed by the Philadelphia Parking Authority, the underground garage is still there, south of Arch Street.

Getting back to PATCO, an immense deserted station, the largest on the entire line, exists under Franklin Square. The stop opened in 1936 with the Philadelphia-Camden Bridge Line and remained in use for three years. Low patronage shuttered the station, and the Philadelphia Transportation Company found that it could shave a minute off the trip to and from the city by eliminating the stop.

Franklin Square Station may have reopened briefly during World War II and positively reopened for a while in 1952. PATCO reactivated the station yet again during the U.S. Bicentennial but shuttered it in 1979 on account of low ridership. (On July 4, 1976, however, almost twenty-three thousand riders exited there!) Fears about crime and homelessness doomed the shabby station. But given recent population growth and development in Old City, Callowhill, and Northern Liberties, there is reason to believe that the station will reopen once more.

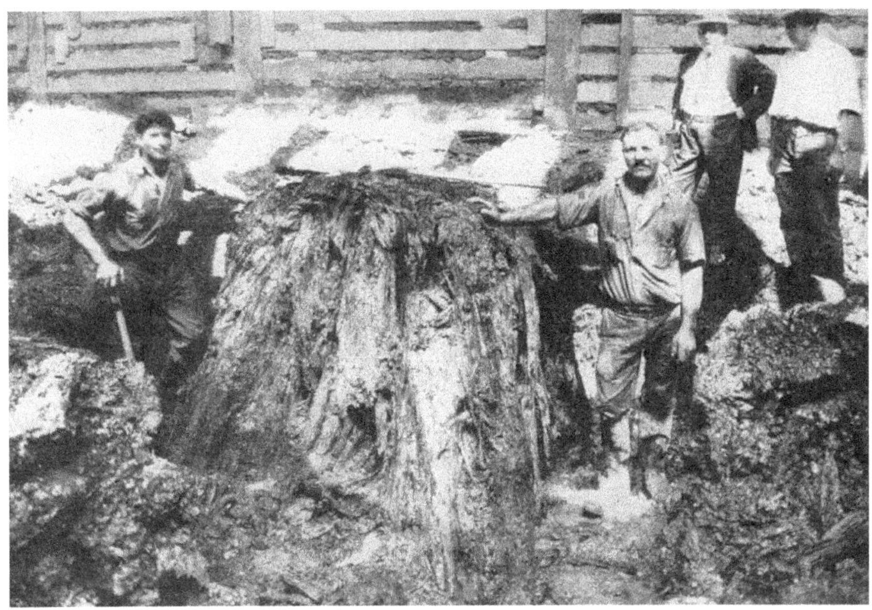

In 1931, Locust Street Subway excavation unearthed the remains of a cypress tree that was estimated to be up to 100,000 years old. The trunk had a circumference of seventeen feet and was found forty feet below the surface at 8th and Locust. The find proved that the Philadelphia region was once a land of swamps. This photo, bright as it is, confirms that the tunnel under Locust Street was built using the cut-and-cover method of subway construction. *From the December 1932 issue of* National Geographic Magazine.

In the meantime, Franklin Square Station is a favorite for urban explorers and graffiti artists, and its dim, graffiti-scarred platforms are visible to riders entering and exiting Philadelphia on PATCO trains. Other than a few ventilation grates and manholes with "DRJC" markings, there are no traces of the ravaged station aboveground.

Franklin Square had the reputation as a place of itinerant and indigent workingmen throughout the mid-twentieth century. Reputed then as "Bum's Park," it was the gateway to Skid Row—between Race and Callowhill Streets, along Vine Street—and it encompassed the red-light zone of Chinatown. The first thing motorists would see upon crossing the Ben Franklin Bridge into Philadelphia was a place filled with dozens of men reclining on benches or lined up for soup and salvation. The area was, in effect, the predecessor of the heroin market—"El Campamento"—miles away in Kensington.

Urban renewal efforts of the 1960s and '70s eliminated this Tenderloin ward, but the Callowhill neighborhood remained a depressed sector. The barren square mile of territory, with Reading Viaduct crossing overhead, has been called the "Eraserhood" after David Lynch's 1977 absurd film *Eraserhead*, which was inspired by the bleakness of the locality. Paperback author David Goodis also set many of his 1950s crime novels in Philadelphia's Skid Row, chronicling the despair of the area and its dwellers. Happily, the western portion of the Callowhill and Chinatown North neighborhoods are in the midst of a development boom, impelled by the creation of the highly anticipated Reading Viaduct Rail Park.

Franklin Square Station is not the only underground activity at Franklin Square. In 1776, a powder magazine was built in the northwest quadrant of the commons for the Quaker City's gunpowder supply during the War for American Independence. This partially below-ground structure held four hundred casks of gunpowder and had space for four hundred more. By 1791, a substitute powder magazine had been built elsewhere, and the one at Franklin Square was used to store whale oil for the city's streetlamps.

An earlier below-grade powder magazine was situated a few blocks away, around New Market Street and Artillery Lane. Built in 1724, this was the first ordnance storage structure in Pennsylvania, if not the Western Hemisphere. Artillery Lane was between Noble and Green Streets and was afterward renamed Duke, then Dana, and then Nectarine Street. It has long been removed, and I-95 now runs over the powder house site.

From 1741 until 1836, the northeastern half of Franklin Square was used as a burial ground for Old First Reformed Church. Members of that congregation—located at 4th and Race and still home to the descendent fold, United Church of Christ—were not able to include an adjoining cemetery at their church when it opened in 1747. The nearest sizeable tract of open land was Northeast Square (Franklin Square's initial designation).

William Penn's son Thomas had granted a portion of the square to First Reformed for use as a burial ground in 1741, and the church began using the space within a few years. As many as 3,100 bodies were interred in Franklin Square's northeast quadrant. The necropolis lasted there for almost a hundred years before the city sought to return the square to recreational use exclusively. In 1835, the Pennsylvania Supreme Court ruled that Thomas Penn's conveyance of public land was invalid, so First Reformed Church was ordered to move the bodies and vacate the park. Many graves were moved, but some remain to this day, since the headstones were merely laid atop the caskets and covered with soil.

General knowledge of the graveyard did not prevent the digging of a sewer through Franklin Square in 1915. And in the 1930s, it did not prevent the excavation of two subway tunnels (one for eastbound trains and the other for westbound trains), not to mention Franklin Square Station itself between them. Workers building the Bridge Line callously dug through the old cemetery without calling attention to what they surely discovered.

The headstones were left in place after an archaeological investigation in 2006. Today, Franklin Square is administered as a tourist attraction by Historic Philadelphia Inc. A miniature golf course sits on the footprint of Old First Reformed's onetime burial ground. Human remains were reburied in a tomb under the park, marked by a memorial plaque near the graveyard's original location.

Chapter 14

Subways that Were Never Built in the Quaker City

A. Merritt Taylor (1873–1937) was the first commissioner of the newly created Department of City Transit in 1912. Appointed to peruse mass transit expansion in the city, he released his recommendations the following year. Although Taylor was a competent planner, it could be said that he was a dreamer and perhaps a tad subway-happy.

Among others in just about all sections of the Quaker City, the "Taylor Plan" suggested subways along Chestnut, Walnut, and Arch Streets; a subway loop to distribute Broad Street Subway riders around Center City; a line along Benjamin Franklin Parkway to points north; and a subway branch into Northeast Philly via Roosevelt Boulevard. But the majority of Taylor's planned routes never came to be. The blame for why Philadelphia's public transit system did not develop as anticipated can be spread around pretty wide.

First of all, A. Merritt Taylor was succeeded in 1916 by a more pragmatic transit commissioner, William S. Twining (1865–1937), who took exception to many of Taylor's ideas. Whereas Taylor saw transit as a stimulant of urban development, Twinning sanctioned building lines only where there was already demand.

Moreover, World War I severely affected the development of Philadelphia's transit system, as labor became scarce, construction costs skyrocketed, and materials were in short supply. Then the city spent inordinate sums of money on several projects leading up to and into the 1920s:

- acquiring land for and building the Benjamin Franklin Parkway
- extending Roosevelt Boulevard northward
- erecting the Delaware River (Benjamin Franklin) Bridge
- constructing the Philadelphia Museum of Art
- constructing the Free Library of Philadelphia (Central Branch)
- hosting the Sesqui-Centennial Exposition of 1926

Furthermore, there was persistent wrangling among the mayor and Philadelphia's City Councils as to which subway lines should receive priority. Endless studies of the lines (and their expected profitability) and the incessant rearranging of routes slowed transit expansion to a crawl.

Legal complications with the awarding of contracts made matters worse. Much of that trouble arose from the Philadelphia Rapid Transit Company (PRT), which was at constant odds with the city government for one reason or another. Its president, Thomas Mitten, thwarted much of the proposed subway system that Commissioner Taylor championed, expressing a disinterest in building any subway line that was potentially unprofitable or that would compete against PRT's trolley routes. (PRT was so heavily invested in trolley lines that it did not want any competition from municipal subways.) This issue came to bear even when the city offered to build subway lines at taxpayer expense, with PRT merely operating them. And the City of Philadelphia never mandated additional subway routes as part of Philadelphia Rapid Transit's franchise.

These delays gave Philadelphia a late start in building the subway lines that were eventually agreed on. By the time decisions were made in the 1920s, the age of the private motor car had overtaken the age of the subway and the trolley.

The Depression then killed many latent subway lines, since the city was barely solvent during the 1930s. And unlike New York City, Philadelphia did not pursue subway expansion as a way to alleviate unemployment. When prosperity returned to the Quaker City after World War II, public transit projects took a back seat to highway construction and urban renewal efforts.

It is a shame that most of Commissioner Taylor's proposed subway lines did not come to fruition. The Market-Frankford El and Broad Street Subway were to have been the commencement of a citywide transit system that would confound modern-day Philadelphians. A description of some of the more important lines not constructed (or partially constructed and then dropped) in Center City and elsewhere in Philadelphia follows.

A Chestnut Street subway was supposed to have traversed west under Chestnut Street and then turn south at 42nd to become an elevated line on Woodland Avenue heading toward Darby, Pennsylvania. The route would have started in Camden, New Jersey, and continued into Philly via a tunnel under the Delaware River.

The thought of a subway along Chestnut Street hearkens back to 1906, when the Philadelphia & Western Railroad (P&W) proposed such a line to compete with PRT's Market Street Subway. After all, the Market Street Line, then being built, was predicted to reach capacity by 1940. (Philadelphia & Western was a high-speed commuter railroad in the western suburbs of Philadelphia.)

Nothing came of P&W's proposal, although a *city*-built line under Chestnut was seriously discussed into the 1920s. Such a subway seemed like it really would be constructed until opposition by the Chestnut Street Association doused the proposal in 1928. Merchants of this business consortium objected because construction of the line would disrupt their retail establishments. One member stated that the line would "cheapen one of the finest business thoroughfare in America."

Chestnut Street *did* have an electric trolley line on its surface, tracing its roots back to December 7, 1831, when an early omnibus line called "Boxall's Accommodation" was inaugurated. The service consisted of a single horsecar that made hourly trips between 2nd and 16th Streets, picking up passengers at any point along Chestnut. The owner and lone driver of the glorified stagecoach was James Boxall, who was also the line's ticket agent and conductor. Later, horse-drawn and electric streetcars on rails operated on Chestnut Street until buses came into use. (Thanks to the National City Lines, the street's trolley tracks were paved over in 1956; a segment of preserved tracks was exposed during road construction near 31st Street in early 2018.) It could be said that Boxall's Accommodation was the forefather of SEPTA bus Routes 21 and 42 on Chestnut Street.

An *augmented* trolley line for Chestnut Street was also proffered during the 1920s. Under the plan, electric streetcars would operate via subway in West Philadelphia and connect to the city's streetcar network at 42nd Street. Moving east, trolleys would run on the surface of Chestnut until about 7th Street, where they would turn north toward the Delaware River (Ben Franklin) Bridge to take riders to Camden.

The enhanced streetcar route would have included moving sidewalks inside tunnels under the surface of pavements on both sides of Chestnut. The innovative moving platforms would run on three individual tracks at three, six, and nine miles per hour. Yet, in the end, no subway or moving platforms were built along Chestnut Street.

The Chestnut Street Transitway (CST) could be regarded as the legacy of these plans. The CST opened between 6th and 18th in 1976 as part of the city's Bicentennial celebration. It was the idea of city planner Edmund Bacon, who had envisioned open-air electric trolleys traversing both Chestnut and Walnut Streets between the Delaware and Schuylkill Rivers. The trolley would serve a twelve-block outdoor mall that was intended to reinvigorate Chestnut Street by prohibiting cars from the road, making the street and its stores more pedestrian-friendly.

Yet Philadelphians wondered what to make of this strange thoroughfare, with its all-too-spacious sidewalks, cumbersome street furniture, and peculiar streetlamps (of luminous plastic globes). No trolleys were ever made part of the project; only SEPTA buses lumbered along the street. And they lumbered very fast, treating the roadway as an exclusive highway and scaring pedestrians crossing at crosswalks.

Instead of becoming a pleasant pedestrian promenade with electric streetcars, the CST became a thruway for noisy diesel buses—as many as a thousand a day! Upscale stores closed or moved away, replaced by discount stores and the like. Chestnut Street became a place that people on foot avoided; urban planners and others deemed the CST a fiasco.

Automobile traffic was allowed on Chestnut in the evenings after 1981 and was permitted entirely in the 1990s. The city afterward restricted the right lane to bikes and buses (and automobiles making right turns), since construction funds would otherwise have had to have been repaid to the federal government. But the right lane is seldom used for those purposes. Traffic barrels along Chestnut Street as it did in the old days.

A subway delivery loop in Center City was the most intriguing and implicitly useful of Taylor's transit proposals. This loop was to have been part of the Broad Street Subway and would have run from Broad and Fairmount down Ridge Avenue to 8th Street and then south to either Walnut or Locust, where it would continue west to 19th and then turn north to Arch and east again to reconnect with the Broad Street Line. The subway loop would have collected riders from North Philadelphia and distributed them around Center City's shopping and business precinct. At least five downtown stations were planned.

The proposed sub-way route was later shortened into a compact ring around Center City by relying on Arch Street rather than Ridge Avenue. Sections of tunnel were excavated under both Arch and Locust Streets in

1915 before work was halted for want of funds. The Locust Street Tunnel was eventually completed, but the tunnel under Arch was not, as World War I wound up condemning the loop project. Just two short sub-way segments were excavated under Arch Street before the war: one between 12th and 13th Streets that is 263 feet long and the other between 10th and 11th Streets that is 126 feet long. Two metal grates in the Arch Street sidewalk are the only entrances into these discarded tunnel sections.

Lore has it that the Trocadero Theatre (normally called "The Troc," at 1003 Arch Street) had an emergency exit into one segment during its seedier days. Having opened in 1870, what may be the only intact Victorian theater in the United States predated the Arch Street excavations by decades. In addition, the renowned Chinese Friendship Gate straddling 10th Street was not assembled precisely at the intersection of 10th and Arch because the tunnel under Arch Street could not support the forty-foot-tall structure's weight. Philadelphia's is the first authentic Friendship Gate ever constructed by Chinese artisans outside of China.

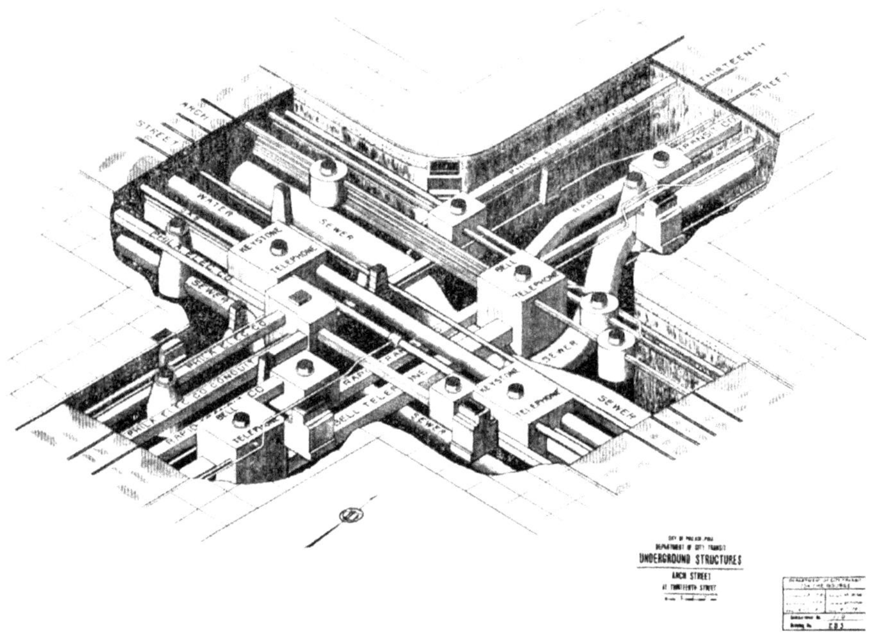

This isometric view of underground structures at 13th and Arch Streets shows how congested a typical Center City intersection can be, with water, gas, and sewer pipes and telephone, electrical, and other utility conduits—and manhole access into them—all vying for space. And this is from 1914! The diagram was apparently prepared for the proposed Arch Street subway. *From* Annual Report of the Department of City Transit of the City of Philadelphia for the Year Ending December 31, 1914 *(1915)*.

There have been proposals to use the Arch Street sub-way tunnels as vehicular parking space or as an underground approach to the Ben Franklin Bridge, but these ideas failed to generate any attention. The two passages are still under Arch Street, minus any tracks or trains.

In the 1970s, the Delaware River Port Authority proposed constructing a Center City subway loop from 8th and Arch, up Arch Street (using the tunnel sections just described) to 19th Street, then connecting by way of 19th to the PATCO Hi-Speedline under Locust Street. This loop plan was comparable to the scheme set forth by A. Merritt Taylor sixty years earlier, albeit larger. Mayor Frank Rizzo bluntly rebuffed the $120 million plan because it would allegedly filch riders from SEPTA.

While the downtown *subway* loop did not come to pass, the concept of a *highway* loop around Center City was promoted beginning in the late 1940s. The Vine Street Expressway (I-676), Interstate 95, and the Schuylkill Expressway (I-76) were elements of this plan and were ultimately built. The unbuilt Crosstown Expressway of the 1960s and '70s would have formed the southern portion of this loop, connecting I-95 and the Schuylkill Expressway along the line of South Street. It would have taken out a block-wide swath of the city in between the Delaware and Schuylkill Rivers, separating South Philadelphia from Center City much as I-676 separates North Philadelphia from Center City.

The Crosstown Expressway's last incarnation was a broader plan that would have placed the highway underground. Dubbed Southbridge, the $750 million urban development project would have included thousands of housing units, approximately 2.8 million square feet of office space, about 200,000 square feet of commercial real estate, and some fourteen thousand parking spaces inside several parking garages. An elevated light-rail system was also to have connected the Southbridge development with the Broad Street Subway and area bus lines. The monstrous project was slated for completion in 1982, but Mayor Rizzo canceled it in 1973 after environmental concerns and community opposition, especially protests of the African American community that would have been displaced.

Getting back to subways, Commissioner Taylor also suggested a subway line under the Ben Franklin Parkway. The Parkway-Roxborough (or Northwestern) subway-elevated was to have been an extension of the yet-to-be Broad Street Subway. Starting at City Hall, it would have proceeded under the Parkway to 29th Street, where it would then have continued as an elevated line to Henry Avenue, following that road north past Wissahickon Creek. Space for the transit line was incorporated into the bridge over

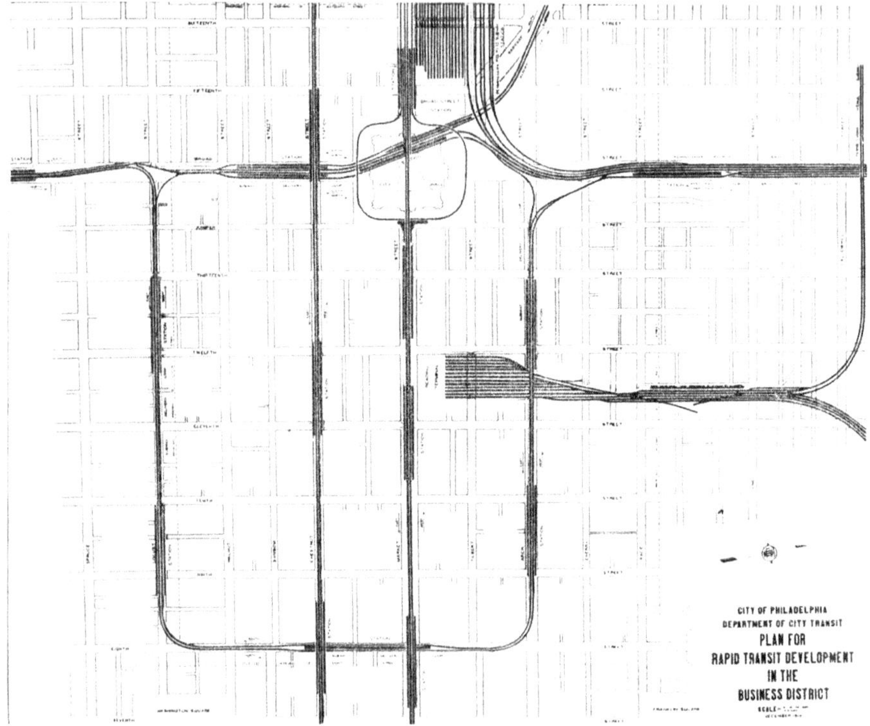

An unfulfilled 1914 plan of the underground downtown subway loop, showing the projected tunnels under Arch Street, 8th Street, and Locust Street and connecting to the yet-to-be Broad Street Subway. Also shown is the never-built subway under Chestnut Street and a spur leading to the never-built subway under the Benjamin Franklin Parkway that would have gone to Roxborough. Furthermore, the plan includes the Pennsylvania Railroad's never-built tracks leading to Broad Street Station. These tracks were to have brought the Pennsylvania Railroad's Northeast Corridor all the way from North Philadelphia Station into (and through) Broad Street Station by traveling under Broad Street for three miles! In addition, the diagram shows that as far back as 1914, the Market Street Subway was planned to cross directly under City Hall rather than go around the building. That alteration happened in the 1930s. *From* Annual Report of the Department of City Transit of the City of Philadelphia for the Year Ending December 31, 1914 *(1915).*

the Wissahickon; never-used box-tunnels are within each flank of the Wissahickon Memorial Bridge.

A cavernous subway station was built on the ground level of the Philadelphia Museum of Art for this proposed line. The expectation was that visitors would arrive at the museum via this below-grade "Art Museum Station." With its limestone walls and vaulted ceiling, the space was probably created as a gallery and was foreseen as a grand entrance to the museum, with elevators to upper floors. The actual subway was likely planned to pass underneath this space.

The 640-feet-long corridor was roughed out of the base of Faire Mount before construction began on the museum. It still exists, running below the building's southeastern foundation, under the iconic "Rocky Steps" (up which fictional fighter Rocky Balboa triumphantly ran) and close to the Rocky statue (properly titled *Thunder in His Heart*). Never-used entrances were built at both sides of the museum to provide access into the "Art Museum Station."

Closed to the public and used as storage space for generations, the "station" is currently part of the museum's campaign to create sixty-seven thousand square feet of new public space and twenty-three thousand square feet of gallery space. The subsurface expansion will serve as an entrance to the main building (as originally designed) through new space that will be opened up by the removal of the museum's auditorium. Next will come excavating additional gallery space underneath the "Rocky Steps." A controversial plan of punching skylights into the stone steps is still on the table. Work is scheduled for completion in 2020.

In 1923, Mayor J. Hampton Moore lobbied for utilizing the Pennsylvania Avenue Subway and Tunnel as the route to Roxborough. In this way, the Ben Franklin Parkway could be spared from a major construction undertaking that would have ruined the boulevard-like panorama that was so desired when it was built. The Reading Railroad no doubt put a stop to the mayor's notion since the Pennsylvania Avenue Tunnel would need to be widened to manage subway traffic that would accompany freight traffic already using the City Branch.

In any event, the Parkway-Roxborough subway-elevated route was never built. And too bad, as a rapid transit line passing by the Manayunk section of Philadelphia would be quite popular today.

The intersection of Broad Street and Erie Avenue, where the Broad Street Line's Erie Station is, was to have been a major transportation interchange under Commissioner Taylor's 1913 plans for rapid transit lines. Erie Junction would have provided access to a subway-elevated line to Philadelphia's Germantown district. Never completed, this would have allowed for a Broad Street Subway spur route that would have served the maturing Oak Lane neighborhood. Additional tunneling and trackwork under Broad Street does exist in the vicinity of Erie Avenue, but Erie Junction was not finished.

An extension of the Broad Street Subway was also to have been placed under Roosevelt Boulevard to cater to Northeast Philadelphia, connecting to the subway at Erie Junction. But nothing came of this or any of the other studies and proposals (including an elevated line) for adding rapid transit along Roosevelt Boulevard. The expense of building any such line—estimated to be between $3 billion and $4.6 billion—has always been a chief stumbling block. Community opposition has always been another.

A primordial segment of the Lincoln Highway, Roosevelt Boulevard runs southwest from the Philadelphia-Bucks County line to Hunting Park Avenue, near Broad Street. Its first division, a four-lane parkway named "Torresdale Boulevard," opened in 1903, with subsequent sections completed in later years and decades. At first also called "Northeast Boulevard," the road was renamed "Theodore Roosevelt Memorial Boulevard" in 1919 to honor the ex-President. It was designated US 1 eight years thereafter.

The twelve-lane Boulevard is the most congested and pedestrian-hostile traffic artery in Philadelphia, so wide that it contains an eighty-foot median built specifically to facilitate a subway (or even an elevated). Motor vehicles zoom along the thoroughfare as though it was a freeway, making for hair-raising experiences when trying to walk (more accurately, *run*) across the roadway at one of dozens of intersections. Pedestrian deaths have routinely occurred along Roosevelt Boulevard, whether or not those crossings are used. The Boulevard has some of the most treacherous traffic intersections in the United States.

Plans for a Bus Rapid Transit system have been suggested for years for the Boulevard's median. SEPTA in 2017 launched "Boulevard Direct," an express bus service in the regular travel lanes with several features that reduce travel time between Northeast Philadelphia and Center City. For instance, Boulevard Direct's buses make faster runs by making eight stops rather than the eighty stops of the Boulevard's existing Route 14 buses.

Despite the absence of a Roosevelt Boulevard subway, an underground transit station was built in 1967 near Adams Avenue and the Boulevard. The Adams Avenue Station would have served the Sears Building at that intersection, as well as the surrounding Northeast Philadelphia neighborhood. A parking garage was erected atop the station for Sears, and a pedestrian tunnel was installed under the width of Roosevelt Boulevard for the convenience of shoppers. A later plan would have routed the subway through Northeast Philadelphia by way of the never-built Northeast Expressway.

The unopened Adams Avenue Station was built speculatively by Sears to ensure that the oft-proposed subway would stop at the Sears Building. It was intended to become a significant transit terminal for burgeoning Northeast

Philadelphia and was to enable entry into the lower retail level of Sears, much like the Market Street Subway permitted ready access to the "bargain basement" levels of department stores lining Market Street.

The implosion of the Sears Building on October 31, 1994, was a sorrowful event in the history of Northeast Philadelphia. The parking garage was demolished at that time too. Parts of the station and the pedestrian tunnel under the Boulevard remain sealed and unseen today. Crime concerns made the Boulevard tunnel dicey during the short time it was open.

Roosevelt *Expressway* (US 1, aka the Roosevelt Boulevard Extension) was built to connect Roosevelt Boulevard to the Schuylkill Expressway by means of a divided highway that runs west from Hunting Park Avenue. Completed in 1961, the throughway descends westward into a canyon of concrete embankments with numerous streets crossing above. One overpass carries Broad Street and the Broad Street Subway (within a box structure). Almost all Philadelphians know the bridge as the one with oversized signs cautioning highway traffic that clearance is fourteen feet.

Chapter 15

Franklin's Tunnels, the Underground Railroad, and Other Downtown Subterranean Passages

The prominence of the Quaker City and its institutions are tied to the legacy of Benjamin Franklin (1706–1790). "No other town, burying its great man, ever buried more of itself than Philadelphia with Franklin," wrote Carl Van Doren in his 1938 biography of Franklin. And never has one done so much for his adopted hometown in terms of infrastructure.

Benjamin Franklin's house once stood within a large courtyard in the middle of the block between 3rd and 4th and between High (Market) and Chestnut. Dating from the 1760s, the house at Franklin Court was razed in 1812 after Franklin's descendants redeveloped the site. A street was run through the tract and remained there for 150 years. It was removed when the National Park Service conducted comprehensive archaeological excavations at Franklin Court in the 1950s and '60s.

The attraction includes a row of townhouses along Market Street that Franklin owned and which today serve as an eighteenth-century print shop, an archaeological exhibit ("Fragments of Franklin Court"), a working colonial-themed post office, and a postal museum (as befitting the first Postmaster General under the Continental Congress; Franklin began his postal calling as Philadelphia's postmaster in 1737). The buildings bestraddle a covered walkway through which Ben Franklin passed in the years before he died. Under this corridor is a series of vaults installed at Franklin's direction.

In 1959, a worker inside the Franklin property at 316 Market Street discovered a fossilized mastodon tooth buried in the dirt-floor basement. Ben Franklin owned this and other fossils that had been sent to him through the years. According to his correspondence, Franklin was interested in mastodons, comparing this ancient specimen with the teeth of African elephants. Fossils like this made him question the hierarchical structure of life believed to have been decreed by God. The grapefruit-sized molar is in the collection at Franklin Court.

The architectural highlight of Franklin Court is a full-sized skeletal framework of Franklin's home on the spot where it once stood, together with glass-covered portals that peer into the ground and show Ben Franklin's privy pits, wells, and some foundations of the house.

Directly beneath the steel "ghost structure" is a twenty-two-thousand-square-foot underground museum that illustrates Franklin's life and times. The architectural firm of Venturi, Scott, Brown took great care in constructing a museum and auditorium compound under the remnants of Franklin's house without disturbing those archaeological remains. The museum's ceiling is only inches below house footings from the 1760s. Benjamin Franklin would be fascinated by this subterranean engineering feat.

Franklin's grave is a few blocks away, at the southeast corner of 5th and Arch, visible through an opening in the wall enclosing Christ Church Burial Ground. Thousands of tourists come from around the world every year to pay their respects to Ben Franklin. Coins lie about the marble slab tombstone, as per the local custom in which tossing small change will bring the tosser good luck.

Founded in 1824, the Franklin Institute lionizes Franklin's intellectual memory by being one of the oldest centers for scientific education in the United States, as well as the nation's first institute of applied sciences and mechanical arts. The institute joined with the Poor Richard Club of Philadelphia around 1930 to establish both a contemporary science museum and national memorial to Benjamin Franklin. The resulting edifice opened on January 1, 1934, at 20th and the Benjamin Franklin Parkway. (Note that the institute's director in 1937 suggested to Mayor Samuel Wilson that renaming the "Fairmount Parkway" after Benjamin Franklin would be a good idea.)

Beneath the museum's "Train Factory" (formerly "Railroad Hall"), there is a commodious room in which diverse bridge construction technologies hold up the ceiling—and the heft of steam locomotives on display on the first floor above. The assorted post and beam, truss, and arch support structures were intended to show the many modern ways that heavy loads could be supported by bridges. The room is not open to visitors despite plans for it to be a museum attraction when the building was built.

One of the locomotives on display is the famous Baldwin 60,000. Weighing approximately 350 tons (including tender), this experimental 1926 model employed new technologies to ascertain the gain in efficiency of using high pressure steam. As it turned out, old 60,000 was deemed too complicated and too heavy in actual operation. Baldwin sold the locomotive to the Franklin Institute for one dollar in 1933, and it was dragged to the museum atop city streets around the Ben Franklin Parkway.

A 250-foot-long tunnel underneath Race Street once connected the institute to the Franklin Institute Research Laboratories building at the southwest corner of 20th and Race. Put up in the 1960s to conduct government-funded research and testing, the lab closed in the 1980s and has since become a senior community. The institute had stored old displays and equipment in the tunnel under Race Street until the passage was sealed.

The Benjamin Franklin Bridge is the largest symbol of Ben Franklin in Philly. Leaders from Pennsylvania and New Jersey had talked for years about constructing a tunnel or bridge between Philadelphia and Camden. Considering the number of railroad and highway tunnels that had been excavated (or were planned) around New York City in the early 1900s, it was soundly presumed that a tunnel would be constructed. But in 1919, legislation was passed in both states to build a (less expensive) bridge across the Delaware River.

Construction of the then-named Delaware River Bridge began on January 6, 1922, and it opened on July 1, 1926, just in time for the nation's Sesqui-Centennial Exposition being held in Philadelphia. It cost $37 million and has been characterized as the "first distinctly modern suspension bridge built on a grand scale." The structure's 1,750-foot-long center span made it the world's longest single-suspension bridge for a while. Attracting thirty-five thousand vehicles a day to cross the Delaware at twenty-five cents a crossing, the Delaware River Bridge was an instant success.

St. George's Church, the oldest Methodist church in America (founded in the 1760s), stood directly in the path of the bridge and faced demolition. After a countrywide protest in which St. George's became famed as "the church that moved the bridge," plans were modified to save the structure. Vehicular traffic and PATCO trains now pass just fourteen feet south of the venerable church's walls. Plus, the lowering of 4th Street to pass under the bridge compelled the addition of stairs up to the main entrance.

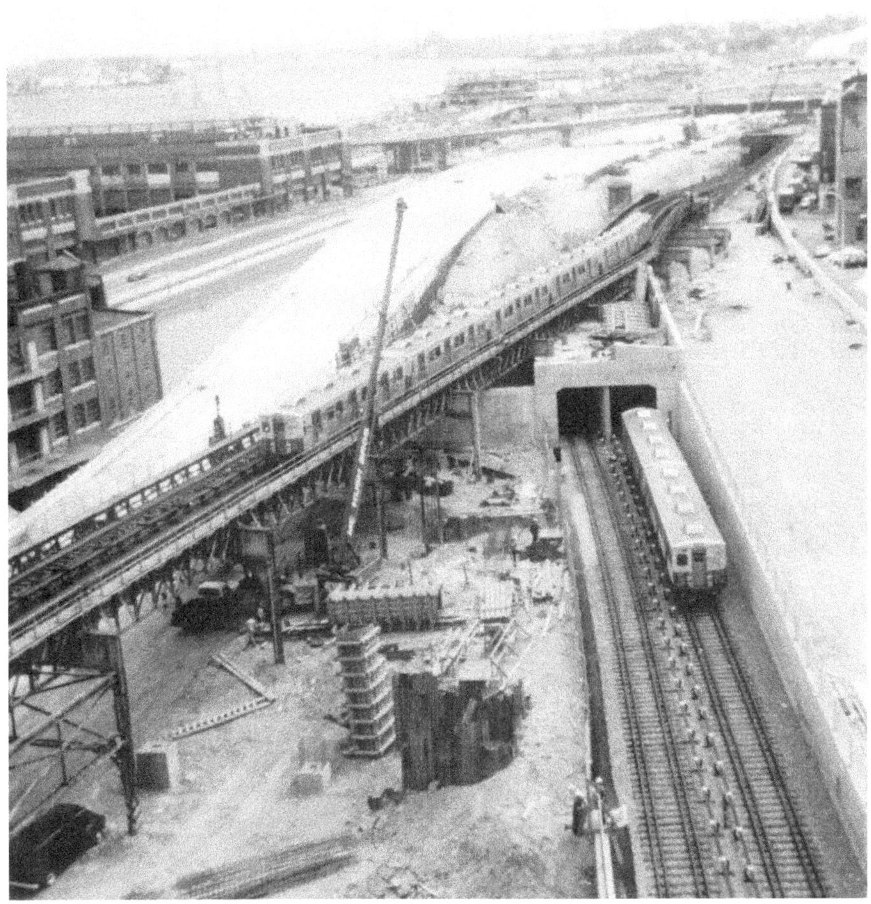

Taken during the heavy-handed threading of Interstate 95 through Penn's Landing in the mid-1970s, this dynamic photograph shows two eastern transition portals for the Market Street Subway: the original (demolished) one located along between Front Street and Water Street in the upper right and the new one (still in use) that was built to lay within the I-95 median. The long Market-Frankford El train is descending into the subway, soon to make a hard right turn to proceed west under Market Street. The shorter train is presumably a test train. The photo was apparently taken from the southern walkway of the Benjamin Franklin Bridge. *Joel Spivak's collection.*

Likewise, St. Augustine's Catholic Church across 4th Street was affected by the street's depression during the 1920s. A scar in the brickwork can still clearly be seen where the church's doorway was lowered to the new street level. St. Augustine's was incorporated in 1804 as the first permanent establishment of the Augustinian Order on American soil. On May 8, 1844, after three days of anti-Catholic rioting, a mob burned down the place of worship. Architect Napoleon LeBrun designed the present church, completed in 1847.

Designed by Paul Crét, the bridge's anchorages support the span and are huge riverfront monoliths on either side of the Delaware. The Philadelphia Anchorage extends between Columbus Boulevard (Delaware Avenue) and Front Street, and its foundations go down sixty-three feet to bedrock. The bridge's final engineering report states that "hewn oak timbers 24 inches square and parts of a barge or boat framed with wooden pins were removed" during the work. This indicates that the Philadelphia Anchorage was built over an area that was once within the Delaware channel and that boats that had sunk into the river at riverside wharves were afterward covered by the city's development as soil and rock was amassed atop the river to make new land. ("Made-earth" is the proper term for such man-made land.)

Images of the Philadelphia Anchorage site just before construction show the basements of demolished commercial buildings that were located between Delaware Avenue and Front Street. These 1920s photographs plainly reveal brick-arched vaults that extend westward beneath Front Street. Used for storage, the cavities were undoubtedly the remnants of caves that settlers used in the 1690s. The Quaker caves were dug into the riverbank precisely where the eastern sidewalk of Front Street came to be. All evidence of these openings was eliminated with the construction of Interstate 95 in the 1970s.

As for the bridge's 382-foot-tall towers, laborers ("sand hogs") had to work 69 feet below the river surface in Philadelphia and 82 feet below the surface in Camden to reach bedrock. They toiled in chambers at the base of caissons to remove mud, sand, and rock from inside the chamber, causing the caisson to slowly sink into the riverbed. The sand hogs had to spend time in decompression chambers prior to leaving the caissons or they would suffer caisson disease ("the bends").

East of 2nd, Race Street was shifted roughly thirty feet north during Interstate 95's construction. The Delaware River Waterfront Corporation enhanced the highway underpass in 2011 with wider sidewalks and multicolored lights. The "Race Street Connector" project now entices pedestrians to use this once unappealing vehicular pathway as a means of getting to the Delaware River from Center City. Access to the Race Street Pier was an important aspect of this project. The once abandoned municipal pier was turned into a verdant riverside park in 2011.

Another "connector" was executed in 2016 for the dingy I-95 underpass at Spring Garden Street. The "Spring Garden Connector" added bright lights and flower-shaped metal scrims inspired by the street's name. Other connector projects for I-95 overpasses north of Center City are likewise in the works.

A twenty-foot-wide tunnel carries 5th Street traffic below the entrance to the Ben Franklin Bridge from just south of Race Street (in front of the U.S. Mint) to Callowhill Street. The Fifth Street Tunnel is one of two former trolley tunnels in downtown Philly that were built around the same time and share similarities, not the least of which is that they both own their existence to something named "Benjamin Franklin."

The Fifth Street Tunnel is the second tunnel built under the bridge's eastern entrance. Plans for the first passage came about when it was realized that trolleys on 5th Street would have difficulty traversing crosswise through the Philadelphia approach to the Delaware River (Ben Franklin) Bridge. After the bridge's completion in 1926, northbound streetcars and vehicular traffic on 5th Street crossed the plaza at grade (as did southbound traffic on 6th Street), causing congestion with east–west bridge traffic. Newspapers of the day continually reported on this and other bridge-related traffic woes.

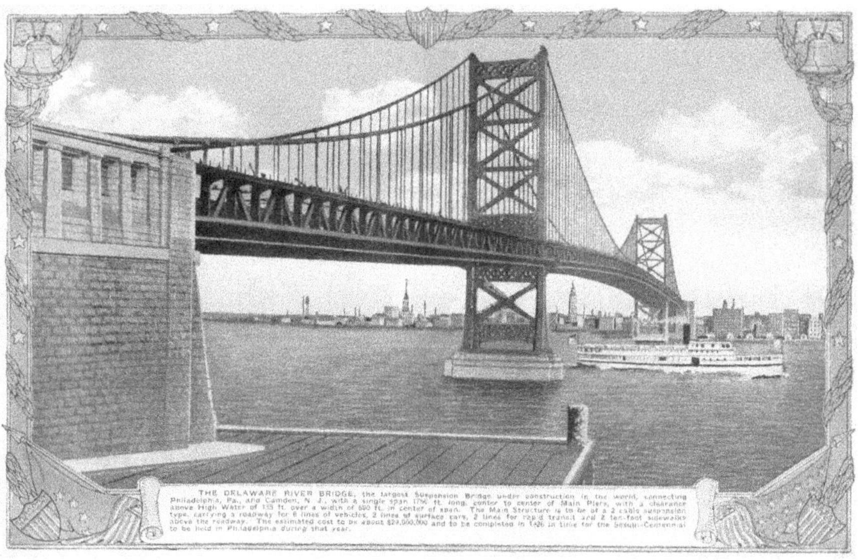

This large undated postcard of the Delaware River Bridge was produced for the Sesqui-Centennial International Exposition of 1926. Fifty years later, the span's name was changed to "Benjamin Franklin Bridge" to mark the 250th anniversary of Franklin's birth and to distinguish it from the newly constructed Walt Whitman Bridge. The Delaware River Port Authority manages this and other spans over the Delaware, as well as the PATCO Hi-Speedline, which uses the bridge to access Philadelphia. *Harry Kyriakodis's collection.*

After four years of this intolerable situation, the Delaware River Bridge Commission finally constructed an underpass to convey local trolley and vehicular traffic on 5th Street, between Race and Vine Streets, under the bridge approach. The tunnel opened in May 1930. Unfortunately, it was not deep enough to enable tracks of the future high-speed rail line—today's PATCO Hi-Speedline—to pass overhead.

When the Philadelphia-Camden Bridge Line crossed over the bridge in the mid-1930s, the Fifth Street Tunnel had to be substituted with a deeper and longer excavation some thirty feet east of the original tunnel. The second underpass opened on May 28, 1935, and is still in use. All this explains its peculiar location—not on the line of 5th Street. Its placement allowed it to be built fourteen feet deeper than the original tunnel so as to permit the Bridge Line to pass above. There is no surface vestige of the original Fifth Street Tunnel, but much of it still exists parallel to the current passage, sealed off.

Trolleys shared the 1,200-foot Fifth Street Tunnel with vehicular traffic until SEPTA stopped running trolleys on 5th Street in 1980. Buses took over until SEPTA discontinued the route entirely five years later. As of late, the one-way underpass has been improved with better lighting and a buffered bicycle lane. Motorists and bike riders get a glimpse of the sky through a section of open roof approaching the northern portal at Callowhill Street, as do pedestrians who at times walk along the bicycle lane. In 2018, murals were painted inside the tunnel, on the walls, by the Philadelphia's Mural Arts Program.

The bridge's Philadelphia Plaza, nowadays called Monument Plaza, was envisioned as a major transit interchange for the Philadelphia region. A trolley terminal was installed there for streetcar lines that were expected to cross the bridge on their own dedicated lanes. Trolleys from New Jersey were to have descended into the lower level of Philadelphia Plaza before crossing back over the bridge. The station never opened, since streetcar service was not implemented on the bridge due to track gauge issues between Philadelphia and Camden, among other problems. The plaza's western zone, facing Franklin Square, contains shuttered openings that would have led into the station at trolley level. Trolley lanes on the bridge were converted into traffic lanes for cars and trucks by 1950.

Monument Plaza these days is encircled by rivers of traffic and is virtually inaccessible to pedestrians, but it does prominently exhibit the sixty-ton sculpture *Bolt of Lightning: A Memorial to Benjamin Franklin* by artist Isamu Noguchi. The Pennsylvania Horticultural Society has recently developed plans to redesign the plaza into a more user-friendly space.

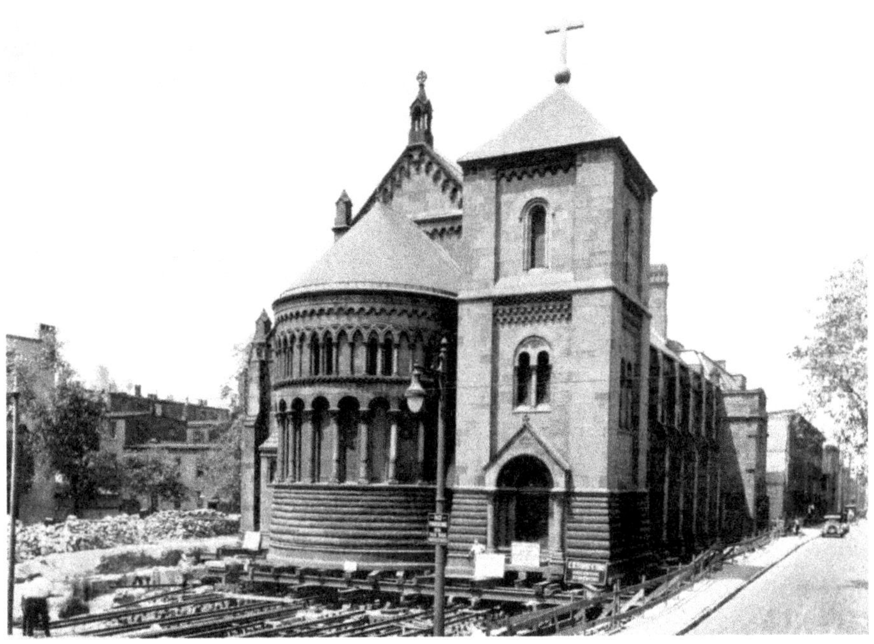

A church about a block away from the Franklin Institute has some interesting ground-based history. St. Clement's Episcopal at 20th and Cherry was erected in 1859 but was repositioned forty feet to the west seventy years later for the widening of 20th Street due to construction of the Benjamin Franklin Parkway. On July 19, 1929, the 5,500-ton building was lifted onto steel beams, shifted on tracks, and placed on a new foundation. No evidence of this move is discernable today. *From* A Memorial on the Moving of St. Clement's Church *(1929).*

A short underpass that allows pedestrians to cross from one side of the Ben Franklin Bridge to the other is a few paces from the southern portal of the Fifth Street Tunnel. There is not much to say about this passageway, other than it has been somewhat chancy in terms of criminal activity. But conditions have improved after the Philadelphia Mural Arts Program painted murals on the walls in 2018. Various underpasses cross below the bridge approach in Camden too.

In the 1990s, surface space under the bridge in Philadelphia was being prepared for use as a parking lot to help alleviate parking congestion in Old City. Security concerns after the 2001 terrorist attacks put an end to that.

A passageway on the west side of Center City is like the Fifth Street Tunnel in both construction, semblance, and onetime use. Spring Garden Street Tunnel brings Spring Garden Street's westbound traffic to the Spring

Garden Street Bridge over the Schuylkill River into West Philadelphia. Note that this 950-foot excavation should not be mistaken with Fairmount Park Tunnel or the so-called Art Museum Station discussed in previous chapters and both a stone's throw away.

The Spring Garden Tunnel opened on December 20, 1925, for trolley use exclusively after the Benjamin Franklin Parkway and the Philadelphia Museum of Art were constructed. Philadelphia Rapid Transit had concluded that streetcars heading both east and west on Spring Garden Street could not safely traverse the intensive traffic amid Fairmount Plaza (the precursor to Eakins Oval). Moreover, museum administrators did not want trolley traffic, wires, and poles in front of the new "Parthenon on the Parkway" and doubtlessly used their influence to get the tunnel built.

As far back as 1938, Keystone Automobile Club advised changing the two-track tunnel to motor vehicle use, based on complaints about the number of cars and trucks passing in front of the museum. In 1946, two trolleys collided inside the tunnel, injuring more than thirty people. Seven years later, a trolley derailed inside the tunnel, snarling traffic for miles on Spring Garden Street. The tunnel's low ceiling prevented the Philadelphia Transportation Company from using a crane to right the streetcar, causing more delays.

Streetcars stopped using the Spring Garden Tunnel on July 4, 1956, when National City Lines unexpectedly converted the one-way route to bus operation. Three years later, motor vehicles traveling westbound began using the passageway. The narrow right (northern) lane was put into service alongside the equally narrow left (southern) lane, separated by steel beams supporting the ceiling.

The tunnel's fourteen-foot-high roof is five feet below the surface of the plaza in front of the Philadelphia Art Museum's "Rocky Steps." A sealed doorway halfway through the passage leads to a mechanical room beneath the easternmost fountain in Eakins Oval, and a separate service tunnel for cabling and other official access runs from Eakins Oval to the plaza area.

The Spring Garden Tunnel was closed for repairs in 2000 after a tall truck damaged the overhead lights. The northern lane was barricaded at that time. Following September 11, 2001, the entire passage was off-limits for security reasons, as it runs near the basement of the Philadelphia Museum of Art. Reopened since then, the tunnel saw construction when the museum created new space for a loading dock near the western portal. Also, its eastern portal was realigned in 2016 to enhance safety at the intersection with Pennsylvania Avenue.

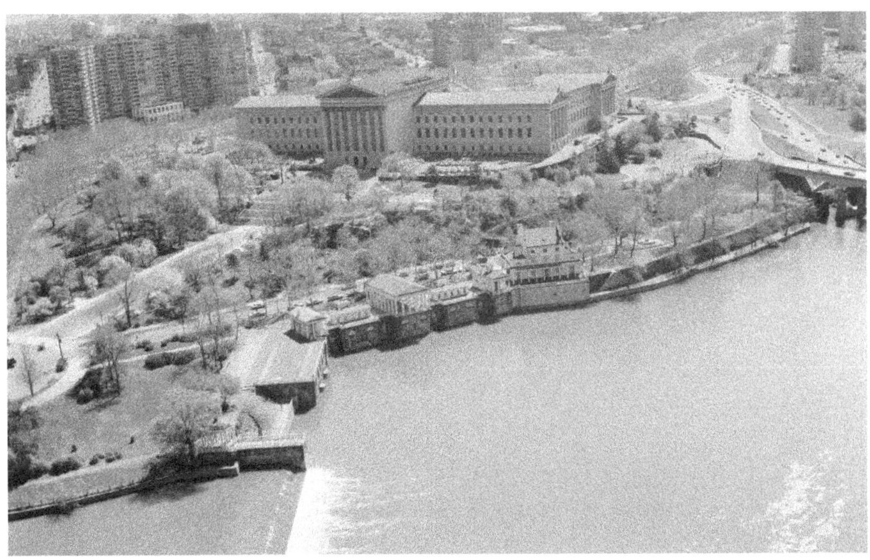

The buildings of the Fairmount Water Works appear below the Philadelphia Museum of Art in this 1978 photograph. The museum was built atop the hill (once called "Faire Mount") on the site of the reservoirs of the Fairmount Water Works. This scene belies the immense amount of railroad infrastructure around the "Parthenon on the Parkway." Fairmount Dam is also visible. *Library of Congress.*

Even with these improvements, Spring Garden Street Tunnel is possibly the scariest public underground space in Philadelphia. Graffiti covers its interior walls, trash is strewn about the unused northern lane, and cars typically scream along on the southern lane. In spite of these drawbacks and a placard warning "Passenger Cars Only," intrepid bicyclists often utilize the tunnel as a shortcut toward West Philadelphia. Using it this way is not recommended, in view of the southern lane's uneven sewer grates and unrelenting traffic. Conversely, there has been chatter of reopening the northern lane for use as a bike path into West Philadelphia.

Benjamin Franklin Parkway becomes Kelly (formerly East River) Drive at the Philadelphia Museum of Art. About a mile north is Kelly Drive Tunnel, a four-lane vehicular passageway that penetrates an outcropping of solid stone along the Schuylkill River's east bank. The striking formation, dubbed Promontory Rock, is a mound of Wissahickon schist that engineers blasted through to unite two distinct portions of East River Drive. Philadelphians all over the city in 1871 heard nocturnal explosions during the months it took to burrow 140 feet through the rock. In present times, thousands of speeding cars and trucks squeeze through Kelly Drive Tunnel every day.

Another tight squeeze is the Schuylkill Expressway (I-76) as it passes through the eastern edge of West Philadelphia between Arch and Walnut Streets. The artery dips below street level and hugs the west bank of the Schuylkill River in what is, in effect, a tunnel. The half-mile stretch of freeway has only two lanes in each direction since it threads between the river and railroad tracks under 30th Street Station. Room was so tight when I-76 was constructed in the 1950s that this section required moving the Schuylkill's edge eight feet eastward by driving pilings into the riverbed. As discussed in Chapter 3, Fairmount Dam Canal was also eliminated during this work.

This length of I-76 is not a true tunnel since the passage's eastern wall is open to the Schuylkill River. Such a vista *should* afford pleasing views of Center City, but the presence of all too many steel beams supporting Schuylkill Avenue overhead makes I-76 perilous at this point. Then again, looking westward while passing through provides tantalizing glimpses of the

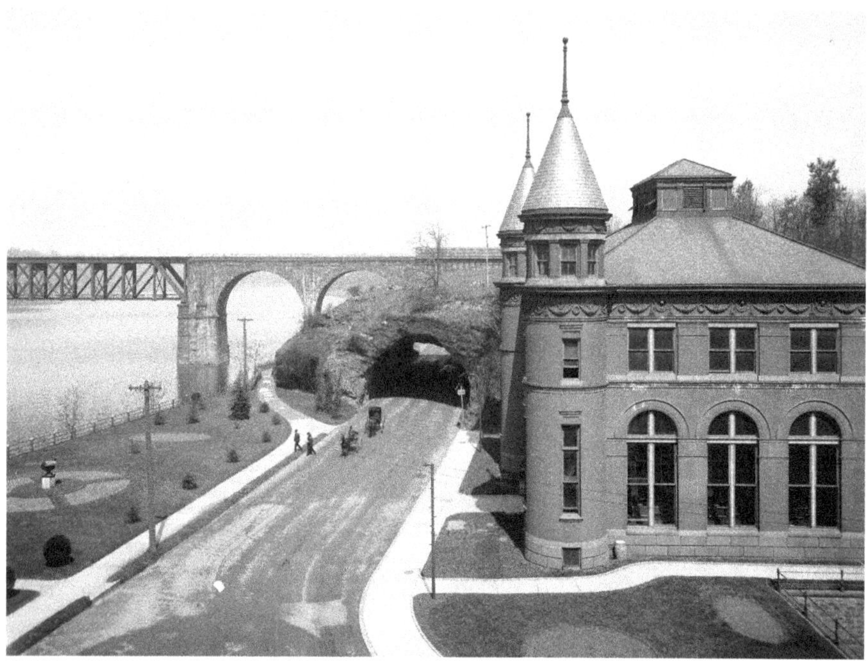

The John B. Kelly Drive Tunnel (aka Promontory Rock Tunnel) in East Fairmount Park, 1905. The bridge in the background was built by the Pennsylvania Railroad to carry tracks the over the Schuylkill River and is still used today by Amtrak, although it was rebuilt in 1910 as an entirely stone structure. The building on the right is part of the Spring Garden and Northern Liberties Water Works, no longer standing. A few ruins remain at Glendinning Rock Garden. *Detroit Publishing Company; Library of Congress.*

convoluted subterraneous rail activity under 30th Street Station and the ex–Main Post Office.

The perception of there being subsurface passageways under Old City and Society Hill related to the slave trade or liquor smuggling has long absorbed local historians. While corroboration of this is lacking, there are inklings that a few tunnels once in the oldest sectors of town were used to secretly usher fugitive slaves to freedom via the Underground Railroad.

After its use as a pirate hideaway (Chapter 1), the tunnel under what became Starr Garden Playground at 6th and Lombard connected a tenement house on the site to a vault in the graveyard of the long-gone Colored Presbyterian Church on nearby Rodman (formerly St. Mary) Street. The house was a known station on the Underground Railroad, and the tunnel ostensibly helped escaped slaves find refuge. Following the Civil War, the passage was employed by neighborhood bandits and then sealed before the playground's appearance.

Other African churches in the Society Hill district apparently had interconnecting tunnels relating to the Underground Railroad. Since these houses of worship usually had adjoining churchyards, fleeing slaves were in all likelihood transported inside coffins.

There is some oral history about a tunnel for runaway slaves between Mother Bethel Church and Wesley African Methodist Episcopal Zion Church. Founded in 1787, Mother Bethel was the world's first African Methodist Episcopal Church and a principal stop on the Underground Railroad. It stands on the oldest parcel of land continuously owned by African Americans in the nation. Meanwhile, Wesley Church was housed at 521–27 Lombard, ninety feet from Mother Bethel, in the mid-1800s. A sealed door and archway in Mother Bethel's basement crypt is intriguing, but there is no conclusive evidence.

The attractive colonial house at 415 Pine might be connected to this reputed tunnel network. Completed in 1795 by James and Mary Moyes, ardent Quaker foes of African enslavement, the residence did conceal slaves fleeing north. Fugitives were sheltered in the Moyeses' attic, and they could access the roof and run across the rooftops of adjoining homes to elude capture. Plus, a tunnel in the basement connected to Old Pine Street Church across the street. Organized as the Third Presbyterian Church in 1768, Old Pine was a center of abolitionist activity in the nineteenth century and is among the oldest continuously used Presbyterian churches in America.

Not far away, at 9th and Lombard, was the home of Robert Purvis Sr. (1810–1898), a mixed-race abolitionist born in South Carolina. Slave rescue meetings were convened at Purvis's house, and fugitives were sometimes sheltered in a basement hideout accessible via trapdoor. Purvis estimated that he helped one slave achieve liberty every day from 1831 to 1861.

While Purvis is remembered as the "president" of the Underground Railroad, William Still (1821–1902) was an African American widely considered to be the "father" of the network of covert routes and safe houses. A clerk for the Pennsylvania Anti-Slavery Society, Still kept detailed records—preserved in his book *The Underground Railroad* (1872)—of every escaped slave passing through the Quaker City. A dramatic episode in the chronicle is Still's reunion with his brother, who had been sold into slavery forty years earlier. Still's small home at nearby 625 South Delhi Street, recently rediscovered, was perhaps the most important Underground Railroad way station in the region from 1850 to 1855. Abolitionist and former slave Harriet Tubman is said to have arrived in Philadelphia there.

Many other Philadelphia dwellings outside the downtown area were safe houses for Underground Railroad. Belmont Mansion in Fairmount Park comes to mind, as does the Johnson House in the city's Germantown section. All of these houses and churches proudly attest to the City of Brotherly Love's predominant role in the Underground Railroad, helping countless slaves escape to freedom.

Newspaper articles in 1909 asserted that several east–west underground passages had been sporadically revealed in Old City/Society Hill by that time. The tunnels reportedly led from the Delaware River and stopped hundreds of feet inland. They may have been related to the Underground Railroad, or they may have provided early tavern owners an easy and cool (temperature-wise) way of moving food and alcohol from ships to their barrooms. And it is conceivable that these dead-end passageways were subsequently used to furtively store and transport kegs of bootleg liquor during Prohibition, although, again, evidence for this is scant.

The Man Full of Trouble Tavern at 2nd and Spruce, near Dock Street, is an old Philadelphia pub containing the remains of a tunnel that once ran from the basement kitchen to the edge of Dock Creek. The passage certainly brought food and drink into the saloon, but it was also probably used to smuggle stolen goods. Opened in 1759 (along with the abutting house), Man Full of Trouble is the only surviving colonial tavern in the city. The low-ceilinged building was on the verge of collapse before a private organization restored it as a museum in 1965. It's been closed to the public since 1996.

Bistro Romano at 120 Lombard Street showcases its vaulted wine cellar as part of a network of tunnels that might be related to the Underground

Railroad. Built in the early 1700s, the building was at one time a cider and vinegar factory and then was turned into a seed warehouse before being transformed into a restaurant. The clandestine chamber, resembling more a coal vault, is available for romantic dining.

An existing tunnel under Sansom Street connects the Curtis Publishing Center with the Public Ledger Building across the street. Occupying the block bounded by 6th, 7th, Walnut, and Sansom, the Curtis Center was built in 1910 for publisher Cyrus H.K. Curtis, who in 1937 erected the Public Ledger Building between Sansom and Chestnut Streets to print the *Public Ledger*. The tunnel likely connected the two office-plants so that newspapers could be swiftly moved to delivery trucks at the Curtis Center. Both of these buildings across from Independence Square are now residential.

There is some kind of underground passage leading from the basements of select jewelry shops along the 700 block of Sansom Street (Jewelers Row). Going out past the sidewalk to under the street itself, the excavation appears to be connected basement vaults possibly used by turn-of-the-century jewelers to protect their wares.

The background of Jewelers Row might shed some light here. Structures on the south side of Sansom Street were designed and built by architect Thomas Carstairs from 1799 to 1820 as part of a housing development created by merchant/investor William Sansom, one of the nation's earliest developers. Then called Carstairs Row, this block of twenty-two identical dwellings was one of the first speculative residential developments in America. The structures were America's first row of houses erected simultaneously from a single design—the primordial Philly rowhome development. Perhaps the tunnel interconnected the cellars of individual homes from the outset of construction.

The street was primarily occupied by printing and publishing companies by the 1870s. At the turn of the twentieth century, the block had started its evolution into what it is today: Jewelers Row, America's oldest diamond district. Only 700, 730, and 732 Sansom endure as recognizable fragments of Carstairs Row.

The Pennsylvania Bible Society—the first and oldest Bible association in the United States, founded in 1808—is headquartered a half block away in a comely building at the northwest corner of 7th and Walnut. The society acquired the property from William Sansom's daughter, Hannah, in 1853. A sealed basement opening is said to lead under 7th Street, seemingly connecting to the passageway supposedly under Jewelers Row, although there is no sign of this opening today.

Chapter 16

John Wanamaker's Pneumatic Philadelphia

Following Benjamin Franklin's lead, Philadelphia merchant John Wanamaker (1838–1922) was appointed U.S. Postmaster General in 1889 by President Benjamin Harrison. Wanamaker launched several advancements in the U.S. Post Office system, such as commemorative stamps and Rural Free Delivery. But the most engaging of his initiatives was pneumatic mail, an unconventional delivery system that carried letters and small packages under city streets via pneumatic tubes.

The first pneumatic dispatch system arose in England in 1853, linking the London Stock Exchange to the city's main telegraph station. Twelve years later, the tube-equipped Rohrpost was built in Berlin, and Paris created a pneumatic system in 1866 that survived until 1984.

John Wanamaker advocated for a pneumatic mail delivery system based on his experience at Wanamaker's Grand Depot at 13th and Market. His department store was the world's first to install pneumatic tubes as message and cash transporters. The Grand Depot had a network of more than 250 pneumatic stations connected by twenty miles of tubes by 1880. This was the same store that had seen the installation of arc lamps and telephones a few years before.

Wanamaker proposed a citywide pneumatic tube system in several reports to Congress, stating that he "should like to see [pneumatic mail systems] in cities like Philadelphia, St. Louis and others of importance…as a necessary step in the march of postal improvement." He then arranged for a Congressional grant of $10,000 for experiments in the Quaker City.

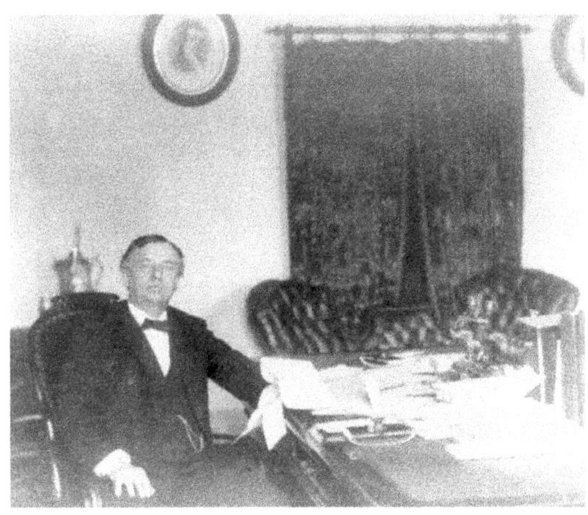

An 1890 photograph of Postmaster John Wanamaker, taken at his desk in Washington, D.C., by Frances Johnston, an early American female photojournalist. Wanamaker was so beloved and respected in Philadelphia that schoolchildren donated $50,000 in pennies to help erect a statue of him on the east side of City Hall, across from his famous department store and virtually on top of the tunnel for the Green lines. The bronze commemorates him with a single word: "Citizen." *Library of Congress.*

The agreement between Pneumatic Transit Company and the U.S. Post Office Department was that the Post Office could utilize the Philadelphia line for one year free of charge and then could rent, purchase, or reject it. The company installed two tubes—one in each direction—between the city's Central Post Office, then at 9th and Chestnut, and East Chestnut Street Station, a postal branch a half mile away at 323 Chestnut. Appropriately enough, *the* branch post office was located practically within the footprint of Postmaster Franklin's former property at Franklin Court.

The work was done in late 1892. Pneumatic Transit buried cast-iron pipes that were 6.5 inches in diameter within trenches between two to six feet below Chestnut Street, alongside much other city infrastructure. The company had to light bonfires atop city streets to thaw the ground in order to remove paving stones and to facilitate trench excavation.

Wanamaker himself inaugurated the system at 4:18 p.m. on March 1, 1893, as one of his last duties as Postmaster General. At East Chestnut Street Station, he placed a Bible wrapped in an American flag into a canister that went flying (underground) to the Central Post Office with a loud *whish*. The ardently religious Wanamaker sent a message with the package reading, "First use of the pneumatic postal tube in the United States is to send through it a copy of the Holy Scriptures, the greatest message ever given to the world. Covering the Bible is an American flag, the emblem of freedom of 65,000,000 happy people."

After this successful trial, postal officials tested the system with miscellaneous items, including eggs, oranges, shoes, and even a lit candle. All this was regarded as an exhibition of the possibilities of the modern age, just before the twentieth century.

A continuous stream (or pressure) of air—not vacuum—from a steam-powered compressor in the Central Post Office's basement generated six pounds per square inch and pushed specially designed cylindrical mail canisters ("carriers") between the two stations along Chestnut Street. Each eighteen-inch-long steel canister could hold several hundred letters; about five hundred carriers were dispatched daily from each station. Mail moved between them in about a minute—about thirty-five miles per hour. This compared favorably to the fifteen minutes the trip took by horse and wagon or trolley along crowded Chestnut Street.

Philadelphia's pneumatic mail system was extended from the Central Post Office to Broad Street Station and Reading Terminal in 1898. In that era, about 65 percent of all mail passing in and out of Philly—some 550,000 letters each day—came and went by way of trains that stopped at Broad Street Station. All this mail was handled through the Broad Street Station tube, except for mail arriving and departing the city between 12:30 a.m. and 2:00 a.m. when the tube was shut down for maintenance.

Further expansion around Center City followed, as well as a tube all the way to the Pennsylvania Railroad's North Philadelphia Station. The city eventually had 19.9 miles of underground tubes operated by Pneumatic Transit Company. The system's capacity could move 240,000 letters an hour; more than 35 million letters were carried in the first four years. Tubes with a 6.5-inch-diameter bore were used until 1898 when 8-inch tubes became common.

At a later demonstration of the enlarged system, invited guests were offered hot refreshments sent through the tube from a point miles away. The system also demonstrated that living animals could be whisked at high speed for miles underground. Cats, puppies, monkeys, rabbits, guinea pigs, roosters, and an aquarium of goldfish braved the subsurface journey with no harm.

The idea of conveying people in this manner was then posited. Of course, the eight-inch tube network was too confining, and there was fear of suffocation if the carrier became stuck. Nevertheless, it was felt that such human transport would become viable, even commonplace, after twelve-inch tubes were outfitted as the next manifestation of the tube system. It was seriously suggested that a small boy could be used for an experiment of this kind when the time came. But the larger pneumatic system was never realized; a Congressional commission in 1900 recommended that the standard-size pipe would remain eight inches in diameter.

In the late 1890s, it was suggested that Philadelphia should be grid-ironed with subterranean pneumatic tubes so that mail, telegrams, and packages

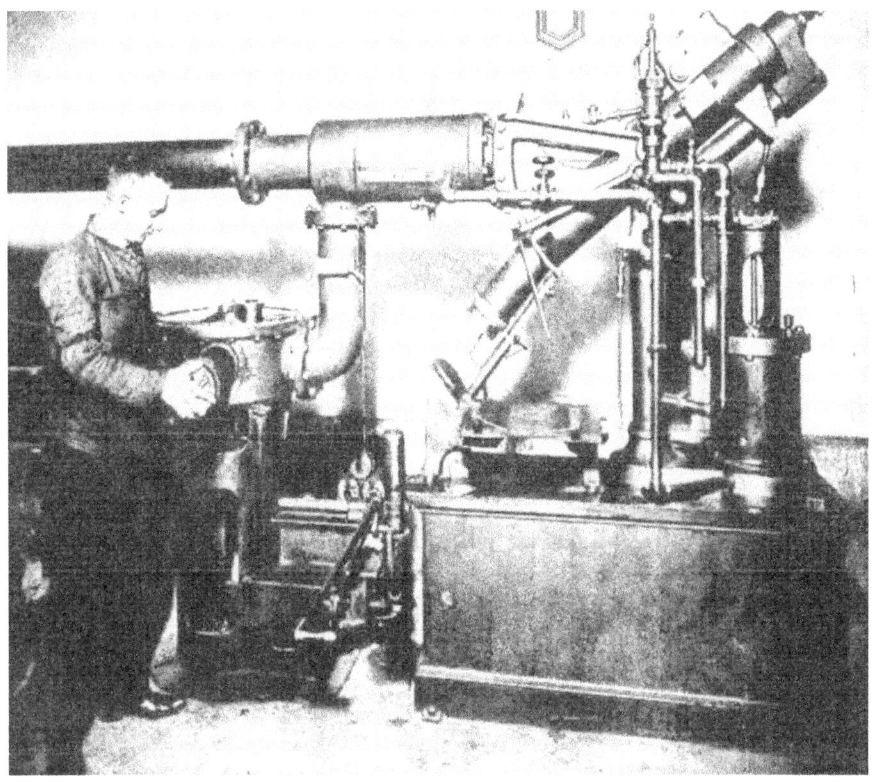

This is a rare photograph of the receiving and sending apparatus used at the East Chestnut Street post office during the first few years of pneumatic tube mail service in Philadelphia. An operator is inserting a pneumatic carrier, perhaps stuffed with mail, into the pneumatic sending device. The photo's right side shows the carrier receiving mechanism. *From* The Pneumatic Despatch Tube System of the Batcheller Pneumatic Company *(1897), by B.C. Batcheller.*

could be dispatched instantly to any section of the city in any direction from anyplace. There was to be a main air pumping station somewhere near the newly opened City Hall, and tubes were to radiate from the building in all points of the compass. The aim was to give Philadelphia the best pneumatic delivery system in the world.

While Philadelphia's pneumatic mail system was the first of its kind in the country, the system enjoyed its greatest success in New York City. That city, Boston, Chicago, and St. Louis adopted pneumatic delivery systems by 1898. Within a few years, it was proposed that pneumatic tubes could be employed to deliver mail *between* cities. Another U.S. Postmaster General predicted that all American households would be interconnected by means of pneumatic tubes one day. Even notions of a pneumatic delivery system between North America and Europe were canvassed.

But pneumatic tube systems lost their appeal when they became too expensive to maintain. Moreover, the systems could not keep pace with the ever-changing movement of municipal business centers. The tubes were also inefficient: about 90 percent of the power generated for the air pressure was wasted in pushing the air through the tubes. Motorized delivery trucks also came into use and were much more efficient for transporting mail in urban centers.

The U.S. Post Office suspended pneumatic service during World War I to save money for the war effort. Afterward, Postmaster Albert Burleson was against reinstating the tubes and saw to it that funding for them was struck from the 1918 Post Office Appropriation Bill. Furthermore, a

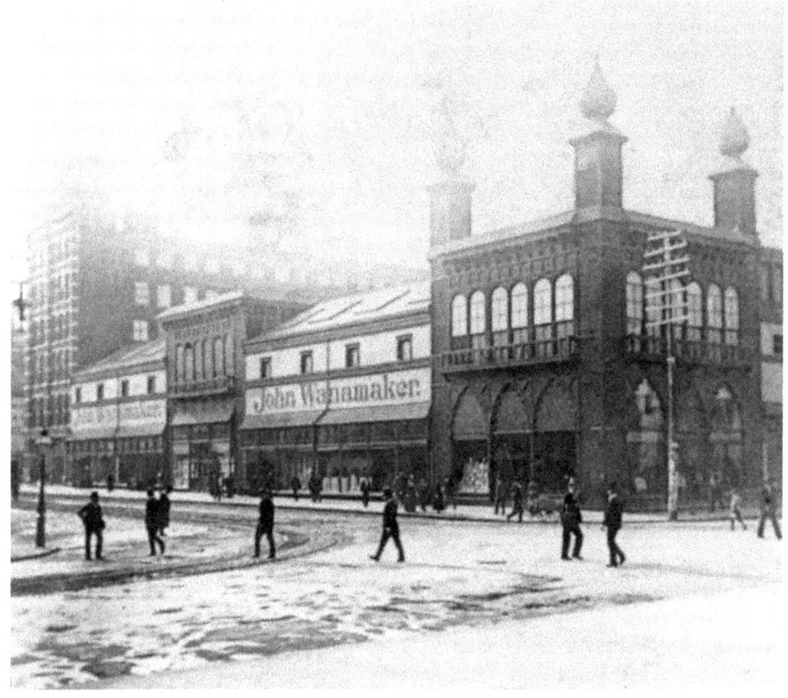

In 1875, John Wanamaker bought the Pennsylvania Railroad's old freight station at the southeast corner of 13th and Market. There, he opened Wanamaker's Grand Depot on March 12, 1877, and so gave birth to the phrase "department store." The Grand Depot was a place that offered "Everything from Everywhere for Everybody." Wanamaker also pioneered electrical and telephone service at this store, as well as pneumatic tubes as carriers for cash and messages. His later store, now a Macy's, still occupies the same spot. *Library of Congress.*

Congressional committee had ascertained that the use of the pneumatic tubes cost $17,000 per mile every year, with rental charges for the tubes an "exorbitant, unjustified and an extravagant waste of public funds." Without financing, pneumatic mail delivery ceased in Philadelphia and elsewhere on June 30, 1918.

Limited operation resumed in New York City and Boston in the 1920s due to increased mail volume, but service was suspended nationally on December 12, 1953. Construction crews in New York occasionally come across old pipes marked "U.S. Post Office Department," but there has not been a sighting of such pipes in Philly in decades.

Pressurized air delivery is still seen as fast, reliable and cheap, and the concept still comes up on television and in real life. Banks use small-scale versions of pneumatic carrier systems for their drive-through windows. Other pneumatic delivery systems are in use or are being installed in factories, railyards, hospitals, libraries, and other places around the world. Business magnate and inventor Elon Musk has proposed a mode of passenger and freight transportation that would propel pressurized pods inside near-vacuum tubes, magnetically levitated and exceeding airliner speed. This underground "Hyperloop" system might one day connect New York and Washington through Philadelphia. Amazon is also looking into building a subterranean network of vacuum tubes and conveyor belts for package delivery.

Upon John Wanamaker's death in 1922, his body was interred within the Wanamaker Memorial Bell Tower in the graveyard of the Church of St. James the Less, a National Historic Landmark that is a short distance from Laurel Hill Cemetery. The merchant-king had a profound influence on the Quaker City, and his genius truly came into play in the case of underground delivery of mail. Wanamaker would be pleased that the topic of pneumatic delivery tubes is still the subject of discussion and implementation a century after his demise.

Chapter 17

The Dock Creek Caper and Willie Sutton's Escape

Many people assume that Manhattan's Wall Street has always been the center of the American financial system. But the first leading U.S. monetary quarter was in Philadelphia, centered on lower Chestnut Street. The Quaker City's financial district ruled the nation's fiscal system until the 1830s.

It was in this vicinity that an underground robbery attempt occurred at the Philadelphia Bank (or Bank of Philadelphia). The bank building was designed by Benjamin Latrobe (of Water Works fame) and was erected in 1807–08 at the southwest corner of 4th and Chestnut. The handsome brick and marble edifice, built atop stout arches flanking the culverted Dock Creek, was the first American commercial structure in the Gothic style.

On April 16, 1821, two men tried to rob the Philadelphia Bank by rowing a boat through the Dock Creek Sewer from the Delaware River and digging under the bank's foundations to get into the money vaults. Several bank clerks heard the subterranean excavation and gave chase as the thieves came into the basement. The men retreated through the opening they had dug without securing any cash, having missed the vaults by a few yards.

Two clerks dashed outside to a nearby sewer inlet, surmising that the robbers would come out there. One heard voices and saw the thieves place their hands on the iron sewer grate. He aimed a blow with his truncheon at the men's hands, causing the thieves to fall back. The other clerk, who had gone for a weapon, later saw a man covered in filth walking as if to avoid detection at 4th and Market. He gave chase and apprehended the man, taking him to the bank, where it was determined that he was one of the robbers. This was the only person arrested for the attempted crime.

Dock Street and 4th Street in front of the bank were dug up the next day and examined. It was speculated that the thieves had pursued their plot for two or three weeks, excavating in the daytime when street noise prevented them from being heard.

The building under which this robbery attempt took place was demolished in 1836 when the Philadelphia Bank built a replacement structure on the same spot. The site is now green space beside the Second Bank of the United States.

The captured Philadelphia Bank thief may have been imprisoned at the Walnut Street Prison/Jail (Goal), not far from the bank. Standing at 6th and Walnut from 1775 to 1835, the jail served as a brutal military prison for both sides during the Revolutionary War and then underwent change in 1790 when the Pennsylvania Assembly passed a succession of prison reform bills. Novel practices of confinement included separation of juveniles from adults and the creation of distinct prisons for debtors and felons. Walnut Street Jail's system of prison discipline made Pennsylvania a leader in modern penology.

The Philadelphia Athenæum, a not-for-profit library and museum founded in 1814, is located on part of the jail site. In 1973, the Athenæum's plans to extend its basement vaults beneath the garden behind its building led to an archaeological excavation. The dig uncovered more than seven thousand artifacts that presented evidence of the prison's inmates and the corrective efforts directed toward them. The Walnut Street Prison was closed by 1835; the Athenæum has occupied the site since 1845.

Overcrowding at the jail led Pennsylvania officials to erect Eastern State Penitentiary in Philadelphia County. Local prison reform activists instituted a new system of prisoner isolation at Eastern State—as opposed to the prevalent method of corporal punishment. Proponents of the Quaker-inspired "Pennsylvania System" believed that criminals, left in absolute silence to think about their criminal behavior, would become sincerely penitent. One of the most unique philosophies of penal treatment, the system coined a new word: penitentiary.

Eastern State was built along the north side of Coats Street (later Fairmount Avenue) in the Spring Garden District of Philadelphia County. This area was far outside the developed territory of the city of Philadelphia, a region not even part of town until 1854. The prison was referred to as "Cherry Hill" because the site had once been a cherry orchard.

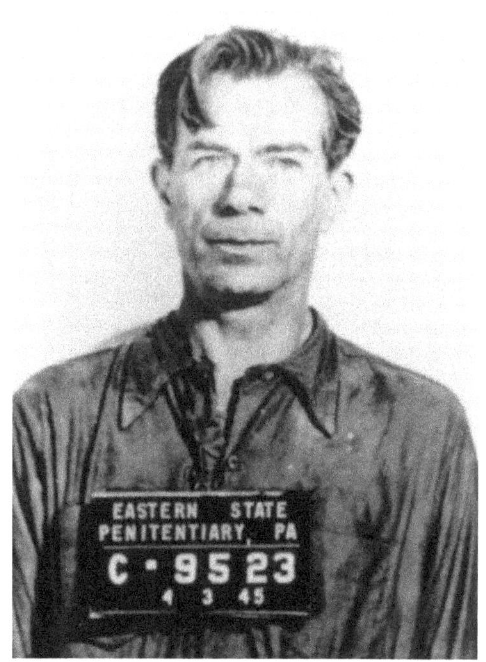

After his doomed escape from Eastern State, Willie Sutton was sentenced to life imprisonment as a four-time offender. He was transferred to Philadelphia's Holmesburg Prison, but successfully escaped from there in 1947. Nabbed (yet again) in 1952, he was incarcerated in New York's Attica State Prison. Long after his release in 1969, Sutton reputedly replied to a reporter's inquiry as to why he robbed banks by saying "because that's where the money is," although he later denied having said this.

Opened in 1829, the penitentiary was the most expensive American edifice of its day and soon became the most preeminent prison in the world. Architect John Haviland's plan of seven cell blocks radiating from an inner surveillance rotunda may represent the first modern building in America. Each chamber placed an inmate in his or her own private cell, with running water, a flush toilet, and a skylight. The prisoner had only illumination from the skylight (the "eye of God"), a Bible, and honest work (shoemaking, weaving, and the like) to lead to penitence.

During the decades following Eastern State's construction, delegations came to study the Pennsylvania System and the penitentiary's design. What's more, like Fairmount Water Works, the place became an attraction for tourists. In the 1830s and '40s, some ten thousand people came annually for a prison tour. Charles Dickens was one of them, visiting in 1842. He and others expressed doubt as to the effectiveness and humanity of the Pennsylvania System. Was it not cruel to hold prisoners in silent isolation, without visitors, letters from home, or any other contact with the outside world? Prisoners often went insane as a result of incarceration at Cherry Hill.

Due to this skepticism, as well as overcrowding, the system of solitary confinement at Eastern State fell by the wayside and was officially dropped by

1913. Windowless subsurface cells, nicknamed "The Hole" and "Klondike," were thereafter installed for solitary confinement, but these chambers were for punishment, not redemption.

The aged prison experienced riots and needed costly repairs by the 1960s. The Commonwealth of Pennsylvania closed the facility in 1971, and the City of Philadelphia purchased the site in 1980. Plans for redevelopment—options included a condominium, a supermarket, and a restaurant/nightclub—were successfully petitioned against. Eastern State Penitentiary persevered and opened, in a semi-decayed state, as a historical tourist attraction that now rivals San Francisco's Alcatraz.

Some of America's most notorious criminals were held at Cherry Hill. Gangster Al Capone was sentenced to a year there in 1929. He spent his time in relative comfort in a cell brimming with antiques, oriental rugs, and oil paintings. But it was bank robber William "Slick Willie" Sutton (1901–1980) who was Eastern State's most infamous prisoner. Along with eleven other men, Sutton escaped by way of a tunnel under the penitentiary walls in 1945.

More than a hundred inmates had managed to escape from the penitentiary through the years, and some thirty tunnels had been discovered in the 1930s and early '40s. In 1934, five prisoners jumped down a sewer grate in the prison yard and emerged at 21st and Hamilton before being snared fairly quickly. Then, in 1940, nine long-termers were implicated in burrowing two passages that were about to connect to a nearby home's basement. But the 1945 breakout was sensational and threw the Quaker City into a tizzy during the closing days of World War II.

The underground escape was planned by prisoners Clarence Klinedinst and William Russell, who shared cell no. 68, the chamber at Cellblock 7's southwest corner. Over a period of eighteen months, Klinedinst dug into the cell wall and then dug twelve feet down to avoid the prison wall along Fairmount Avenue. He then burrowed ninety-seven feet out toward the street, before digging fifteen feet up to the surface. By April 3, 1945, the ninety-seven-foot-long tunnel was ready.

Klinedinst and Russell had used a trowel and an ice pick and found knives to dig out the tunnel. They excavated two hundred cubic feet of dirt, gradually depositing it in the prison yard, throwing it down sewer grates, and flushing it down the toilet. The prisoners also had to dispose of several cubic feet of rock from Cell 68's wall, likely using the penitentiary's trash detail and friendly inmates—some who became escapees. They further shored the tunnel with timber bracing and equipped it with lights powered by a long electric cord.

The exit point was a grassy patch by the corner of 22nd and Fairmount Avenue, purposefully close to the corner watchtower so that the opening was veiled by the prison. Klinedinst and his excavation crew had broken to the surface during the night of April 2 but chose to wait until the next morning to make their escape. This turned out to be a mistake.

On the way to breakfast the next day, Willie Sutton joined a group of inmates to participate in the escape. A fugitive from New York state's Sing Sing Prison, the Brooklyn-born Sutton, who had a penchant for escaping and being caught, was serving a twenty-five- to fifty-year sentence at Eastern State for a 1934 bank robbery in which he used a machine gun to flee with $10,000.

After crawling through the slender passage and an underground stream of foot-deep water, twelve inmates emerged from the exit point and scattered into the neighborhood, trying to look inconspicuous. But a witness raised an alarm after seeing the men, covered in mud from head to toe, climbing out of the ground. City and state police organized a manhunt, and the streets around Eastern State were soon patrolled with officers sporting automatic rifles.

All escapees were recaptured at length. Klinedinst was out for only three hours, and Russell was shot seven times and apprehended when he walked into a trap at a girlfriend's home. Another fugitive returned to the main prison gate after eight days, hungry and exhausted from his time on the run, and rang the bell by the door to surrender. He received twelve years added to his prison term for his trouble.

As for Sutton, he was arrested at 24th and Wallace within minutes of escaping. He initially denied having been involved in the plot, but when prison supervisors and newspaper stories conjectured that Sutton was the mastermind, he subsequently claimed credit for the tunnel's design and construction, even though he had participated in neither.

Prison officials declared the prison break as one of the most ingenious in the annals of Eastern State Penitentiary. State authorities ordered an investigation into the escape, which was seen as proof that the facility was too old and decrepit to still be used as a prison, especially in such a teeming urban environment. (The built city had long expanded to incorporate the open area of Cherry Hill.) The 1945 breakout amplified demands for the prison's abandonment, although that did not transpire for a quarter century.

In 2005, Eastern State Penitentiary Historic Site conducted an investigation of the archaeological remains of the "Willie Sutton Tunnel"—filled with ash from the prison incinerator—as part of a commemoration of the breakout's

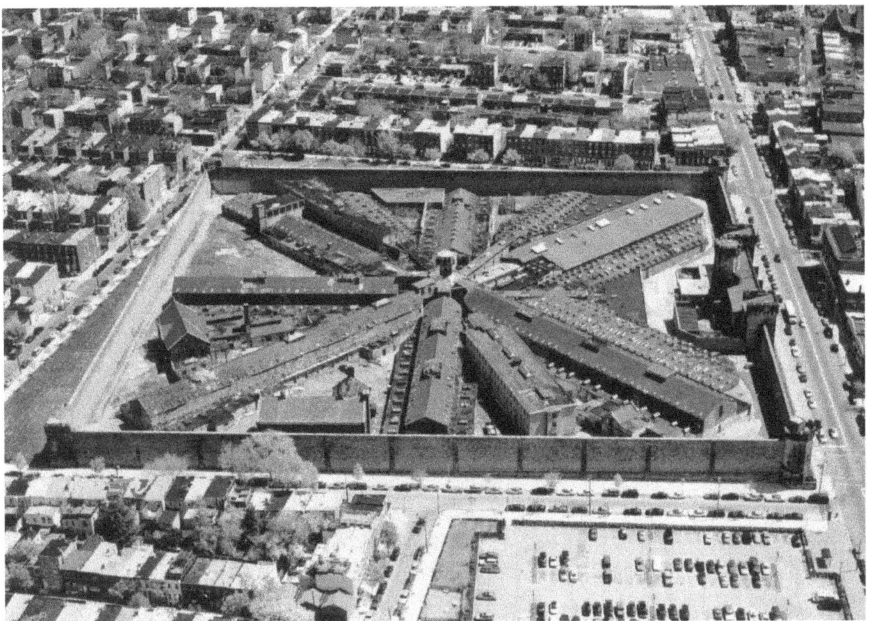

This 1990s overhead shot of Eastern State Penitentiary shows the size of the prison facility. Architect John Haviland designed an austere Gothic exterior, complete with an intimidating medieval façade that implied (incorrectly) that physical punishment occurred behind the grim walls. More than three hundred penitentiaries in Europe, South America, Russia, China, Japan, and across the British empire were based on Haviland's plan. *Library of Congress.*

sixtieth anniversary. Ground-penetrating radar located the excavation and remote cameras entered an intact section to view the escape passage. Tunnel remnants still run from Cell 68 to the penitentiary's front terrace.

The crimes described in this chapter did not involve physical harm to others, unlike the "basement of horrors" case of 2011, in which five defendants were convicted for kidnapping, murder, and sex trafficking after four mentally disabled people were found locked in a filthy subbasement of a home in Philadelphia's Tacony neighborhood. Their captivity over several years was part of a plot to collect disability checks.

The defendants may have taken their cue from Gary Heidnik, who kidnapped, tortured, and raped six women and held them prisoner in his basement in the 1980s. He was sentenced to death for his crimes, which encompassed murder and cannibalism in his "House of Horrors" at 3520 North Marshall Street. Heidnik was put to death by lethal injection in 1999, the last person to be executed in Pennsylvania.

Not unlike Eastern State Penitentiary, the Federal Metropolitan Detention Center (FMDC) at 7th and Arch contains 628 prisoner cells, each with a five-inch-wide window. Erected in 1999, the facility houses detainees who are under the jurisdiction of the U.S. Marshals Office and who await trial, sentencing, or transfer to a correctional institution. A 120-foot-long tunnel leads from the Detention Center's basement to the U.S. Courthouse across 7th Street to allow for the safe movement of prisoners. In fact, the City Planning Commission agreed to locate the FMDC on this prime commercial site because doing so would avoid the necessity of moving prisoners to the courthouse by van. About 30 feet below the street, the 14-foot-wide passage cost $2 million to dig—by hand, due to space issues. The FMDC's tunnel also had to meet the special security concerns of the Federal Reserve Bank of Philadelphia; the two facilities are catty-corner from each other.

The architect of Eastern State Penitentiary, John Haviland (1792–1852), has some atypical underground doings connected to him. According to Nicholas Pappas, who has led a multi-year search for Haviland's grave site, the architect was first entombed in a crypt at St. George Greek Orthodox Cathedral. This house of worship at 256 South 8th Street was originally St. Andrews Episcopal Church, designed in 1822 by Haviland himself.

In 1937, fifteen years after the building became St. George's, the mortal remains of those interred there were moved to the Divinity School of the Episcopal Church at 42nd and Locust. They were transported for a second time to St. Paul's Episcopal Church in Exton, Pennsylvania, in 1976. There, the well-traveled architect presumably rests. Plans are afoot, however, to rebury Haviland's relics, once again, at a more prominent location, along with a fitting monument.

Chapter 18

Digging Up Graves in Center City

Philly Archaeology

Until the middle of the twentieth century, archaeology had been viewed as something pertaining to primitive cultures or lost civilizations, usually carried out in remote or undeveloped settings. Historical archaeology in America until that time had been restricted to rural or abandoned sites like Jamestown and Williamsburg in Virginia. But archaeological excavations at Independence National Historical Park in the 1950s made Philadelphia the nation's first large urban center to be archaeologically examined. Since then, the Quaker City has received more archaeological attention than any other North American metropolis.

Digs at Independence Park in the 1950s and '60s were meaningful to the professional archaeological community, for it had been assumed that metropolitan sites were too disturbed to produce reliable results. But the park showed otherwise, becoming a laboratory for archaeology and its interpretation, not to mention a place where archaeologists honed their skills and developed new tools of the trade. Likewise, the digs showed everyday citizens that the past might be revealed under the ground on which they walked and lived.

The work prompted the adoption of the Philadelphia Historic Preservation Ordinance and formation of the Philadelphia Historical Commission, both in 1955. The city thus became a pioneer in the field of historic preservation. More importantly, though, digging at Independence Park inspired the enactment of two federal laws for the protection of archaeological sites: the National Historic Preservation Act (NHPA) of 1966 and the National Environmental

Policy Act of 1969. With its numerous historic places, Philadelphia was a prime beneficiary of this legislation, chiefly the 1966 act, which authorized the National Register of Historic Places to designate "districts, sites, buildings, structures, and objects significant in American history, architecture, archeology, and culture."

The federal laws mandated an archaeological investigation prior to construction of any project involving federal funds. Archaeologists were thus able to survey some of the Interstate 95 corridor during the freeway's construction through Philadelphia's central waterfront in the late 1960s.

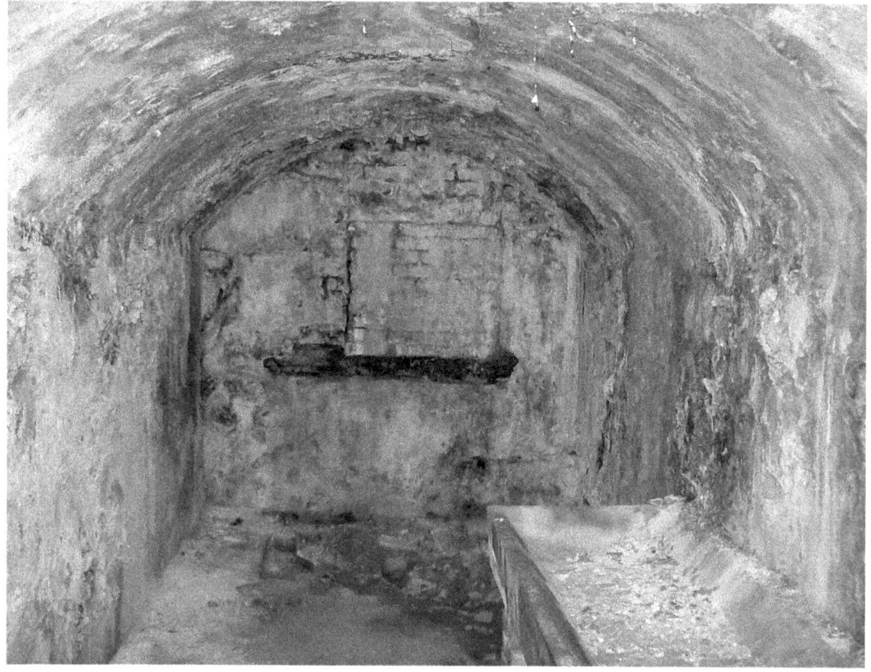

Philadelphia physicians had been associated with body-snatching since colonial days. Dead bodies were typically delivered to medical schools, where they served as cadavers on which students applied their studies. However, Dr. Philip Syng Physick, the "Father of American Surgery," may have autopsied bodies in the basement of his mansion along South 4th Street. Cadavers could have been brought to this vaulted space under the sidewalk of Cypress Street. Its far end is bricked up, and it might have been part of a tunnel leading blocks away. Then again, the hypogeum was likely built by the 1786 home's original owner, Henry Hill, a wealthy importer of Madeira wine, who could have used it for wine transport or storage. Nevertheless, the chamber is peculiar in that it contains an ancient stone table (*at right*) with a hole—a hole that could have been used to drain blood. The Hill-Physick House is open for tours (go to PhilaLandmarks.org), although the basement is off-limits. *Photograph by Harry Kyriakodis.*

They dug into the archaeological site as wrecking balls knocked down forsaken warehouses and rowhouses around them. At the same time, collectors looking for bottles and pottery would scour the great gorge as darkness fell. Artifacts not pillaged were pulverized by bulldozers or reburied under tons of concrete.

Archaeological investigation is occurring under I-95 these days in accordance with the NHPA. Long stretches of the highway are being rebuilt in the course of the ongoing "Digging I-95" highway reconstruction project. Privy pit finds have brought to light more than five thousand years of local history, and the project has come across Leni-Lenape (Native American) artifacts dating back some nine thousand years. A pair of eyeglasses unearthed at 1026 Shackamaxon Street may very well be the oldest spectacles ever found archaeologically in the United States. The "Shackamaxon Spectacles" were probably made in Spain sometime between 1650 and 1700.

Speaking of privies, the practice of non-archaeologists exploring these wood- or brick-lined shafts for artifacts has become popular in Philadelphia. About twenty amateur archaeologists in the region can be hired to excavate backyard outhouses, a pastime that hearkens back to when day laborers routinely cleaned out privies around town. Trained archaeologists, however, maintain that privy diggers are destroying potential archaeological sites and are fulfilling personal pursuits instead of contextualizing the past.

The Sheraton Society Hill Hotel opened at Front and Walnut, next to Interstate 95, on July 4, 1986. As archaeological investigations of construction sites had become customary by then, professional archaeologists recovered more than 130 prehistoric artifacts there before highway construction.

Moving west a few blocks, the Free Quaker Meeting House was raised in 1783 at the southwest corner of 5th and Arch and is today part of Independence Park. The Free Quakers splintered from the pacifist main body of the Society of Friends to support the American Revolution, even though they knew they would be "read out" (expelled) for doing so. About two hundred Free Quakers worshiped at this, the first Free Quaker Meeting House in the world. They met there until 1834, when participation waned. Betsy Ross was one of the last two members.

The structure then became a library, followed by a warehouse. Just before it was restored in the mid-1960s, the meetinghouse was physically moved about twenty feet west to its present location so as to enable the widening of 5th Street during the creation of Independence Park. The building is now an interpretive center; its original basement vaults may still lie under the intersection of 5th and Arch.

Betsy Ross died in 1836 and has been laid to rest at three different locations in Philadelphia: a Free Quaker graveyard at 5th and Locust; Mount Moriah Cemetery in Southwest Philadelphia; and in the courtyard of the Betsy Ross House on Arch Street since 1975, in preparation for the Bicentennial celebration. So Betsy Ross wandered after death as much as John Haviland. Note that no remains were found beneath Ross's tombstone during the last move, so bones from elsewhere within the family plot were reckoned to be hers and were reinterred in the current grave.

In 2005 or thereabouts, an eight-inch cannonball was uncovered in the ground steps away from Betsy Ross's grave site. A metal works previously occupied the courtyard of the Betsy Ross House, so the discovery is odd yet not outlandish. In addition, the sidewalk along Arch Street fronting the yard contains several large slabs of flagstone, each containing what appears to be a coal-hole cover. The pavers were once over what may have been a large basement coal vault for the metals factory taken down to create the Betsy Ross Courtyard. (Perchance the basement is still intact under the sidewalk?)

Archaeological investigations had been done periodically at Washington Square, another one of the five public commons drawn up by William Penn in his 1682 plan for Philadelphia. This area was known as "Congo Square," as it was one of few places in the city to bury African Americans in the 1700s. Additionally, more dead from the War for American Independence are interred at Washington Square than any other place in the nation—more than two thousand Continental soldiers and sailors and British prisoners of war.

The Washington Square Planning Committee in 1954 decided to put up a memorial that honored both George Washington and an unidentified soldier from the Revolutionary War. An archaeological dig in 1956 exposed the remains of a male about twenty years old inside an oak coffin, with the skull showing indications of a likely musket ball injury. This would be the body used for the unknown soldier who would repose in a stone sarcophagus at the feet of the life-size statue of Washington. Yet a nagging question persists: Was this the body of an American rebel or a British soldier? The world will never know for sure.

Archaeologists monitoring the Commuter Rail Tunnel's construction in 1980 happened on a burial ground of the First African Baptist Church near 8th and Vine. Some 140 graves were discovered and showed traits of African burial customs, with plots often holding as many as five bodies. Ten years later, another cemetery of this church or a related one was detected at 10th and Vine during the construction of the Vine Street Expressway.

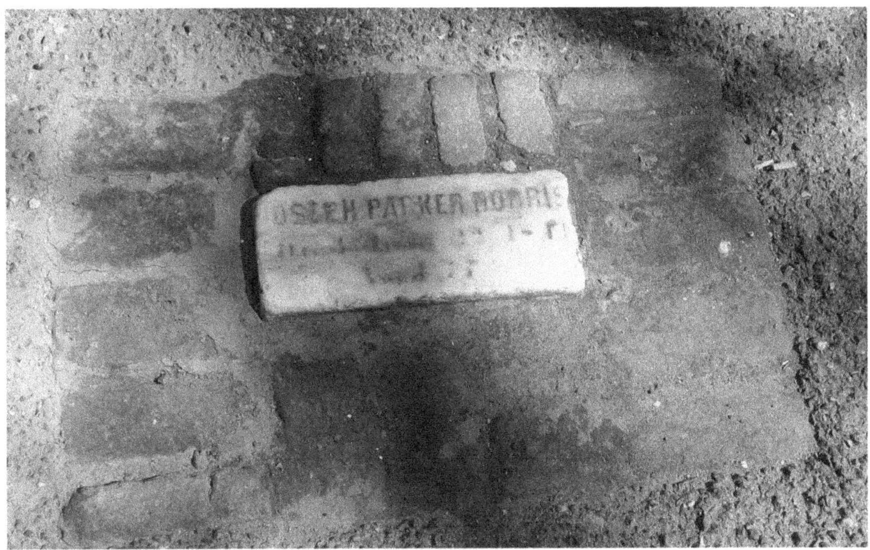

The gravestone of one Joseph Parker Norris is plainly visible within the parking lot at 302–04 Arch Street, along with the markers of others. The Arch Street Friends Meeting House, still possibly the largest Quaker meetinghouse in the world, was built on top of the first burial ground for Quakers in Philadelphia. Interments had been taking place there since the 1680s, although William Penn did not officially confer the ground to the Society of Friends until 1701. Not only were graves not moved when the meetinghouse was erected atop the graveyard in 1804, but they were also not moved from parts of the burial ground that were subsequently sold and developed along Arch Street. And that's the reason for the ignominious parking of cars over Joseph Norris. *Photograph by Harry Kyriakodis.*

These digs provided a glimpse into free African American life and death in nineteenth-century Philadelphia. Remains were reinterred in Eden Cemetery, the nation's oldest black-owned burial ground, in Delaware County, Pennsylvania.

The archaeologists who worked on these Philadelphia projects included John Lambert Cotter, Daniel Roberts, and Michael Parrington. Together, they authored *The Buried Past: An Archeological History of Philadelphia* (1993), the first general archaeological synthesis for any major city in North America. Indeed, John Cotter became the primary founder of urban archaeology in the United States by virtue of selecting the city of Philadelphia as his laboratory. He also taught a series of courses at the University of Pennsylvania that explored Philadelphia as an archaeological site. First offered in the 1960–61 academic year, Cotter's "Problems and Methods of Historical American Archeology" was the nation's first course in American historical archaeology. Between 1963 and 1978, the city's historic estates, churches, taverns, factories, prisons, and neighborhoods were sampled or fully excavated, gradually providing an outline of Philadelphia's archaeological history.

The popularity of urban archaeology in Philadelphia continues in the twenty-first century. More than 1 million eighteenth-century artifacts were unearthed at the National Constitution Center construction site in 2000–2001, leading one archaeologist to call it "the greatest urban archaeological find of our lifetime." Archaeologists there further unveiled the bodies of members of the Second Presbyterian Church, the graveyard of which was located at the northwest corner of 5th and Arch from around 1750 to 1864. Although it was believed that 1,500 burials there had been removed in 1867, eighty-eight sets of relics were encountered in stacked coffins. They were later reinterred at The Woodlands Cemetery.

In 2001, the coffins of nine adults and six children were discovered during the digging of a utility trench for replacing water pipes along the 700 block of Washington Avenue. The ground was once the remote necropolis of Old St. Joseph's Catholic Church, of Society Hill. The cemetery opened in 1824 and closed in 1893, and graves were to have been removed when the land was sold for housing in 1905. The Philadelphia Water Department considered laying new pipes in place over the coffins, as had been done during the original pipe installation, but this was rejected. Volunteers donated time and money to move the remains to Laurel Hill Cemetery by 2004.

What happened to these burial grounds is a familiar story throughout the Quaker City, particularly the downtown area. The likelihood that a cemetery has been wherever one stands in Philadelphia is fairly high—and not surprising for a city that has witnessed so much human history. Experts contend that bodies are buried underneath buildings, homes, streets, and even parks throughout Philadelphia. For example, sixty or so graves were unearthed in 2010 during the revitalization of Sister Cities Park (within Logan Circle), thought to be from when Logan Square was a potter's field in the early nineteenth century.

Another graveyard in the news lately is Mother Bethel Burying Ground, located under parts of Weccacoe Playground in the Queens Village neighborhood. Mother Bethel Church purchased the property in 1810 and used the cemetery until the 1860s. There was reason to believe that not all burials were moved prior the graveyard's eventual sale to the City of Philadelphia for the site's transformation into a community park (Weccacoe Square). Planned renovations raised questions as to whether any intact burials would be disturbed. The Pennsylvania Historical and Museum Commission requested an archaeological examination in accordance with NHPA Section 106. The 2013 investigation not only found that human remains were still on the Weccacoe Playground site but also estimated that more than five thousand bodies rested there! These were men and women who struggled to successfully establish the first major free black community in the North. The graves, only about three feet below the surface, have not been moved.

The site of the Morris House was excavated early this century, and it, too, had a connection to early African American life in Philadelphia. The finest mansion in Philadelphia, it had been built at the southeast corner of 6th and Market in the 1760s and was afterward owned by merchant Robert Morris, then the richest man in America and the chief financier of the American Revolution. George Washington frequently visited Philadelphia during the Revolutionary War and stayed with the Morris family.

The Morrises later lent the dwelling rent-free to Washington while the Constitutional Convention was in session. Washington would later pay Robert Morris $3,000 per year to live there with his family during his time as President of the United States, occupying the mansion from November 1790 to March 1797. The house was thus the nation's first presidential mansion (the original "White House," so to speak).

President Washington remodeled the house, adding a bowed structure with windows to the State Dining Room on the southern façade. The interior of this room was semicircular, so the bow is thought to be the model for the Oval Office in the real White House. Washington may also have added an underground passage between the outside kitchen and the house for use by servants and the enslaved. Remains of this tunnel are under the site.

More than twenty people lived on the premises with the Washingtons in the 1790s, including fifteen white servants and eight black slaves from Mount Vernon. Oney Judge was a female slave who escaped to New Hampshire in 1796 while the Washingtons were having dinner. George Washington made repeated attempts to recapture her, all unsuccessful.

President John Adams lived in the President's House for much of his term before leaving Philadelphia for Washington, D.C., in 1800. The house was subsequently used as a hotel and for mercantile purposes until it was razed in 1832. Stores were then opened on the site, including one that was John Wanamaker's first dry goods emporium ("Oak Hall"). The land was thoroughly cleared in the 1950s when Independence National Historical Park was created, thus removing any trace of the house aboveground.

But below ground, the foundations of the mansion endured. In 2007, the National Park Service undertook an archaeology project to assess the President's House site. A viewing area was set up so citizens could oversee archaeologists at work. The excavation attracted some 300,000

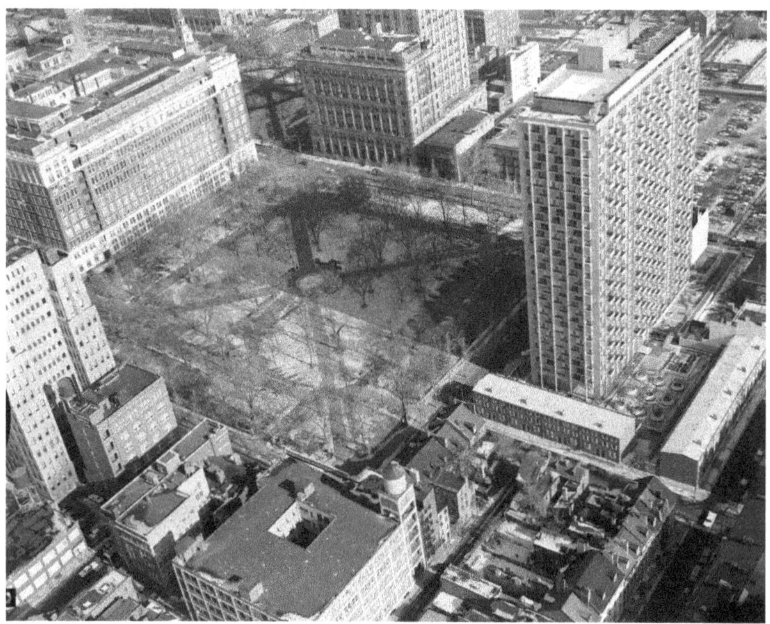

This mid-1960s aerial view of Washington Square looking northeast shows the Curtis Center at top left. The Philadelphia Athenæum is the short structure at top center, located on ground that once held the Walnut Street Prison/Jail (Goal). The grave site of the unknown soldier from the Revolutionary War is situated in this park, beside which stands a statue of George Washington and an eternal gas flame (added in 1976). The Philadelphia Fountain Society's first horse trough is barely detectable in this image, near where the shadow of Hopkinson House condominium first touches the park. Independence Square is in the background. *Library of Congress.*

visitors, captivating Philadelphians and spurring a Congressional mandate to commemorate the house, its use during the Washington and Adams presidencies, and the slaves who toiled there.

The memorial, *President's House: Freedom and Slavery in the Making of a New Nation*, is a pavilion that allows visitors to view the Morris House's remaining foundations. Signage and video exhibits portray the venue's history and the roles of slavery in the Washington household and in American culture. The site, now part of Independence Park, also highlights the early role of Philadelphia in the Executive Branch of national government.

Lastly, archaeologists made national news when they discovered more than twenty colonial-era privies and well shafts filled with eighty-two thousand artifacts during excavation work at 3rd and Chestnut for the Museum of the American Revolution. Found items relating to the Revolutionary War have been on display at the museum since it opened in 2017.

Epilogue

The phrase "Underground Philadelphia" could refer to things other than the subsurface story of the City of Brotherly Love. One may recall the alternative newspapers published in Philly from the 1960s to the 1990s. Dozens of counterculture publications gave readers the opportunity to tap into bohemian currents, learn about up-and-coming bands, and sample the opinions of new writers. Many were free, often published because the editor wanted an alternative outlet for his or her ideas. They followed the trailblazing tradition of another local editor and publisher, Benjamin Franklin.

But returning to subterranean topics, following are just a few of the more substantial underground/infrastructure matters that have preoccupied Center City Philadelphia in recent years.

Two ten-foot-long pine logs with center openings through them were exposed on the 900 block of Spruce Street in May 2017. Installed for water distribution in 1812 or so, they were evidently not removed when iron pipes subsequently replaced wooden pipes throughout the city.

Streets around Rittenhouse Square were closed for days in December 2017 after two separate sections of a water main burst on 18th Street near Locust. The deluge damaged the Curtis Institute of Music's historic building on Locust Street and closed ritzy restaurants facing the square. Colder weather and the pipe's age were contributing factors in both breaks.

A blast in a conduit vault eight feet below the surface of Market Street beside 30th Street Station occurred on May 21, 2016. This explosion was not a PECO-related defect; a cable installed by the Pennsylvania Railroad in 1932 had become corroded and began smoldering. A buildup of gases resulted in the blast. Nobody was hurt.

The Broad Street Subway's Spring Garden Station received a makeover in 2011 with the installation of a public art piece titled *Walking on Sunshine*. As a component of its Art in Transit program, SEPTA commissioned an artist to decorate the platform, transfiguring it with images inspired by Vincent van Gogh's sunflower paintings. Other downtown subway stations have been modernized since the turn of the century.

SEPTA is branding Center City's entire pedestrian concourse network as the "Downtown Link" in 2018.

PATCO budgets of the past few years have earmarked funds for design work in reactivating Franklin Square Station. About $2 million was allocated in 2017 for starting the refurbishment. The station is on track for its next resurrection in 2022, although a reopening is not absolutely certain.

In 2016–17, archaeologists unearthed hundreds of colonial-era coffins about twenty-two feet below the surface of a parking lot on the 200 block of Arch Street (south side, pretty much facing the Betsy Ross House). The graves were part of the First Baptist Church's burial ground, one of Philadelphia's first graveyards. Fifty or so interments were performed there annually in the late 1700s and early 1800s. The coffins were to have been removed to Mount Moriah Cemetery around 1860 (after First Baptist departed the Old City neighborhood), but this obviously did not happen. The find brought construction of an apartment complex—with two levels of underground parking—to a temporary halt. Volunteer archaeologists raced bulldozers and weather to exhume the bodies, which will be reinterred at Mount Moriah after study.

These incidents suggest that Philadelphia's surreptitious subterraneous history will continue to reveal itself with regularity in the twenty-first century. And no wonder: the Quaker City has been at the forefront of utility and transportation infrastructure development for the past three hundred years. And this is besides the saga of the earliest Philadelphians living in caves along the Delaware River and the proliferation of burial grounds throughout the city.

Even the story of the founder of Philadelphia since his death is illustrative. More than 160 years after William Penn's 1718 entombment at Jordans Quaker Meetinghouse in Buckinghamshire, England, the Pennsylvania legislature approved a resolution to relocate his mortal remains to Philadelphia—probably to repose at City Hall. This proposed move was intended to honor Penn's memory by returning him to the state and the metropolis that he brought into existence, and this would have coincided with the bicentennial of Penn's arrival in what would become Pennsylvania. But English Quaker leaders, having met a local delegation in 1881, cited numerous reasons for refusing to sanction such a transfer.

It could be said that Philly's hidden underground experience will always be an essential part of the City of Brotherly Love, like the immortal spirits of William Penn, Benjamin Franklin, Stephen Girard, and John Wanamaker. These gentlemen will surely be joined by Betsy Ross, Benjamin Latrobe, Frederick Graff and his son, Strickland Kneass, Samuel Merrick, Thomas Dolan, Thomas Cornish, A. Merritt Taylor, Edmund Bacon, Paul vanMeter, and others (even Willie Sutton!) who left their mark on underground Philadelphia.

INDEX

C

I

J

K

L

O

P

Q

R

S

T

U

Y

Z

About the Authors

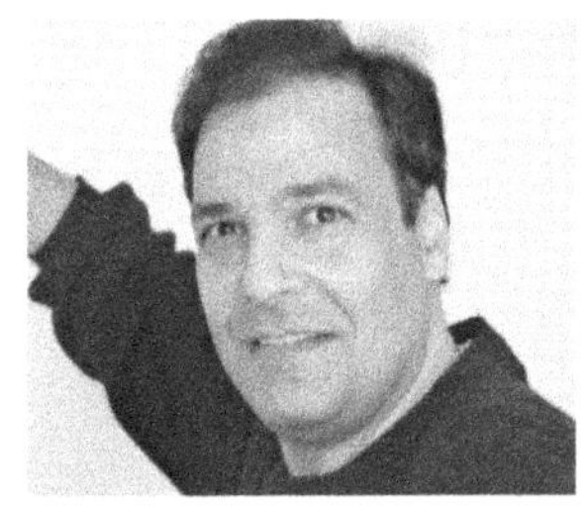

Harry Kyriakodis is a librarian, historian, and writer about Philadelphia and has collected what is likely the largest private collection of books about the City of Brotherly Love—more than 2,800 titles, new and old. He is a founding/certified member of the Association of Philadelphia Tour Guides and gives walking tours and presentations on unique yet unappreciated parts of the city for various groups. Once an officer in the U.S. Army Field Artillery, Harry is a graduate of La Salle University (1986) and Temple University School of Law (1993). He is also the author of *Philadelphia's Lost Waterfront* (2011) and *Northern Liberties: The Story of a Philadelphia River Ward* (2012), both published by The History Press, and *The Benjamin Franklin Parkway* (2014), a postcard history book from Arcadia Publishing. Harry is a member of the Philadelphia chapter of the Society for Industrial Archeology and also writes regularly for the blog *Hidden City Philadelphia*.

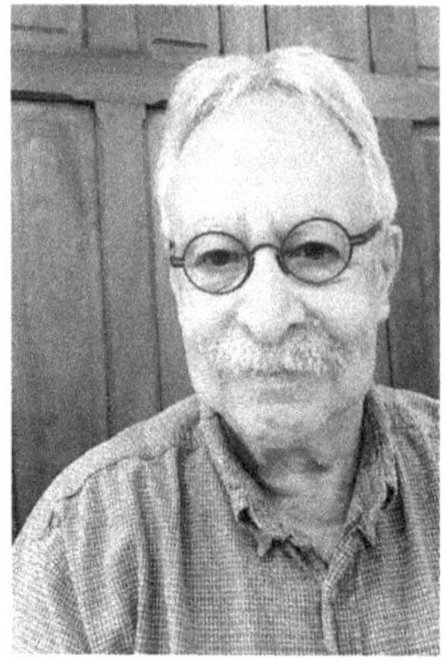

Joel Spivak is an architect, artist, author, and community activist in Philadelphia, where he helped lead the renaissance of South Street in the 1970s and early 1980s by coordinating with artists and builders. He opened his own specialty toy store, Rocketships & Accessories, and in 1992 cofounded Philadelphia Dumpster Divers, an artists' collective. Nicknamed the "Trolley Lama" for his expertise in Philadelphia's public transit history, Joel has a degree in industrial arts and is a member of the Philadelphia chapter of the National Railway Historical Society. His books include *Philadelphia Trolleys* (2003) and *Philadelphia Railroads* (2010), both with Allen Meyers and part of Arcadia's "Images of Rail" series. Joel also self-published *Market Street Elevated Passenger Railway Centennial, 1907–2007* for the 100th anniversary of the El. He originated Philadelphia's National Hot Dog Month celebration, which spotlights both vegan and non-vegan sandwiches. His wife is artist Diane Keller.

www.ingramcontent.com/pod-product-compliance
Lightning Source LLC
LaVergne TN
LVHW052335100826
845147LV00020B/1073